Praise for

SLIP

"In *Slip*, Mallary Tenore Tarpley carves out a "middle place" between acute sickness and full recovery for those of us with eating disorders. Tarpley is the perfect guide for this conversation, as she seamlessly blends memoir, reportage, and research. At all times, *Slip* remains accessible, realistic, and hopeful about the messy and maddening process of recovering from disordered eating. This tremendous book will comfort, inspire, and educate readers. We are lucky that it exists."

—Christie Tate, *New York Times* bestselling author of *Group*

"This is a must-read for anyone affected by the devastation of an eating disorder. Those who have suffered themselves will find a redemptive narrative to guide their recovery. Loved ones will understand more about how to support recovery without expecting perfection. And clinicians, educators, activists, and policy makers may decide their narrative should be less about eradicating eating disorders and more about elucidating them. We need to make space in the middle, in the shadows, where recovery becomes possible, just as Tarpley has shown us."

—Margo Maine, PhD, clinical psychologist and author

"There is no single image of eating disorders in the United States, but so often, we think about eating disorders as a linear journey with a neat and happy ending. Mallary Tenore Tarpley beautifully disrupts this narrative with *Slip*, an erudite memoir that moves us into a new generation in which we're not defined by our disorders. It's an essential addition to a canon of memoirs that shift paradigms and push us toward a new idea of what it means to recover and to fully, completely live."

—Evette Dionne, author of *Weightless: Making Space for My Resilient Body and Soul*

"*Slip* is a gorgeous, paradigm-smashing book that explores the liminal space between sickness and health where so many of us live. Blending memoir and reportage, *Slip* defies tidy narratives to show us we are not alone when we struggle, when we strive to get better, when we slip."

—Emi Nietfeld, author of *Acceptance*

"Candid, courageous, and meticulously researched, *Slip* is a game-changing addition to literature on disordered eating from the perspective of someone in committed recovery. Tarpley's quest to exercise control in a turbulent world is meaningful and timely, and this book is a necessary read for anyone trying to understand—or grapple with—the dark side of perfectionism."

—Courtney Maum, author of *The Year of the Horses*

"[Tarpley's] uplifting story should raise awareness about eating disorders, reduce stigma, and help survivors and their families stay hopeful."

—Booklist

"For readers who have struggled with disordered eating or for the friends and family who support them, this book will be a welcome balm, reminding them that recovery is not always linear, and that's okay."

—Library Journal

"The book is far more than a traditional recovery memoir—it challenges our either-or understanding of illness and wellness . . . Tarpley's courage in rejecting the tidy recovery narrative in favor of messy, honest truth-telling makes *Slip* an enlightening read."

—*The Austin Chronicle*

"Drawing on hundreds of interviews with patients, clinicians, and researchers, Tarpley reveals how treatment and understanding have evolved, challenging the idea of recovery as a fixed destination. Insightful and hopeful, *Slip* offers a nuanced view of long-term healing."

—KPCW, NPR affiliate

"*Slip*'s most important contribution is putting a name to a phenomenon that many sufferers of chronic illness will know intimately: the middle place. That's ultimately the greatest lesson from *Slip*: That the middle place is attainable, and preferable, to active illness, and that there's no shame in living there."

—*Hippocampus Magazine*

"Mallary Tenore Tarpley argues that our lexicon for eating-disorder recovery is woefully narrow. American medicine has a tendency to slot patients into one of two boxes: acutely sick or entirely healthy. But when you speak to real people touched by eating disorders—and Tarpley did, conducting hundreds of interviews with patients, family members, and clinicians—their rehabilitation stories emerge as anything but black and white. The persuasive power of Tarpley's thesis—that recovery is a matter of degrees, not absolutes—comes from the resounding crescendo of her many interviewees."

—Washington Independent Review of Books

SLIP

Life in the Middle of Eating-Disorder Recovery

Mallary Tenore Tarpley

SIMON ELEMENT

New York Amsterdam/Antwerp London

Toronto Sydney/Melbourne New Delhi

SIMON
ELEMENT

An Imprint of Simon & Schuster, LLC
1230 Avenue of the Americas
New York, NY 10020

Some names and identifying characteristics have been changed. Some dialogue has been recreated.

First Simon Element paperback edition August 2026

SIMON ELEMENT is a trademark of Simon & Schuster, LLC

Interior design by Lexy East

Manufactured in the United States of America

10 9 8 7 6 5 4 3 2 1

Library of Congress Cataloging-in-Publication Data has been applied for.

ISBN 978-1-6680-3501-6
ISBN 978-1-6680-3502-3 (pbk)
ISBN 978-1-6680-3503-0 (ebook)

To my father, for never giving up hope.
I owe so much of who I am, and where I am today, to you.

Life can survive in the constant shadow of illness,
and even rise to moments of rampant joy,
but the shadow remains, and one has to make space for it.

—Diane Ackerman

Contents

Author's Note

I was twelve when I developed anorexia nervosa, less than one year after my mother died of metastatic breast cancer. After years of treatment I got better, but not *all* better. I spent my early adulthood hoping the day would arrive when I would feel as though I had achieved the fullest expression of recovery. The truth is, though, that day hasn't arrived. I'm further along than I ever thought I would be, but my disorder isn't gone.

My recovery has been messy and maddening, and it is not redemptive in the ways our society hopes illness narratives will be. On one end of the spectrum of how we talk about this disease, there is sickness. On the other, full recovery. I live my life in the in-between, in what I've come to call the middle place. It's the liminal space that many of us inhabit as we work our way toward wellness. And it's an alternative to black-and-white thinking that bifurcates the world into two halves without exploring the beauty in between. In the middle place, hope and hardship coexist, slips are expected, and progress is possible.

As I've moved through the middle place, people have asked: What helped you get better? It's a difficult question to answer. It took me years to realize that I had to work toward recovery first and foremost for myself. Intrinsic motivation is an important part of the process, and studies show that it can yield more positive outcomes. But I couldn't do it *by* myself. No one can. I needed a team of people helping me, step by step, to get to where I am today. I was lucky to have the support of family and medical providers who cared for me and treated me over the course of five hospitalizations and a year and a half of residential treatment. It was only after getting help that I was able to begin the recovery process.

Recovery, I learned, is not a return to who you once were so much as a retrieval of all you lost while you were sick: pleasure, possibility, some semblance of peace. It requires a ruthless commitment to hard work. It's an accumulation of slow steps, with an acceptance that some steps will lead to slips. And it's a promise that you'll be honest about the slips, knowing they are an inevitable part of progress. You can't slip, after all, if you're standing still. As you move forward, you may or may not reach full recovery, but you emerge as someone who can lead a fuller life.

Slip isn't a tidy narrative about defeating my disorder but, rather, an intimate look at what it means to live with its imprints. By framing this book around the middle place, I hope to show what it takes to engage with the world even as I traverse the space between sickness and full recovery. I don't mean to suggest that full recovery is not possible; for many people, it is. Nor do I want to imply that people in the middle place aren't trying hard enough or are somehow settling. Living in the middle place isn't about giving up on full recovery; it's about viewing recovery as an ongoing process rather than a final destination.

To better understand my own story as a woman in the middle place, I poured through old therapy workbooks and medical records. I read the hundreds of journal entries I wrote while in treatment, and I interviewed former staffers and patients to corroborate my memory. I traveled back to the places where I was treated, where I relapsed, and where I got better.

While resurfacing painful memories, it sometimes felt like I was climbing an emotional Mount Everest. I ascended with caution as I taught myself how to revisit my past without getting lost in it. Along the way, I arrived at a telling truth: it's hard to be sick, but it's even harder to fully recover.

When it comes to eating disorders, "full recovery" is complicated. Clinicians have varying thoughts on what it means, and those with lived experience are often left to grapple with the elusiveness of a term that has not been adequately defined. The middle place provides a framework that is more inclusive of people who don't see themselves as fully recovered. Some people in the middle place meet all the BMI and body-weight criteria associated with someone who's fully recovered, but they may still have distorted thoughts that dictate their choices regarding food and exercise. Some of us struggle silently, fearful of sharing our stories and ashamed that we aren't "all better." It's easier to keep our secrets hidden if we don't fit the stereotypical mold of someone with an eating disorder.

I've written this book with an awareness that people of all different sizes, races, ethnicities, genders, ages, and socioeconomic statuses can struggle with eating disorders, and with a deep sensitivity to the fact that many people are overlooked or denied treatment because they don't match the stereotype. I am also sensitive to the fact that some of the childhood thoughts and writings I share may come across as fatphobic. I have spent my adult years trying to unlearn diet culture's harmful anti-fat messages. I recognize the damage that weight stigma and discrimination have caused, and I believe diet culture hurts everyone.

Slip follows my own story, but it is not my story alone. The book features diverse perspectives from others with lived experience and from clinicians and researchers who have helped broaden my scope of understanding about eating disorders, the treatment of them, and recovery from them. As part of my reporting, I spoke with dozens of experts who are quoted throughout the book. I also created a survey that I shared with communities of recovered individuals, eating disorder support and recovery groups on social media, clinicians, and treatment centers. Respondents were asked to consider a variety of topics, including the factors that contributed to their eating disorder; whether they ever received treatment (and if they considered it effective); and the biggest obstacles they faced while working toward recovery. I also introduced respondents to the concept of the middle place, knowing that I wanted to explore the recovery process through this frame. The survey ultimately reached 718 people from forty-four states and thirty-seven countries. About 71 percent of respondents indicated they were still struggling with an eating disorder, while the remaining 29 percent said they were fully recovered or in recovery. Of all respondents, 85 percent said they've been in the middle place.

To expand my understanding of this in-between space, I interviewed nearly 170 survey respondents, clinicians, and researchers. My interviews were conducted between 2021 and 2024, so some details from people's personal stories may have naturally changed since then. In some cases, I have used first-name pseudonyms for sources who were willing to share their stories with me but did not want to do so publicly. In other cases, I left out details from people's stories (and my own) when I thought they would be too triggering for readers. It is a tricky balancing act as a writer—to reveal the hard truths of one's personal narrative and to determine which details are better left unsaid. It is an even trickier one when you're telling another's narrative. Whenever interviewing people with lived experience, I asked them each the same question: How would you like me to describe where you're at in your recovery process? I want to honor the language we each use, however far along we may be. And I hope that by naming the middle place, I can help people put words to this prevalent but often overlooked part of recovery.

This book is for my fellow travelers in the middle place. It's also for people on either end of the spectrum—those who are acutely sick and those who consider themselves to be fully recovered. I hope this book will arrive like a knowing friend to families dealing with the ravages of eating disorders and that it will be of service to medical providers, educators, legislators, and others who want to deepen their understanding of how and why eating disorders take shape and what it takes to recover.

The story that follows marries memoir and journalism. Each chapter starts with my own story, told from the perspective of my younger self. That opens to my writing from my present-day self as a daughter, mother, wife, professor, and journalist living in the middle place, with stories and insights from others woven in. This structure, with its mix of narrative, research, and reflection, has enabled me to write intimately about my past and then examine all that has changed in the eating-disorder field in the twenty-five years since I was in treatment—and all the work that remains to be done.

Chapter One

The Trigger

On Saturday mornings, before the sun awoke, Mom would come into my bedroom and tell me it was yard-sale time. We would dress, buckle up in our 1986 Mercury Grand Marquis, and head to the first yard sale on our list. We always arrived early, on the hunt for toys, books, and costume jewelry to add to my childhood collections. If I found something I wanted, I knew my mother would never let me pay full price. "Ask them if they'll take fifty cents for that book," she would say, staring at the price tag on the book's cover. "Then see if they'll knock one dollar off that Checkers set." If the sellers didn't want to bargain, Mom would intervene and threaten to leave behind all the goods. Most of the time, she got what she wanted.

I was in awe of my mother and her brazen bargaining skills. Her family didn't have much while she was growing up; they lived a paycheck-to-paycheck life, and food did not end up on the dinner table easily. This piece of my mother's past seemed to stay with her. Even after she had settled into a middle-class suburbia lifestyle as an adult, she was always searching for sales and free food.

After our yard-sale outings, Mom and I would go to the bank in downtown Holliston, the small Massachusetts suburb where we lived. On Saturday mornings, a table was set up across from the tellers' station with free coffee and Dunkin' Donuts Munchkins. Mom would pour herself a cup of coffee with generous amounts of sugar and cream, then stick half a dozen donut holes in an empty cup for us to take home. I would hold it and stand by my mom's side as she chatted with the tellers and deposited the checks from her job as a medical records clerk. Glass bowls of lollipops sat at each teller station. Mom would reach inside the nearest one and give me a big handful of suckers as I smiled, wide-eyed with delight. Over time, the tellers came to know Robin, the lady who loved free donuts and Dum-Dums.

Mom was bold, fearless. But there was one thing she did fear, from as far back as I can remember: cancer. I grew up in the 1990s, when the pink ribbon had emerged as a ubiquitous emblem of breast cancer awareness. Mom saw that little pink ribbon as a warning that we needed to be careful of cancer and all its potential causes. "Don't stand in front of the microwave," she first told me when I was five or six years old. "Don't microwave anything in plastic containers. Don't ever buy a house under high-tension wires, and don't stay in someone's house if it's under those wires. Don't ever smoke cigarettes." These were rules never to be broken—by her or by me—lest we both end up with cancer. I thought that if we followed the rules, if our pact stayed intact, we'd be safe. But cancer had other plans.

In April 1994, when my mom was thirty-six years old, she was diagnosed with breast cancer. I was just eight and too young to fully comprehend the gravity of her diagnosis. I thought that when cancer showed up at our doorstep, it would be a temporary roommate confined to the basement. But during the three years my mother was sick, cancer became a permanent houseguest, roaming our halls like it owned the place. In the face of its threat, my parents became bearers of unwavering optimism. Even when my mother's body no longer seemed like her own, she would often tell me she was "a soldier in a battle" and was "strong like a warrior." She compared herself to the Little Engine That Could, repeating the well-known refrain, "I think I can. I think I can. I know I can." "I'm going to get over the other side of that mountain," she would insist.

My father clung to the same plotline. "Mom is the strongest person I know," he would tell me. "She's going to be perfectly fine. Nothing bad is going to happen. Believe me." And so I did. These narratives appealed to me as a young child. A lover of fairy tales, I knew there was evil in the world, but I always thought that good would prevail and that characters who endured hard times would end up where they belonged: with the ones they loved. Hansel and Gretel would return home safely to their father. Jack would cut down the beanstalk and live prosperously with his mother. A kiss would awaken Snow White, and then she and the prince would wed, promising to love each other for all time.

Now I see my family's fairy tale unfold in the pages of old journals, which I started keeping when my mother got sick. I always loved the written word, and as an only child who lived in a neighborhood without many kids my age, I spent a lot of time reading and writing by myself. I would climb the Japanese maple tree in our front yard, where I wrote short stories and journal entries. I read countless books there, propping my body up against the strongest limb and losing myself in other worlds. I devoured *The Secret Garden*, *A Little Princess*, *Tuck Everlasting*, *Bridge to Terabithia*, and *A Wrinkle in Time*, wishing I could make my favorite characters come to life. I pretended to be the protagonist from *Harriet the Spy*. In the book, Harriet is an eleven-year-old aspiring writer who spies on her classmates, friends, and neighbors and writes down observations in her notebook. I saw myself in her, as a young girl who was about the same age and had the same dream of becoming a famous author. Like Harriet, with binoculars in hand, I would often spy on my neighbors from high up in my tree and write down activities I deemed suspicious. (*Man walking dog stopped and looked up into the sky . . . Car drove down the street slowly . . . Truck just sped by without any apparent reason.*) I'd jot down these observations (and a slew of random license plate numbers) in my fluorescent pink Lisa Frank notebook. My neighbors came to know me as Mallary the Spy, and they found my detective skills endearing.

When my mom got sick, spying started to feel like a lonelier endeavor—an act of looking into other people's worlds for the mere purpose of escaping my own. I started journaling more, writing about my mom. "I went to the hospital to pick up my mother," I wrote one week after my ninth birthday. "It was good, and I was happy that I could see my mother. She was a little weak, but she was fine and is always going to be. The only thing is that I hope my mom's not hiding anything from me." Whenever doubt crept into the tale, as it did here, I'd squash it and then turn my attention back to soldiers standing triumphantly and little blue engines that could.

My father and I were convinced our positive outlook had worked when Mom went into remission. In June 1995, a little over a year after her initial diagnosis, the doctor's records noted that she was "coming along beautifully. Her spirits have improved, her attitude towards life is better, and she feels as though she can get on with everything." In September, the doctor declared: "Robin has recovered very nicely from chemotherapy. She appears to be free of disease." But less than three months later, my mom started experiencing pain in her spine. Her medical records suddenly took on a graver note. An MRI of her spine, femur, shoulders, pelvis, and skull revealed "metastatic disease in virtually every bone examined," with the doctor noting that "the disease process is ubiquitous." A month later, the cancer spread to Mom's liver.

One day, not long after the cancer came back, I was standing next to my mother in the bathroom as we got ready for the day. My parents and I lived in a 715-square-foot house and we all shared one tiny bathroom, so we were used to squeezing in front of the mirror together. On this day, Mom was topless and wasn't wearing her wig or prosthetic breast. She stared at her reflection with blue eyes that looked cold and piercing. "Mal," she said, turning to me, her little ten-year-old. "Do you think I'm beautiful?"

I didn't know how to respond. I felt like I had suddenly been thrust into adult territory, as though Mom were addressing me not as a mother but as a friend in need of reassurance. I looked at her and longed for what she used to look like, with her strong body, thick brown hair, and a smile that seemed to stretch across her entire face. Now, smiling took energy my mother no longer had. She was bald and jaundiced, with one breast and a mastectomy scar that scowled at me. It looked like a cross, a sign of cancer's curse disguised in a symbol of faith. I stared at it and felt the pressure of having to convince my mother that cancer had not altered her beauty. "Of course, I think you're beautiful, Mom!" I responded, feeling deeply ashamed about wishing she looked different.

Mom had always been my barometer of beauty. She taught me how to dress up, how to do my hair, how to match my clothes. And she showed me that beauty comes not just in the shape of a body but also in the curvature of a smile, in the tenderness of a heart. She didn't succumb to the diet fads of the 1980s and 1990s, and I don't remember her ever buying fat-free or low-fat foods, which were all the rage then. Instead of demonizing treats, she ate them alongside me. Our favorites were mocha-almond chip ice cream, Yodels devils food cakes, and Jiffy Pop popcorn (except for the times when she would accidentally burn it and set off the fire alarm). When we went on our weekly mother-daughter outings to Burger King, we drank vanilla milkshakes and devoured 99-cent Whoppers. I would sink my teeth into the sesame bun. Ketchup and mayonnaise would ooze out the side, covering my fingertips and falling onto my shirt. Mom and I would shake our heads and laugh. We both knew that, had my father been with us, he would have been disgusted by all the sauce. He was, and still is, a plain McDonald's hamburger kind of guy. I can still picture and hear him placing his orders at McDonald's: "No pickles, ketchup, mustard, or onion. Just a plain burger with nothing on it, please." Whenever the cashier got his order wrong, Dad would roll his eyes and sigh as he scraped the condiments off his burger and into the trash.

Some weeks, Mom was too tired to take me to Burger King, but she always tried to have an after-school snack waiting for me—Ritz Crackers 'n Cheesy Dip, store-bought cupcakes, strawberry-flavored Toaster Strudels, a bowl of frozen green grapes. Mom was home every day when I walked in the door from school, and we would spend a couple hours together before she left for work at 4:30 p.m. She worked in the medical records department at the local hospital where I was born and where she was treated. My father was the director of housekeeping at a Catholic nursing home. They worked opposite shifts because they couldn't afford childcare, and they liked the idea of one parent always being with me. Most days, as my father pulled into the driveway on his way home, my mother was pulling out. They would exchange a quick kiss, then transition from work to home, home to work, barely seeing each other on weekdays.

We had a very small family that couldn't be called on to babysit. My maternal grandmother would sometimes watch me when my mom was sick, but for the most part my parents took me with them everywhere. When school was out for the summer, my mother brought me to her oncology appointments. She never wanted me to hear what the doctor had to say, so I would sit in the waiting room during her appointments and look at all the other cancer patients. Many had no hair. Some were in wheelchairs. Others looked like they could barely muster the strength it took to walk from the entrance to the reception desk. I would smile at each of them politely, as though unfazed, but I was terrified to see what cancer could do. Later, at night, in hopes of forgetting what I saw, I would cradle my head and silently say: "Erase it from my mind, erase it from my mind." I did this a lot when my mother was sick, sometimes multiple times a day. And a little part of me believed it worked.

As Mom's cancer metastasized, she mostly stopped leaving the house. I would come home from school to find her in the living room, lying down on the couch. I would give her a kiss, then put my backpack away, knowing it would make her upset if I left it on the living room floor.

Ever the neatnik, my mom taught me to clean up my messes and keep the house as tidy as possible. When I didn't measure up, she scolded me. Once, when I was eight or nine, she asked me to clean our bathroom toilet with "the brush." I assumed she meant the dirty old toothbrush under the sink. I meticulously scrubbed the side of the toilet bowl with it, trying to wipe away all the icky spots and make my mother proud. When she came into the bathroom a few minutes later and saw what I was doing, she yanked the toothbrush out of my hand. "WHAT do you think you're doing?" she snapped, as if I had just committed an unforgivable mistake. "Why would you ever think you're supposed to use a toothbrush? You use a toilet bowl brush!" She grabbed the foreign object from beneath the sink and slammed it down in front of me before storming out. I blamed myself for my mother's outburst and scolded my stupidity. Kneeling on the bathroom floor, I scrubbed the toilet bowl as fast and as hard as I could with the proper brush, trying to erase the mess I had made.

After that day, I was afraid to clean the toilet and decided to stick with other tidying tasks I had mastered, like "fixing the quilt." The living room couch where my mother spent most of her days was one of the first new pieces of furniture my parents had ever purchased. My mom wanted to protect it from dirt and stains, so she kept it covered with a massive quilt that she had bought in the Amish country during a family road trip to Pennsylvania. The quilt was a patchwork of art, with intricate floral designs in each sewn square. Mom didn't think the designs matched the living room's decor, so she would only display the underside, which was a solid seafoam green. Every day, she had me line the quilt neatly against the couch and smooth out any wrinkles. She would supervise over my shoulder, making sure I did it just right. "Tuck in that corner on the left more. . . . Pull it down a little more in the front. . . . Even it out on both sides . . . just like that. There you go."

My mother never told me I *needed* to be perfect, but in moments like this I sensed she *wanted* me to be. There was the precision of the quilt, the line of questioning whenever I got an A- instead of an A+, the look and sound of anger whenever I lost something. One day while eating lunch at school, I put my retainer in a crumpled-up napkin and accidentally threw it away. By the time I realized what I'd done, it was too late to retrieve the retainer from the trash. I was afraid to admit my mistake to my mother, so I told her I had "misplaced" my retainer. She assumed I lost it somewhere at home, and she made me search for it until late into the night. "How could you be so careless, Mallary?" she asked, shaking her head in disbelief. "That retainer was expensive!" I wanted so badly to please her, so I kept looking. But it felt futile, like searching for a teardrop in the ocean. Mom ended up buying me a replacement, and I could never bring myself to tell her what happened to the original. I did eventually tell my father, though. He was always my protector, the one who often told my mother, "Robin, she's just a child. Please don't be so hard on her."

The sicker Mom got, the more I wanted to be perfect for her. I diligently tended to my daily chore, pulling up the green quilt if it had fallen off the cushions and tucking it in around the sides. On nights when my mother didn't have enough energy to get up off the couch, I would wrap the quilt around her frail body. Often, her waning energy was a sign she didn't have enough platelets in her blood. Chemotherapy treatments had destroyed the stem cells that form platelets, or "platelifts," as I used to call them. I didn't really know what they were; I just knew my mother needed a lot more of them. One afternoon, Mom's platelets were so low she could barely move. I reached for her hand and tried to pull her up, but the cancer was stronger. I wanted my mother back—the one who used to go bike riding with me, who did arts and crafts by my side, who drove to the store and bought me that must-have, hot pink Pogo stick I'd been asking for. Time had put a frame around those memories, and they were always on display in my mind.

That summer night in 1996, my father called 911. He whispered into the phone so I wouldn't hear the details. They were to be kept hidden from me, even though I could see them unfolding right before my eyes. When the paramedics came, they lifted Mom onto a stretcher and wheeled her out of the house. Her gaze was empty, her face a road map of pain and shame. She was in her late thirties, but cancer had aged her to the point where she seemed barely recognizable.

"Mal," Mom said from the stretcher, reaching out for my hand just before she was wheeled into the ambulance. "I'll see you and Dad at the hospital. I love you." My dad and I trailed the ambulance in his 1993 Ford Tempo and drove the nine miles to Leonard Morse Hospital. There, the doctors told us my mom had developed thrombocytopenia—the medical term for abnormally low blood-platelet counts. Normal platelet levels are in the 150,000 to 400,000 range; that night, hers were under 20,000. As we sat by my mother's side, watching the platelets drip from an IV bag, down a tube, and into her implanted mediport, we tried to encourage her. "You are so brave," I told her, embracing my parents' warrior language in the presence of a mother who looked defeated. In moments like that, I sometimes wondered how long it would take my mom to win. But I never thought she would lose.

The first day of my mother's hospitalizations was always the hardest. On day two, she would usually feel well enough to request an orange sherbet. We would curl up in her hospital bed and watch TV—Mom in her medical gown and nonslip socks, me in my Oshkosh overalls—and savor the treat, slowly spooning out bites until there were none left. "Andy, go sneak us two more sherbets," my mom would tell my dad. He would wince a little before walking down the hall to get more, as though fearful he was going to get caught. My rule-following father is a man of restraint who tiptoes around desire. My mother always walked right up to it, swift and sure-footed. Until she no longer could.

By January 1997, Mom's body had stopped responding to chemotherapy treatment, and she was hospitalized with a high fever, forgetfulness, inappropriate word use, and a stiff neck. The cancer, we learned, had spread to her brain. Within a week or two, Mom started having trouble talking. She would use the wrong word to describe something, or she would forget in mid-sentence what she was saying. I tried to fill in the gaps, like a game of Mad Libs. Soon, every other word my mom uttered seemed like a fill-in-the-blank space, a guessing game that left me searching for meaning. The mother who had taught me how to speak was suddenly without words. As confusion settled over my mother like a deep fog, I tried to be her sunshine. While Mom was in the hospital, I wrote her a letter on a piece of notebook paper adorned with bunny stickers. "I miss you so very much, but you'll be home in no time, and you will be better in no time," the letter read. "I love you, Mom!" She was discharged a few days later, and I was hopeful.

But by the end of January, my mom was admitted to the emergency room, having barely consumed any food or liquid for days. After uncovering her medical records years later, I would learn that the doctors had diagnosed her as "positive for anorexia." They were referring to the literal definition of *anorexia*: "without appetite." It's a clinical term that medical providers sometimes use to describe individuals who stop eating due to acute illnesses, often as they near the end of life. Being "positive for anorexia" is different from anorexia nervosa, the latter defined as "nervous loss of appetite" and a disorder of both the body and mind. At the time, I had never heard the word *anorexia* used to describe my mother, and if someone had mentioned it to me, I would not have known what it meant. But I did know my mother's appetite had waned, slowly then rapidly. She looked so skinny and frail, like she might break if I hugged her. She didn't want any sherbet, and I couldn't bring myself to eat any without her.

"Why do good people have to have something bad happen to them? Why, diary, does this happen?" I journaled after my mother returned home to hospice care. "Mom is the best person in the world to me. I don't want to lose her. I hope that I can look at this diary entry of mine—forty, thirty years from now—and be thankful that I still have my mother. I really do."

Ten days later, on February 9, 1997, Mom died at home in bed. She was forty years old, and I was eleven. Cancer had murdered her, but anorexia was a likely accomplice. At the time, no one would have suspected that I would later be hospitalized with an anorexia of my own.

Fourteen hours after my mom died, I walked alone to middle school. A wintry wind numbed my ears and nose. The snow glistened like glitter, and ice crackled under my boots. I knew that route well, having walked along it every day in the sixth grade. My father had offered to drive me to school that morning, but I turned him down, secretly wanting everything to stay the same.

I pretended to read a *Baby-Sitters Club* book as I walked, hoping to find refuge in its pages. But the words blurred through teardrops that fell onto the page. I shielded the tears with my book as I walked into school and toward the bathroom, where I hid in a stall. *Erase it from my mind*, I told myself, closing my eyes as I shook my head from side to side. *Erase it from my mind.*

The school bell rang. I wiped my eyes dry and told the tears to stay away. *I'm okay. Everything's fine. I'm okay. Everything's fine.* I shoved that tear-stained book into my L.L.Bean backpack, looked in the mirror, and smiled. Then I walked off into my new world. *Mom would want you to be strong*, I kept telling myself. *Show her how strong you can be.* I sat in class and raised my hand to answer my teacher's questions as I would on any other day. I didn't speak a word about my mother until afternoon recess, when I told a friend what had happened. She broke the news to my teacher, Mrs. Fallon, who hadn't yet been notified about my mother's death. She pulled me aside and asked how I was doing. She would later tell me she was heartbroken not only by the news but also by how composed I seemed. *This little girl's mother has just died*, she kept thinking. *Her mother just died . . .*

"I'm okay," I told her with a meek smile. "Really, I'm fine." I kept telling myself to stay *cool, calm, and collected*, repeating the same words I had once heard a nurse tell my mother after she had been hospitalized for a platelet transfusion. I thought about my mother throughout the day, fixating on the fact that she had been alive less than twenty-four hours earlier. I kept replaying the previous day in my head, wishing I could hit Rewind, then pause the moments forever. I would have settled for stagnancy if it meant I could have Mom back in my life.

I walked home alone from school that day, and when I opened the front door, I half expected to see my mother on the couch. I stared at the seafoam-green quilt in that empty living room, realizing I would be alone for the next two hours until my father came home from work. The lights and TV were off. There was no after-school snack on the table, and I didn't make myself one. I walked to my parents' bedroom—where my mother had died in bed—and started looking through her dresser drawers. It had been a long time since I opened those drawers, which I used to rummage through in search of dress-up clothes. I opened the top one and spotted the prosthetic breast she sometimes wore after her mastectomy. I thought about the first time I saw my mother slip that silicone into her bra, an attempt to fill a newly formed void. Placing it in the palm of one of my hands, I ran my fingers over the top, pressing them into the softness. The silicone felt squishy, like the green slime I liked playing with. I tried sticking it inside my training bra, but it slipped out the top and bounced onto the floor. I opened a big Ziploc bag where my mom kept her wigs, took out the shoulder-length brown one, and placed it on top of my head. I looked in her bedroom mirror, hoping to see a resemblance. But all I saw was eleven-year-old me with Mom's empty bed in the background. It was the most tragic piece of furniture in our house.

The silence in that house sounded like sadness, so I turned on *Arthur*, my favorite cartoon about the friendliest of aardvarks. The rest of the week, during those lonely afternoon stretches, I spent most of my time watching *Arthur* and reading. I read handwritten notes that my teacher had asked my classmates to write. Most didn't know what it was like to lose a parent, let alone what to say.

"I'm very sorry to hear about your mother," a classmate named Adam wrote. "Don't be depressed." From John: "I'm really sorry that your mom died, and I hope you're alright. I didn't know her, but she probably had a nice life, I hope. I would hate to have my mom die." I felt older as I read their notes, as though suddenly aware that my mother's death was forcing me to grow up faster. My favorite note was from my friend Eliza, who recognized the strength I had been trying to display all week. "You are being very brave," she wrote. "I wouldn't have been able to go to school the next day."

Channeling this bravery, I crafted a eulogy for my mother's funeral. I wrote most of it by hand on scrap pieces of paper while sitting on the floor underneath our kitchen table. There was a vent there, and I loved feeling its warmth whenever the heat would turn on. I filled the eulogy with inspirational guidance about how to find strength in the aftermath of loss. The words sounded like they came from a preacher extolling the afterlife—not from a young girl who had just lost her mother. I had tried to adopt an adult voice when writing my mother's eulogy, imagining the language she would use if trying to console me and my family in the aftermath of loss. I edited the final version carefully with a red pen, tweaking words and phrases to make them sound as perfect as possible. Looking back, I wish I could have put the pen down and cried.

At my mother's funeral, I stood tearless before the congregation and read her eulogy. I explained that "we should always keep my mother, Robin, in our hearts, but we cannot let her death bother us for the rest of our lives. We can't keep going back to that old chapter but look forward to the new chapter in our lives and just hope that it brings us the best of luck and much happiness." Family members and friends came up to me afterward and told me how proud they were. They called me "amazing" and said I did "a phenomenal job." Unsure of how to help me navigate loss, my family kept feeding me praise as I secretly starved my pain, hoping I could lay it to rest.

When I reflect on all that transpired after my mother's death, I'm struck by how proudly I wore my rose-colored glasses. I never realized how much they blurred my vision of grief. No one had ever told me how to grieve or for how long. In my mind, grief was something you felt for a few days—a fleeting sadness you had to get over in order to move on. I had assumed that since I cried the day my mother died and then wrote her eulogy, I was done grieving.

In the days that followed, I remember wanting to see my father cry. *If he cried*, I remember thinking, *then that would mean I could, too*. But his cheeks remained dry whenever we talked about Mom, and so did mine. It seemed we were both trying to deny the death that had just upended our lives.

I've since read research showing that when parents avoid conversations about death, their children have an increased risk of experiencing anxiety, depression, and what's known as complicated (or prolonged) grief. With complicated grief, people experience intense longing and sadness, usually accompanied by persistent images or thoughts of the deceased and an inability to come to terms with the reality of death. I've also learned that children who have experienced death often mimic the loss response of their closest surviving family member. It makes sense, then, that I thought my grief should be as minimal as my father's appeared to be. What's been harder to understand is the way my family downplayed death. Why did my dad send me to school the day after my mom died, and then let me come home to an empty house? Why didn't anyone tell me it was okay to be sad? Had no one thought to question my perpetually cheerful demeanor? I sat with the weight of these questions for a long time, fearful of asking my father for answers. The daughter in me wanted to protect him from all the poking and prodding. But the memoirist in me wanted answers, even if they yielded painful truths. One day, nearly twenty-five years after my mom's passing, I decided to probe.

"Did you ever see me cry in the days and weeks after Mom died?" I asked my dad, unsure of how he would react.

"Not in front of me . . ." he said, trailing off.

Silence sat between us.

"I think if you had broken down," my dad said, "or if you would have started to cry, we would have both been sitting in the living room crying our eyes out. But I kind of took your lead when it came to my reactions."

"How come?" I asked, perplexed. As a child, I had been trying to take *his* lead.

"I think in some ways we both tried to bury it. I didn't know what to do because I was new to it. And I thought, *Gee, Mallary lost her mom, she needs some foundation*. I worried that if I broke down, then I wouldn't be strong for you," my father said in a tender voice. "I wasn't just someone who lost a wife; I was someone who was now a mom and dad. I put my emotions aside because the most important thing was being strong."

Dad is the only person I know who cries when he's happy but not when he's sad. He loves watching romantic comedies and cries during Hallmark movies. When he recounts a happy memory, his soft voice cracks with emotion, and he sometimes has to pause to keep his composure. He has always measured strength not by the amount of sorrow you can shoulder, but by the amount you can shovel and then bury.

I asked my dad why he stayed so positive after Mom's death and throughout her sickness, when it was clear she wasn't going to make it.

"As long as Mom was breathing, I thought there was hope," he told me. "It seemed like everyone else had given up on her. But Mom was a hard fighter, and if she only had one supporter, it was going to be me. And actually, Mom had two supporters—*you* and me. We were always going to be there for Mom, and we were. We were not wrong to think she would make it."

Dad had tried so hard to protect me from the seriousness of my mother's illness, not realizing that truth is often the best armor. For so long I had blamed him for shielding me from reality. But now, I considered the possibility that he had been exposing me to it all along. The difference was that *his* reality wasn't reflective of the difficult truths I've come to appreciate as an adult—the ones that confront you with news you'd rather not hear but deserve to know. They're not the stuff of fairy tales but of real life, replete with unpredictable plotlines and endings. Complicated truths help us grow in ways that sugarcoating seldom can; they make us more attuned to gray spaces by widening our view of the world beyond black or white, positive or negative.

"When it comes to how we think, 'negative' is not the only alternative to 'positive,'" wrote author Barbara Ehrenreich, who dedicated much of her life's work to studying the ills of positive thinking. "The alternative to both is realism—seeing the risks, having the courage to bear bad news, and being prepared for famine as well as plenty . . . We ought to give it a try." In the 1990s, when my mother was sick, the concept of positive thinking had emerged as a predominant pillar of cancer care. Breast cancer patients like my mom (and their families) were told to "stay positive!" and "look on the bright side!" as though a positive mindset alone could lead to better health outcomes. Families like mine adopted the medical community's language, using warrior verbs like *battling* and *fighting* and adjectives like *fiercely* and *bravely*, hoping we could speak and write our way toward a happy ending. Women who were lucky enough to go into remission were deemed full-on "survivors."

"Positive thinking seems to be mandatory in the breast cancer world, to the point that unhappiness requires a kind of apology," Ehrenreich wrote in her book *Bright-Sided: How Positive Thinking Is Undermining America*. And yet, countless studies have since shown that positive thinking doesn't yield better outcomes for breast cancer patients. University of Pennsylvania professor James Coyne studied roughly 1,100 cancer patients and found no evidence that bright-sided thinking led to changes in survival rates. In one pivotal study, published in 2010, Coyne concluded that positive psychology in cancer care perpetuates "a storyline resistant to evidence." For my family, it perpetuated the notion that our thoughts were somehow stronger than a deadly disease.

Also prevalent in the 1990s was the view of grief as a linear, sequential process—an idea that Sigmund Freud first popularized in his paper *Mourning and Melancholia*. In Freud's view, grieving was to be done internally, without help from others. To successfully mourn, he said, one must relinquish all psychic and emotional ties to the deceased. By severing these bonds, people could have the capacity to reinvest energy in new relationships and move past grief. Freud's paper was published in 1917, in the midst of World War I and one year before the start of the Spanish flu—two major events when the speed at which people were dying made it difficult to keep up with the lengthy, public mourning rituals that were commonplace at the time.

Freud's work set the foundation for our collective understanding of grief in the twentieth century, when the dominant theory was that maintaining bonds with a loved one was pathological. Freud's linear views on grief inspired many other leaders in the field, including psychiatrist Elisabeth Kübler-Ross, whose work resulted in the Five Stages of Grief: denial, anger, bargaining, depression, and acceptance. Kübler-Ross first articulated these stages in her groundbreaking 1969 book, *On Death and Dying*. She had developed the stages for people who were terminally ill, as a way of helping them cope with impending death. But by the 1980s, the stages had morphed into a go-to model for how to grieve in the United States. These stages gave people mile markers for dealing with grief. They also grossly oversimplified the grieving process and furthered the idea that it was something to be quickly overcome in a linear fashion.

Over the past twenty years, grief theory has shifted toward a greater emphasis on "continuing bonds." A trio of grief experts—psychologists Phyllis Silverman and Dennis Klass, and psychiatrist Steven Nickman—introduced the theory in 1996, just one year before my mother died. In their book *Continuing Bonds: New Understandings of Grief*, they and other colleagues argued that it's healthier to maintain ongoing bonds with deceased loved ones than to detach ourselves from them. In Klass's words, "a bond is, in common parlance, love." Keeping these bonds alive, then, is a way to preserve our love for people we've lost. This frame would go on to transform the way modern-day practitioners and researchers understand bereavement. If Freud's views on grief were a straight arrow, pointing down a linear path toward a final destination, Klass's were more like a circle that shrinks or grows in size depending on life's ebbs and flows. It may get bigger on certain occasions—when Mother's Day arrives; when we graduate or get married or have kids; when we surpass the age our mother was when she died. And sometimes it may shrink, on days when the load of loss feels lighter. But the circle remains, the loss always lingers.

Loss loomed large one summer afternoon when, in the midst of writing this book, I searched for my old journals. My father had already uncovered twenty-seven of them in previous searches, but I knew there were still three missing from the immediate aftermath of my mother's death. I hunted the attic of my childhood home, opening up boxes that revealed the bric-a-brac of childhood: my collections of Trolls, costume jewelry, and *Baby-Sitters Club* books. Then, buried in the bottom of a tattered box with my father's collectible Matchbox cars and old tax filings, I found the long-lost journals. I cradled them in my hands, feeling like I had just unearthed the keys I needed to unlock a part of my past. I knew they would contain details—not only about what I was doing and thinking in the days following Mom's death but also about how desperate I was to stay connected to her.

The first journal I opened had a picture of Claude Monet's *The Artist's Garden at Giverny* on the cover. One of my sixth-grade teachers had given me the journal a few days after my mother died and suggested I use it to record memories of her. I remember staring at the journal's cover and wishing I could slip into that garden; I wanted to smell the powdery scent of irises, to feel the sun's dappled light on my skin, to be somewhere far away. Instead, I had tried escaping into the journal's pages.

As I made my way through decades-old entries, I noticed all of them began with "Dear Mommy." I read about what I was eating for dinner ("I'm going to have a grilled cheese and tomato sandwich—our favorite!"); about how well I had done in school ("Mommy, I got an A+ on my social studies test today!"); and about the cards I made for my mother and left by her gravestone ("The Valentine's Day card isn't there anymore, but I think you took it up to Heaven with you so that it would not get ruined by the rain. Feel free to do that with any of the cards that I make for you."). I'm sure at the time it was more comforting to pretend Mom had kept the card than to consider the possibility that the wind had whisked it away.

I read on, noticing that in some of the entries, I had written Mom's responses in different handwriting.

"Mommy, it was so nice visiting you at the cemetery today. Tell me, do you like your gravestone?

"Yes, very much."

"Good, I'm glad."

"And that card you made me was beautiful!"

"Oh, thank you, Mommy! It was for a beautiful person—you. I never really told you this straight out, but I always thought you were so beautiful, on the inside and out, but especially on the inside."

Reading this, I couldn't help but think back to the moment when my mother had asked me, topless in front of the mirror, if she was beautiful. I scanned the pages for more blue ink and stumbled upon another entry, written three weeks after my mother died.

"Mommy, I miss you Mommy. You gave me everything that I have. Not a minute goes by when I do not think about you. No one understands. No one, no one at all. You (or I) often wonder how other beings can be so happy and excited when you're so very sad. You often wonder. . . . Well, enough crying for the night, right Mom? I'm sorry, I just can't stop crying."

"That's alright, get it all out of your system. Get it all out."

"Alright."

"CHEER UP, HONEY."

I had used the first person in nearly all my entries in that journal. But in this one, where I admitted to crying, I couldn't commit to it. It seemed easier for my younger self to hide behind the second person—the unidentifiable "you"—than to claim ownership of feelings I didn't think I was supposed to have. In the margin of that entry was an apology, written in near-perfect cursive: ("I'm sorry, Mommy. Please excuse my messy handwriting here; I was crying when I wrote this.").

I was so struck by the journal entries that a few weeks later I reached out to grief expert Hope Edelman to help me parse what I might have been experiencing. Edelman has written several books on mother loss, including *Motherless Daughters*—a book I've referred to often throughout the years.

Was it worrisome, I asked her, that I tried so hard to interact with my mother and pretend she was still alive? "I think it becomes detrimental if the child is refusing to acknowledge that the mother isn't going to come back to the physical world and keeps waiting for her and insisting that she's somewhere else. Under those circumstances, she becomes detached from reality," Edelman told me. "But the way that you described it, I saw it more as an incredibly resourceful child looking for a way to stay connected to her mom." The journal entries, she said, were likely my way of expressing a continuing bond.

In my mind, I had pathologized the entries and viewed them as proof of suppressed grief. And maybe, to an extent, they were. But it had never occurred to me that I was being resourceful as a child. I suddenly felt more empathy toward young Mallary, who was doing a good job with the tools that she had. I wished I could go back in time and let her know she didn't have to put up a brave, flawless front—that it was okay to be sad in front of people and not just on the page.

I told Edelman about the apologies and perfect penmanship I found in the journals. I had always been perfectionistic—about my grades, about my household chores—but "it seems like I became even more perfectionistic after my mother died," I said. Edelman nodded in recognition. "Perfectionism is a way to get external validation because inevitably when a mom dies, it impinges on our feelings of self-worth, our ability to be loved, and our self-esteem," she said. "What happens is that your sense of self-worth can shift from being intrinsic—which ideally is coming from having both parents who love you unconditionally—to extrinsic, which means it's from getting adoration and accolades from other people on the outside." Young motherless daughters, she said, may start pouring all their energy into perfecting their achievement in school—or, as the case became for me—their physical appearance.

The repercussions of loss can be especially challenging for children between the ages of seven and eleven, according to bereavement experts. Children's intellects are developing rapidly during this time, but their emotions aren't maturing at the same rate. Kids in that age bracket have developed an abstract understanding of what death means, and they are old enough to realize that their deceased parent isn't coming back. But they are often too young to know how to handle their feelings and may end up suppressing them as a result. Growing up without a mother feels mysterious and impossible, and children whose grief isn't supported can get "stuck" in childhood. Edelman told me this is particularly true for only children like me, who can't keep memories alive with the help of similar-aged siblings. As an eleven-year-old motherless daughter, I was emotionally mature enough to know that when I put on a happy face, it garnered praise and attention. As the months passed after my mother's death, I mastered the art of wearing that mask—so much so that people couldn't even tell I was wearing one.

Now, as a mother myself, I can see why it's easier for people to praise a child who seems to be dealing well with death than to console one who's actively grieving it. There's a prevailing misconception that children are naturally resilient and can bounce back quickly from adversity. But resilience isn't something we're born with; it's something we learn through enduring, rather than dismissing, hardships. Research shows that the more composed an adolescent appears in the aftermath of death, the greater her risk of experiencing unresolved grief—which can lead to physical illness, depression, and alcohol and drug abuse. "Adolescence is a time of anxiety and exploration anyway, but for the motherless daughter who needs to feel in command of her body or environment, addictive or self-destructive behavior is a common manifestation of suppressed grief," Edelman writes. "Bereaved children often internalize their feelings, but adolescents have more resources for acting out."

My acting-out behaviors would unfold quietly and covertly over time, in ways that were easy for me to disguise and difficult for others to detect.

Chapter Two

The Spiral

Six weeks after Mom died, my dad bought me a subscription to *Seventeen* magazine, hoping it might teach me how to navigate puberty. I sat outside on the stone wall that lined our driveway and flipped through the glossy pages, feeling grown-up as an eleven-year-old with a magazine that I thought was off-limits until you were exactly seventeen. I skimmed the cover stories and ads featuring slender girls with layers of makeup and voluminous hair. They were skinnier than my mom, who fluctuated between size six and eight when she was healthy. With her gone, my vision of what it meant to be beautiful grew blurrier, so I searched for clarity in *Seventeen*.

The April 1997 issue featured cover stories on "Kissing: The Good, the Bad, and the Scary"; "5 Major Makeovers"; "Girls Who Exercise Themselves to Death." The latter story introduced me to a slew of new words: *binging*, *bulimic*, *anorexic*. It featured three girls who were "destroying their lives" by starving themselves and exercising compulsively. It detailed how much they weighed, how many sit-ups they did per day, and how many calories they consumed. "Every day was a challenge—to try to exercise a little more, eat a little less, be maybe half a pound lighter than the day before," one of the girls said. I had no desire to be lighter, and I assumed weight loss was an issue for adults, not kids. I thought about my mother when she was unable to eat and thinner than ever during her final days. "She is a bag of bones," I had declared in one of my journal entries.

Sandwiched between the story and the page break were a slew of diet ads featuring "fat camps" for girls as young as seven, promising they could "lose weight and have fun too!" One of them, advertising a camp for children ages eight and up, promised: "Lose as much as forty pounds and learn to keep it off. This summer, you can become the person you always wanted to be." I read *Seventeen* each month, curious and confused about what the stories and ads suggested—the way they focused on how the body could be changed and controlled. Don't like the way your face looks? Get a makeover. Have frizzy hair? Here's what to do about it. Don't like your waistline? Start exercising (but not *too* much). I took the quizzes ("Do guys rule your life?" "Are you overreacting?" "How romantic is he?"), even though my answers to these questions were always a definitive no or "I have no clue." The how-to stories offered up little guidance, but they made me realize the body could be a problem that girls needed to overcome. In reading stories like "How to Stop Obsessing Over Your Body and Start Feeling Good," I learned that the quest for a perfect body could become a fixation.

Just a few months later, the school nurse weighed me and my classmates in front of one another—a practice that wasn't unheard of in the 1990s, when obesity rates among children were rising. She called us up to that scale one by one, told us our weight, and recorded it on a chart, as if the numbers were grades—but the highest ones were the worst. At least that's how I interpreted it, and as always, I wanted to ace the test. When my name was called, I stood on that little square of terror, feeling like a mannequin on display. I can't recall the number that appeared on the scale that day, but I remember feeling that it wasn't good enough.

Around that same time, I started learning about eating disorders in my seventh-grade health class. Our teacher gave us brief descriptions of anorexia and bulimia, and she explained that they could be dangerous. In an unfortunately timed sequence, the teacher began offering up lessons about "good" and "bad" foods. We learned that we could be "healthy" by eating a lot of fruits and veggies. And we were told to avoid eating too much "junk food"—pizza, hamburgers, ice cream—because such foods could make us "unhealthy." The teacher introduced us to the food pyramid and instructed us to limit our intake of carbs (from the bottom of the pyramid), red meat (from the middle), and fats (from the top). I came away feeling as though very few food groups in the pyramid were permissible. The food pyramid and Nutrition Facts labels had been introduced in the United States just a few years prior, and food packaging had begun carrying a slew of additional labels, including "healthy," "reduced fat," and "fat-free." It became easy for people to demonize food as "unhealthy" based on calorie and fat content alone.

Having watched my mother struggle with sickness for so long, I was afraid of doing anything that was deemed unhealthy. I kept thinking of my mother's warnings: *Don't stand in front of the microwave. Don't microwave anything in plastic containers. Don't ever buy a house under high-tension wires. Don't ever smoke.* . . . I wondered if I needed to add another rule: *Don't eat unhealthy foods.* And as a straight-A student, I thought I needed to follow my teacher's directives.

The health teacher was just one of the many middle school teachers who showed up for me after my mother passed. A lover of theater and music, she took me to see *The Nutcracker* ballet and the Boston Symphony Orchestra. Mrs. Fallon, the sixth-grade teacher who couldn't believe I had gone to school the day after my mother died, shared recipes with me. She had guessed my father might need some ideas about what to cook, and she was right. My math teacher took me mountain-bike riding, and my science teacher took me out for after-school treats. During one of those outings, the science teacher bought me a chocolate cupcake.

I ate it but told her the health teacher would be disappointed in me. I never wanted to let down any of the adults in my life, and in the absence of a mother, I aimed to please them even more.

A few days after getting weighed in health class, I told my father we shouldn't eat burgers anymore because they were loaded with *fat* and *calories* and *cholesterol*. These words were new to my vocabulary, and although I had been learning about them in health class, I still didn't know exactly what they meant. "We can't eat hamburgers, and we need to start eating vegetables with every dinner," I insisted. Dad said eating more veggies seemed like a good idea, but he stayed silent about the burgers.

"Dad, you really need to eat more fruit," I nagged.

"But I drink grape juice every day!" he'd say, half-jokingly.

"Dad, it's not the same; you should know that!"

When one chide didn't seem to work, I would try another.

"Dad, you should stop eating red meat. It's bad for you."

"Dad, when I say we should eat more veggies, I mean *real* veggies. Corn is an unhealthy grain."

"Dad, you should probably cut out your nighttime snack. It's not good to eat food right before bed. It can make you gain weight."

I wanted my dad to do whatever it took to stay healthy and live long. For weeks I tried teaching him how to "eat right," but I soon realized that I couldn't control his food intake. He started cooking a few more vegetables—canned peas and carrots, mostly—but he kept drinking grape juice and eating the occasional hamburger. Many nights, he ate store-brand sugar cookies with a side of Lipton's tea. I snacked alongside him with a growing side of guilt. I started critiquing my body after every nighttime snack, then after every meal. I would look in the mirror and stare at my prepubescent breasts. They looked like little balls of fat, and I didn't want them to get any bigger, afraid of the cancer they might someday contain. I eyed my collarbone, which had always stuck out a little, and began to think the protrusion must be good. I studied my calves, which looked flabby when I sat cross-legged, and wondered if that was okay. I ran my hands along my hips and stomach, contours that could be controlled.

What would happen, I started wondering, *if I cut out bad foods? Maybe that flabbiness would go away. Maybe the round parts would flatten out.* I studied the food pyramid and memorized its parts, fixating on the top: "Fats, oils, sweets. EAT SPARINGLY." The all-caps felt like a warning: If you teeter at the top of that pyramid for too long you may lose your balance and fall right off, proving you never should have been there in the first place.

I started to limit foods from that top group. Instead of a whole bowl of ice cream with toppings, I would eat a small ramekin of it with no toppings. Instead of two cookies, I'd eat one. I worked my way down the pyramid and lowered my meat intake. My family had never been big meat eaters; their idea of a good piece of meat was a well-done steak with ketchup or a dry pork chop slathered with applesauce. I moved further down the pyramid, eating smaller portions here, cutting out foods altogether there. What started as a way to "eat healthy" regressed into restriction within a matter of months. The more I restricted, the more I began to focus on the Nutrition Facts labels, studying the calories and grams of fat in each food as though I were going to get quizzed on them. I started keeping track of the counts at each meal and set goals to lower the amounts each day. I found that calorie counting gave me some semblance of control in the aftermath of my mother's death; I couldn't control what happened to her body, but I could regulate what I put in mine.

I knew that eating fewer calories could make a body smaller, and I could tell my clothes were getting baggier. I liked the idea of staying small; it made me think about staying the same size I was when Mom was still alive. Maybe if I stayed small, I could feel closer to her. Maybe I could remain her little girl. Mom had died less than a year prior, but my former life felt eons distant. The hands on the clock were spinning too fast, and I wanted to handcuff them. I found myself longing for a past that promised preservation of memory, of time, of a mother's love. If growing up meant being without my mother, then I wanted to stay little forever.

My father wasn't sure what to make of my new eating habits. Hoping to spark a change, he tried enticing me with foods he knew I liked.

"Want to go to Burger King?"

"Nah, that's okay," I lied, uncharacteristically.

"Want to go to Papa Gino's tonight? I know how much you like their pizza!"

"I just had pizza for lunch at school today, so I don't really want any tonight. But maybe another day. . . ." I secretly wanted these foods but told myself I didn't need them.

Confused by it all, Dad hoped that whatever I was going through would soon pass. Later he told me he wished he could have turned to my mother and asked her what to do. Her absence felt like a deep hole he had to step into and climb out of every day, without ever getting trapped inside. There was no time for entrapment; he had a demanding job, a household to manage, a daughter to raise. And eventually, he would have a new love life.

About a year after my mom's death, and four months into my food restriction, Dad started dating a woman named Katie. He told me he wanted to "find love again" and was "trying to fill the void" so he could cover up that big hole. The clichés of life after loss had become a reality for my father and a maddening realization for me: He was "moving on," and I was stuck. Wasn't my mother's love enough for him? Wasn't I enough?

My father and I started arguing more, mostly at the dinner table. We fought about Katie and food, and the more we did, the less I wanted to eat. I would stare at my food and push it into piles on my plate, trying to make it seem like I'd eaten more than I had.

"You need to eat more, Mal," my dad would insist.

I would take a few baby bites, then declare I wasn't hungry.

"But you barely ate anything!"

"I had a big lunch at school today. I'm not hungry!"

Dad got the sense that I was lying. It didn't make any sense, though. Why did his daughter, who used to devour ice cream sundaes and pizza and Whoppers, no longer want to eat?

I was still figuring it out, too, unsure of what was happening to me. I just knew I felt a little thrill every time I cut out another food. I became mesmerized by my ability to easily do something that other people found so hard. "I'm on a diet," I had heard people say in passing. "I'm so fat; I need to start watching what I eat." These comments are like the soundtrack of life, ones you inevitably hear as you flip through the channels of each day. Sometimes you stop on the channel and listen for more, but even if you don't, the damage has already been done. The comments start taking hold, tricking you into believing that *you* need to go on a diet, too. When I restricted my food intake, it felt like I was creating my own channel, amplifying a defiant voice I never knew I had.

"I'll start eating normal again if you stop dating Katie," I told my father one night, not long after they had started seeing each other. "But if you keep dating her, I'll stop eating." I felt proud of this ultimatum and naively believed I had found a solution for breaking them apart. My father told me I was being irrational; he wasn't going to press Pause on his love life just because I had demanded it. He understood this was hard for me and said he didn't want to hurt me. But he kept on dating Katie. As a thirteen-year-old, I couldn't shake the thought that he was choosing her over me.

I started restricting more, eliminating all foods except ones I deemed "safe": cottage cheese, bananas, Lender's bagel halves, and fat-free SnackWell's cookies. Starvation numbed me, allowing me to escape the pain of my mother's death instead of having to endure it. I mourned the loss of food but celebrated the loss of weight. I found a scale in my parents' bedroom closet and weighed myself, happy to be getting smaller but still never satisfied with the number that stared up at me. With every pound I lost, I would gain an ounce of control. *It hurts to be beautiful*, I told myself, repeating a refrain I once heard my mother use when she accidentally burned my scalp with a curling iron.

Soon, food restriction alone wasn't enough. I started looking at my walks to and from school as opportunities to burn calories. I'd walk faster than usual, moving my arms and legs in an exaggerated motion, mimicking the way my mother used to powerwalk. I'd hold my *Baby-Sitters Club* book in one hand and wildly swing the other, then switch hands so that I could exercise each arm equally. The exercise-obsessed girls from that *Seventeen* magazine article suddenly seemed more relatable. Before long, I discovered a new form of exercise: jumping. I moved about my day as though I had an imaginary jump rope tied to my body. I would get up in the middle of meals and jump, lowering myself to the ground, touching my knees to my chin, and launching into the air as high as my little body would take me. I meticulously practiced and perfected my form, always in competition with myself. The higher the jump, I told myself, the more calories burned. If my heels didn't touch my butt, the jump didn't count.

I was soon jumping at every chance I got—in the school hallways, in grocery stores, down the aisle to the Catholic church altar where I received weekly Communion. One Sunday, convinced that the Communion wafer had calories, I was too afraid to swallow it. Jumping back to my pew, I kneeled and held it in my hands, which were folded in prayer. My paternal grandma, whom I affectionally referred to as Gramz, was kneeling beside me. When she glanced down and saw the wafer, her eyes widened with admonishment. "Give me that!" she loudly whispered, knowing exactly why I was holding it. She shoved it inside her mouth in disbelief.

People gawked at me as I jumped, but no one could really stop me, and few ever said anything about it. One exception was a middle-aged man at the grocery store one day. He saw me jumping down the bread aisle, and instead of simply staring like everyone else, he spoke up.

"She's quite the jumper!" he told Gramz. "Looks like you've got a bunny on your hands!"

Gramz and I laughed a little in response, as though we both were in need of comic relief.

"I sure do," she replied. "I sure do . . ."

Gramz turned her gaze toward me, looking helpless. I stopped jumping and hugged her. I felt her arms tighten around me and wished I could stay in them forever.

At home, alone after school, my jumping worsened. I would put my backpack down inside the front door, jump all the way to my parents' bedroom, and stare at myself in my mother's oval mirror. Mirrors had become a cruel optical illusion, and the skinnier I got, the fatter I felt. At 3:30 p.m., I would stand next to the green-quilted couch in the living room and jump to the entire opening song of *Arthur*: "And I said hey! What a wonderful kind of day! If we could learn to laugh and play. . . ." I jumped to the beat of the lyrics with increasing force—higher, faster, harder. Every time I landed, the floorboards would creak and the lamp on the glass coffee table would shake, as if motioning me to stop. If those living room walls could talk, they'd whisper condemnations.

Just a year before, I had been jumping on the hot pink Pogo stick my mother bought me. But jumping was no longer child's play; it was an obsession, a warped re-creation of an earlier time. I longed for rest, if only for a moment, but I refused to let my body be still. There was a duality to so much of my life; I was torn between myself and a nameless, intractable force that had taken over my thoughts and actions.

My dad called my school principal to raise concerns about the health class I had taken, saying the "healthy eating" lessons were detrimental. The principal said I had misinterpreted the lessons and that it was my father's responsibility to explain them to me. When he asked the principal if there was anything she could do, she suggested I meet with a guidance counselor once or twice a week. I agreed, but I didn't think I needed any help. "Do you know how embarrassing it is to be called down to the guidance office all the time? I'm sure kids are going to begin to wonder why," I journaled. "Ever since my dad spread the news that I don't eat as much as I used to, all my teachers keep saying 'You've gotten awfully skinny.' Why does everyone keep saying that I've gotten skinner when I haven't? I think I should be the one to know." I was genuinely convinced my body wasn't small enough, and I was baffled that others saw it so differently.

"Step on a scale!" Gramz implored. "Then you'll see the proof: you're losing too much weight." I saw the numbers going down, but that just encouraged me to go further. As I kept my gaze focused on numbers—on scales, on nutrition labels, on the calendars that reminded me how much time had passed since my mother died—I became more and more unrecognizable to my family and friends. I had waded into this existence, dipping one toe at a time into the icy waters. Then I churned faster until I jumped in headlong, numb to the cold.

I jumped through the hallways of eighth grade, drawing stares from classmates and teachers. I joined the cross-country team, hoping running would make me feel closer to my mother, who had signed me up for youth track and field when I was just three years old. She took me to meets every summer after that, and I'd run the 50- and 100-yard dashes, falling into her arms at the finish line, wrapped in the scent of her Halston perfume. But now I was running five miles a day, and what was once a joy turned into a grueling compulsion. Every day, I tried running faster and farther in a body that lacked proper fuel. Exhaustion took up permanent residence in my body and mind, slowing down my ability to function. Some days I would try to eat more and jump less, but the following day I would make up for it by eating less and jumping more. I knew I was robbing myself of needed nutrition, but I was intoxicated at the wheel, plowing through every stop sign in my head. My father pleaded with me, his words like flashing yellow lights warning me to slow down.

"Mallary, can you stop jumping, please? I really need you to stop jumping; it's not good for you."

"I bought you one of those gingerbread cookies you used to like. I thought you might want it? Please try it. You need to eat at least something. Just a few bites. Do it for Dad."

I had trouble eating just a few bites for him, in part because I liked knowing I could control his mood by refusing to eat.

"Why can't you just eat?! You're so smart; why can't you figure this out?" he would lament. My once patient, soft-spoken father yelled—especially during meals. It made me want to eat even less. I felt so misunderstood and so confused: Why couldn't I "just eat?!" A year before, I ate what I wanted, when I wanted, without worrying about calories or weight. Now, every choice about food made me mentally hyperventilate, as though my thoughts could never stop and catch a breath.

My father and I didn't know much about eating disorders. He had heard of anorexia but thought it affected adults, not children. And though I had read about eating disorders in *Seventeen* and learned about them in health class, there was a disconnect between my understanding of the disorder and my lived experience with it. I thought people with anorexia didn't eat anything at all. I was eating a little bit each day and didn't believe I was anywhere near as skinny as the models in *Seventeen. They're anorexic*, I would think, *but not me*.

Much as my father hoped my mother's cancer would disappear, he hoped that whatever I was struggling with would soon fade. My pediatrician, after all, had told us as much. His medical assessment was that my weight loss as a twelve-year-old was a passing phase. But the problem worsened, and we went back to the pediatrician's office a few months later. Even though I had lost more weight, we received the same response. Stunned by the pediatrician's irreverence, my father realized we were at the mercy of a doctor who didn't know what was wrong with me or how to help. My father's efforts to get me medical help proved futile as he watched me—his only child, his precious daughter—slip further away.

No one wakes up one day and decides to develop an eating disorder. These disorders grow out of behaviors that sometimes go unnoticed and, in other cases, get positively reinforced by educators and doctors who are not properly trained to recognize them. Awareness has no doubt improved since I was a child, but eating disorders are still poorly understood in school and medical settings. This lack of understanding has led many people to silently slip into an eating disorder without getting adequate care. Though I tend to think about the middle place in terms of recovery, it's also an apt term for the space between good health and one's descent into an eating disorder. If medical providers, caregivers, and those at risk understood this space better and knew how to detect the warning signs, our collective effort to prevent eating disorders could potentially be much stronger than it is today.

In the United States, efforts to prevent obesity often overshadow the seriousness of eating disorders and can even have the unintended effect of contributing to them. Many school-based initiatives, for instance, tend to center on body mass index, or BMI, which is a deeply flawed measure of body fat that doesn't consider age, muscle mass, gender, race, or ethnicity. A mathematician developed the index about two hundred years ago, based on a sample of white European men, so it does not take into account the different body compositions of women and minorities.

Today, 40 percent of children live in states that require public schools to conduct BMI screenings. The results (or "BMI report cards") are sent to parents. Those screenings, which gather information on an average of 8.3 million children every year, are neither cost-effective nor successful at preventing childhood obesity, according to a 2023 study at Harvard University. The Centers for Disease Control and Prevention (CDC) has also said there's no evidence showing these screenings are effective at reducing or preventing childhood obesity. Indeed, the research suggests that the screenings can actually be harmful. In one study, 30 percent of parents whose children had participated in school-based obesity-prevention programs reported that their children exhibited at least one concerning behavior that could be associated with an eating disorder. And a chart review of young patients treated for anorexia at Boston Children's Hospital from 2015 to 2020 found that healthy-eating education was a trigger for 14 percent of the patients. Early adolescents were especially vulnerable.

The CDC endorses nutrition education as a vital part of health education programs because it "empowers children with knowledge and skills to make healthy food and beverage choices." And some argue that school-based lessons about "healthy eating" are crucial at a time when an estimated one in five U.S. children is obese. But while a good idea in theory, the programs often fall short in practice. Many are rooted in diet culture and anti-fat bias, with an emphasis on "clean eating," food-labeling exercises, and food diaries that require students to track how much they eat and exercise.

"There's even talk in nutrition curricula about teaching kids how to eat for weight maintenance," said Anna Lutz, a North Carolina–based dietitian who specializes in pediatric and family nutrition. "We should never be talking to children about weight maintenance. It makes no sense since children *should be* gaining weight." This issue is exacerbated by the subjectivity that often accompanies nutrition curricula. "It seems to be very common for people to share their own point of view about what children should or shouldn't eat," Lutz said. "It's very much influenced by diet culture and the belief that people in smaller bodies are better than people in larger bodies."

As I spoke with Lutz and others in the field, I realized how little has changed since I was a child, in terms of both health curricula and medical awareness of eating disorders. In 1998, my pediatrician didn't recognize

I needed help, and he didn't seem to know that the young fall prey to eating disorders; although the average age of onset is late teens through mid-twenties, these disorders can emerge in children as young as five or six. My pediatrician passed away before I began working on this book, so I never had the chance to talk with him as an adult. I'd like to think he was doing the best he could with the knowledge he had, but I can't help feeling frustrated by his lack of concern and counsel.

You might assume that the medical community is now more well trained in detecting eating disorders. But in talking with several doctors, I learned that my pediatrician wasn't simply out of touch; he was part of a systemic crisis that remains very much alive. Still today, medical doctors receive little to no training on how to screen for or treat eating disorders. "Your average physician maybe had one to two hours of lecture on eating disorders during their preclinical years out of probably 1,500 hours, if not more," said Brooks Brodrick, MD, an internist and assistant professor of internal medicine and psychiatry at the University of Texas Southwestern Medical School. "The emphasis is more on obesity, overeating, and associated medical conditions, so physicians aren't as aware of the deleterious side effects of malnutrition and underfeeding."

There are also other complicated factors at play. "The traits that predispose someone to an eating disorder (including perfectionism, sensitivity to emotional pain, and intelligence) are also the same ones that tend to facilitate success in certain fields like medicine. As a result, it's difficult for physicians to identify when something has become pathological," said Dr. Brodrick, who is recovered from anorexia nervosa. "And rarely, if ever, do patients come in saying 'I have an eating disorder.' Instead, their complaint is involving either their hair falling out, infertility, orthopedic fractures, gastrointestinal disturbances, or heart-related problems. We aren't trained to ask people about their eating habits when attempting to ascertain the causes of those types of illnesses."

Jason Nagata, MD, who treats eating disorder patients at the University of California San Francisco's Benioff Children's Hospital, agrees that more training is needed. While in medical school, he sat through several lectures on obesity and weight management but not a single one on eating disorders. Dr. Nagata has heard of several stories involving patients whose pediatricians told them they needed to lose weight because of a high BMI, but without providing specific guidance or follow-up. It's not uncommon, he said, for this type of scenario to result in an eating disorder. "The child then goes back for their annual physical and, lo and behold, they've lost fifty to one hundred pounds and they're now medically unstable," Dr. Nagata told me. "That's a pretty common presentation of an eating disorder, where weight loss was taken to the extreme and was actually endorsed by a medical provider or a parent or a coach or a teacher."

It makes sense that physicians like Dr. Nagata would be taught to treat obesity, given that an estimated 42 percent of adults and 20 percent of children are considered obese. But that shouldn't preclude the study or treatment of eating disorders, which are among the deadliest mental health disorders and have been on the rise. According to one report, eating disorder–related health visits among people of all ages increased by 41 percent from 2019 to 2022—a time period that coincided with the Covid-19 pandemic. Among people below age eighteen, the increase was 93 percent. An estimated 9 percent of Americans (roughly 30 million people) will suffer from an eating disorder at some point in their lifetime. And every year, 10,200 deaths are associated with eating disorders in the U.S., with suicide being among the leading causes.

But still, eating disorders get overlooked. Some argue that this is because they are considered to be "specialty disorders" that are "rare" and "niche," despite their prevalence. In a recent editorial, a group of prominent eating-disorder researchers drew attention to this issue, saying that general high-impact journals often reject eating-disorder research and recommend that it be placed in specialty journals instead. "The less eating disorders are discussed in psychiatric training, journals, and conferences, the less exposure professionals receive [on] this topic, which decreases the number of researchers and clinicians knowledgeable about eating disorders," the editorial's authors wrote. In 2021, for instance, eating-disorder samples accounted for fewer than 2 percent of articles in the high-impact *Journal of the American Medical Association Psychiatry*. Eating-disorder research is compelling, but it's not getting the attention or funding it needs.

Similarly, research dollars and illness severity do not align. Funding is notoriously low, even though anorexia is the second-deadliest mental health illness, just behind opioid-use disorder. By most recent estimates, the National Institutes of Health's funding for eating disorders amounted to around $55 million annually. Funding has gone up slightly in recent years; in 2019, the estimated amount was just shy of $50 million annually, or about $9 per person with an eating disorder. That was compared to $239 per person for Alzheimer's disease, $109 for autism, and $69 for schizophrenia. While most eating-disorder funding has come from the National Institutes of Health, new funding sources have emerged in recent years. In 2017, for instance, Congress made research on eating disorders eligible for funding within the Department of Defense's Peer Reviewed Medical Research Program. More recently in 2022, the U.S. Health and Human Services Office on Women's Health funded eating-disorder research for the first time—largely in response to the rise in cases during the Covid-19 pandemic.

"This is all money that would not have been there and wasn't there until the eating disorders community started working together and being really savvy about how to get funding," said S. Bryn Austin, ScD, a social epidemiologist and behavioral scientist who teaches at Harvard Medical School. Dr. Austin founded and runs the Strategic Training Initiative for the Prevention of Eating Disorders (STRIPED)—a program based at Harvard University's T.H. Chan School of Public Health and Boston Children's Hospital. "We have a real pipeline problem," Dr. Austin told me. "The training isn't happening, the research isn't happening because the training's not there, and public health professionals aren't putting eating disorders on the public health agenda because they don't know enough about them."

Under Dr. Austin's leadership, STRIPED created online training aimed at helping pediatric primary care providers screen for eating disorders, recognize symptoms, and learn where to look for referrals. The training is part of the American Medical Association's online education portal, and it is one of the few eating-disorder courses available there. "It's a drop in the bucket compared to what's needed in medical schools, but getting into the medical school curriculum is tough," Dr. Austin said. Continuing education is an easier entry point, even though there's no guarantee that doctors will take, or even come across, eating-disorder–specific trainings.

Only about 30 percent of people with eating disorders seek help from healthcare professionals, and men and minorities are even less likely to do so. It's all the more critical, then, for doctors to implement screening tools and to understand that eating disorders aren't lifestyle choices; they are complicated illnesses that stem from a mix of physiological, genetic, environmental, and neurobiological factors. Dr. Jennifer Gaudiani, a Colorado-based internist specializing in eating disorders, said more doctors need to understand that eating-disorder signs and symptoms can show up among people of all races, genders, ages, and body sizes. "In the medical profession, there's a deep-seated size bias that harms patients of every possible size," Dr. Gaudiani told me. "Medical schools must radically revise centuries-long beliefs about body weight and health. Because even if individuals haven't learned about how to care for those with eating disorders, if they could get rid of their own internalized weight stigma and not have that further baked in as the medical training system currently does, at least they would do less harm to patients. But we're only in the early stages of weight-inclusive, non-stigmatizing care being presented in medical school."

Of the roughly 700 people whom I surveyed for this book, 51 percent said they've faced weight discrimination while receiving eating-disorder treatment and/or medical care. Some described instances in which their doctors didn't think they were suffering from an eating disorder because of their body size. Others said they were denied inpatient treatment because their BMI was considered too high for an eating disorder. These are the types of injustices that can lead people to remain undiagnosed and without adequate care. This is especially true when it comes to lesser-known but increasingly common eating disorders, such as avoidant/restrictive food intake disorder (ARFID) and atypical anorexia.

People with ARFID limit their food intake—not so much because of shape or weight concerns but because of a lack of interest in eating; a sensory aversion to the taste, texture, or smell of food; or fears about possible consequences of eating (such as choking or vomiting). Thirty-year-old Stephanie, who has had ARFID since she was a child, told me: "Food kind of disgusts me, which is horrible because I have to eat it three times a day. I don't like sitting at a table to eat. I don't want other people watching me eat because I feel like they're judging me. And I don't like touching food; it just freaks me out. I work in healthcare, and I would rather deal with somebody's bowel movement than deal with their discarded lunch."

ARFID often leads to nutritional deficiencies and weight loss, as well as psychological and social disturbances. But because it's a lesser-known disorder, those afflicted with it can often feel like they're navigating a lonely terrain. Stephanie said the limited ARFID resources she's come across have mostly focused on children, rather than adults. For a brief period, she tried opening up to others about her experiences, but doing so ultimately felt invalidating. No one seemed to understand the disorder, she said, and people assumed she was just a picky eater. In her hometown of Norfolk, England, Stephanie has yet to encounter a medical provider who has heard of ARFID. "This disorder is debilitating; it has controlled my entire life. But because I'm not massively skinny or massively overweight, people don't take it seriously," said Stephanie. She has wondered, "*Should I make myself super skinny so I can get better treatment? Should I make myself more unhealthy so that people will take me seriously and listen to what I've got to say?*"

These questions are heartbreaking, and I've heard variations of them many times from people who don't fit the stereotypical mold of someone with an eating disorder. This has been especially true with regard to atypical anorexia. The term was introduced in 2013, when the American Psychiatric Association's *Diagnostic and Statistical Manual of Mental Disorders* (*DSM-5*) added the diagnosis after healthcare providers noticed an increase in the number of patients who meet all the diagnostic criteria for anorexia nervosa except that their weight is above or within the normal range despite "significant weight loss." The *DSM-5* categorizes atypical anorexia as an "other specified feeding and eating disorder" (OSFED)—a diagnosis given to people who have symptoms similar to one or more eating disorders but who don't meet all the diagnostic criteria for them. The "atypical anorexia" descriptor has come under scrutiny among eating-disorder specialists, who are finding that many people with anorexia are not clinically underweight. This is true across eating disorders; one study surveyed over 3,000 adolescents with eating disorders and found that only 6 percent of them were underweight. Given such statistics, some argue that the "atypical" descriptor might be better suited for people who are underweight instead of those who aren't.

The same year that the *DSM-5* added "atypical anorexia," it also updated its entry for "anorexia nervosa." For years, it had listed menstruation (specifically, "three or more missed periods") as the diagnostic criterion. Thanks to pushback from eating-disorder clinicians, the *DSM-5* removed the specific criterion concerning menstruation, with the understanding that not everyone with anorexia loses their period or is female. Up to 25 percent of people with anorexia or bulimia are men, and 36 percent of people with binge-eating disorder are men, according to research. The LGBTQ+ population is at increased risk, with multiple studies showing that adolescent and adult gay males are more likely to have eating disorders or report disordered eating behaviors compared to heterosexual males.

In my survey, about 13 percent of respondents said they had experienced gender discrimination when receiving eating-disorder treatment and/or medical care. Among them is Henry, who struggled with atypical anorexia as a teenager and continues to grapple with its imprints in his early twenties. He has lived in a larger body for his entire life and was bullied for it as a child. His mother critiqued his size and pushed him to lose weight, enrolling him in Weight Watchers when he was eleven. Henry followed the program, hoping to please. "I thought, *This is what my mom wants me to do. She's a nurse; she knows what's best for me*," said Henry, who grew up as a competitive dancer. "There was never a moment in my life when my parents were not trying some new diet; they did keto, they did Atkins; there were diet books everywhere in our house." Shortly after starting on Weight Watchers, Henry fell into a pattern of unhealthy food restriction that lasted throughout high school. He lost a substantial amount of weight but never became thin. At times he worried he might be struggling with an eating disorder, but he always convinced himself otherwise, believing he was neither sick nor skinny enough to have one.

During his freshman year of college, Henry's behaviors felt so out of control that he sought medical help, only to find that no one believed him. "I saw a psychiatrist, and the first thing he said was, 'You can't be anorexic because you're not emaciated. You must be binging.' He thought I was lying," Henry told me. "I wasn't really surprised when he said all that because I kind of expected it, and I just used it as fuel for the fire." Henry ended up restricting his food intake more drastically in hopes of losing even more weight and proving he needed care. He said he passed out on several occasions and experienced heart-related issues. This is not uncommon; studies also show that people with atypical anorexia who have lost a significant amount of weight but don't ever become underweight seem to be just as ill as those who lose enough to have a low BMI.

Nine months after Henry's meeting with the psychiatrist, his doctor referred him to an inpatient program, where a provider listened to him describe his behaviors, admitted him, and diagnosed him with atypical anorexia. "To hear a provider say, 'All these people treated you poorly, and you've been neglected by the medical system'—it was sickeningly relieving," Henry said. "I remember thinking, *Finally, somebody believes me*. But I felt sick to my stomach knowing I had been treated so poorly."

Henry is now in recovery and, like me, finds himself in the middle place—that space between acute sickness and full recovery. The term "full recovery" has never resonated with him because it seems too perfectionistic. "A lot of us got into this mess in the first place by striving for perfection, so I think striving for anything other than the middle space would be damaging for me," Henry said. "For me, being in the middle ground means being healthy but informed. I know that I'm never going to have a perfectly healthy relationship with food, but I'm going to do the best I can to keep myself fueled while being aware that I am at risk."

Henry is one of the many people I've interviewed whose stories defy stereotypes about eating disorders. There's a prevailing misconception that anorexia is a "wealthy disease," affecting upper-middle-class white women who can afford treatment. The wealthy-woman stereotype harkens back to the 1880s, when gastroenterologist Samuel Fenwick, MD, described anorexia as "much more common in the wealthier class of society than amongst those who have to procure their bread by daily labor." A century later, psychiatrist Hilde Bruch, MD, referred to anorexia as a disorder that "selectively befalls the young, rich, and beautiful."

But research shows there's no evidence for a relationship between eating disorders and socioeconomic status. A recent study on the topic found that eating disorders present across a range of incomes, and it stressed that there's an "urgent need to prioritize accessible eating disorder treatment."

Another misconception is that eating disorders (and anorexia in particular) only affect "skinny, white, affluent girls" (sometimes referred to as "the SWAG stereotype"). A growing body of research is challenging this long-held stereotype, though. Studies have found that doctors are significantly less likely to ask Black, Indigenous, and People of Color (BIPOC) and transgender people about eating-disorder symptoms, despite statistics showing eating-disorder prevalence in these populations. Black girls are 50 percent more likely than white girls to exhibit bulimic behaviors, and Asian American college students report much higher incidences of restricting and purging compared to their white peers. Transgender college students, meanwhile, are four times more likely to report disordered eating habits compared to cisgender students.

Biases in our healthcare system undoubtedly make it harder for people in marginalized populations to receive treatment, let alone treatment that acknowledges how eating disorders may play out differently across cultures. I spoke about this with Rachel Goode, PhD, who is founding director of the University of North Carolina's (UNC) Living F.R.E.E. Lab, which develops equitable interventions for people of color struggling with disordered eating. "If we're being honest, the eating-disorder screening tools were formed with white populations, so that means we may miss folks because we don't know how eating disorders show up across different races," she told me. "So many people of color have these experiences of invisibility where they are used to not being seen." Dr. Goode, who researches binge-eating disorder among Black Americans, noted that people of color often experience different pathways to sickness. For many Black Americans, she said, eating disorders develop not so much due to weight or shape concerns but as a means of coping with stress, trauma, racism, and/or oppression.

Dr. Goode's colleague, Mae Lynn Reyes-Rodriguez, PhD, told me more research and screening tools need to be developed with minorities in mind so that eating-disorder care won't be one-size-fits-all. "The main limitation in the field is that we are assuming so much," said Dr. Reyes-Rodriguez, a clinical professor in UNC's psychiatry department who works closely with Latino populations. "We need to start conducting more research with diverse populations so that we can have a better understanding of the manifestation of symptoms and treatment responses in diverse populations. Otherwise, we will do the same thing over and over again and won't see any progress in the field."

The myriad cultural misconceptions can lead to confusion and isolation for patients. This was the case for survey respondent Elizabeth, who developed anorexia nervosa in her late teens, after her parents separated.

Even though her menstrual period stopped, and she felt physically weak from restricting her food intake, Elizabeth didn't think she had anorexia. Her parents, who were both from Guatemala, didn't either. Growing up in Minnesota, Elizabeth had only ever heard of white women with eating disorders. She knew that the singer Karen Carpenter died from complications due to anorexia a decade earlier. And in a middle-school health class, she had watched a Lifetime drama, *For the Love of Nancy*, about a young woman struggling with anorexia. The 1994 film portrayed Nancy as a thin, white teenager from a middle- to upper-class family that could afford inpatient treatment. (Interestingly, the actress who played Nancy—Tracey Gold—also struggled with anorexia in real life.)

As a Latina teenager growing up in a lower-middle-class family, Elizabeth couldn't relate to Carpenter or Gold. "I thought to myself, *I don't identify with either of those women; they don't look like me at all*," Elizabeth told me. "I didn't think what I was dealing with could potentially be what they had experienced. I knew something was going on, but I had no idea how to really express that I needed help." She continued restricting, and she experienced dizziness and chest pains. She credits her primary care physician with recognizing she needed help and diagnosing her with anorexia. He admitted her to the hospital on two separate occasions due to low potassium levels and unstable vital signs. After her second hospitalization, Elizabeth began working toward recovery in an outpatient setting. As she looked for a therapist and a dietitian, she found that providers were mostly white and sometimes culturally insensitive.

A new generation of dietitians has become increasingly aware of this issue and has started speaking out about the lack of diversity in the field. They're calling for greater inclusion of different cultures, body types, and dietary preferences; heightened awareness of foods that people do or do not have access to; and support rather than stigmatization of cultural food preferences. But there's still a long way to go. On one occasion, Elizabeth's dietitian recommended that she eat "healthy foods" like kale, without recommending any foods that were part of her culture or that would help her gain weight. Her mother bought kale for Elizabeth, but she wasn't sure how to cook the leafy green. It usually ended up as an unappetizing side dish. Over time, Elizabeth began cooking authentic Guatemalan dishes with her mother and relearning how to feel comfortable preparing them. Enchiladas, *frijoles volteados* (refried black beans), and *ponche de frutas* (fruit punch) were among her favorites. They tasted like home.

Elizabeth eventually got better and now works as a peer mentor for Equip, a virtual eating-disorder treatment program. Every patient who goes through the program is assigned a peer mentor—someone who has recovered from an eating disorder and can provide support and firsthand insights. "When it comes to patients whose culture and background may typically be underserved or overlooked, I'm on the lookout for moments of resistance," Elizabeth said. "If I suggest having an open conversation with a parent, and the patient says that their parent believes they are always right as the head of the family and won't listen, then it wouldn't make sense to say, 'Try it anyway!' So, then we would collaborate to see what might be helpful. It's about being in session and listening to the patient, rather than coming in with the solutions."

Elizabeth, who is thirty-three, now considers herself to be fully recovered. "I am recovered, yes, but with awareness that I need to be active in my recovery so that I don't slip back into old behaviors," she said. "To me, full recovery means living my values, realizing it's okay to be my authentic self, and to treat myself as worthy, no matter what."

Full recovery and early detection are no doubt linked, with research showing that treatment is more likely to be successful the earlier an eating disorder is diagnosed. The more doctors know about eating disorders—and the more we can challenge harmful misconceptions about them—the greater the likelihood that people will get the help they need.

Chapter Three

The Disorder

By the fall of 1998, I had been restricting my food intake for an entire year. My mother had been gone for eighteen months, and I had retreated inward, no longer wanting to interact with friends or family. I had stopped spying and reading—activities that required too much concentration. I climbed the Japanese maple tree in our front yard where I would sit for an hour at a time, longing for Mom. I tried doing my schoolwork in the tree, but I found every assignment took so much more time to complete. My thoughts were fixated on food and exercise; to think of anything else required extra energy that I didn't seem to have. Hunger gnawed at me, leaving me exhausted and irritable.

My father tried everything he could to help. After the dead end with my pediatrician, he called a nurse named Debbie—who had taken care of my mother when she was sick—and asked if she'd be willing to meet with us. My father and I drove to her house together, and when I stepped out of the car, I caught Debbie by surprise. "I took one look at you and said to myself, 'Oh my,'" she told me years later. "You were so thin and so pale, and it was just startling to see how much you had changed in a relatively short period of time. What I saw was definitely somebody who was in need of intensive care." Debbie gave my father what he had been looking for all along: validation that I needed help and advice on how to get it. She suspected I had anorexia and urged us to go to Boston Children's Hospital, which had a respected eating-disorder treatment program. It was the first time we had ever heard anyone use the word *anorexia* to describe my condition. It surprised me, and it scared my father, who took me to the Boston Children's Hospital emergency room the next day.

At the time, I was thirteen and in the seventh grade. My body ached inside and out, and it was crying for help. My legs and feet felt strained from jumping, and my hands were chapped and bleeding from malnutrition. An intake nurse recorded my vitals and noted that I was hypothermic, with a temperature of just 94 degrees. My hands and feet felt cold as ice and had a reddish-blue tinge that classmates noticed. "Why are your hands so purple?" one of them had asked, a look of disgust on her face. I shrugged, not knowing that this type of discoloration is a common condition among people with anorexia, whose bodies instinctively try to keep them warm by heating up the parts that need the most energy and neglecting the rest.

In my records, the emergency room doctor described me as "extremely undernourished" and "wasted appearing," noting the cause ("grief reaction") and the status of my condition ("emergent"). She said my heart rate was "dangerously low" and that I needed to be admitted right away. Had I been healthy, my heart rate would have been somewhere in the range of seventy to one hundred beats per minute. But mine was just forty beats per minute. The doctor explained that cardiovascular issues were common in patients with anorexia; the disorder can cause serious changes in heart structure and function and, in extreme cases, can lead to heart failure.

As a motherless daughter, my body spoke for me. I didn't have to say I wanted to be mothered; the hospital providers could take one look at me and know I needed to be nurtured and nourished. I hoped the hospitalization would help my body, but I doubted its power to cure me. Anorexia had become part of me, tangling itself up with my identity to the point where I barely recognized myself. The young writer in me looked for some analogy, some way to describe this unstoppable force that had gotten ahold of me. I pictured an invisible sea monster that had slowly wrapped itself around my body without my even realizing it. That monster's grip had tightened to the point where I couldn't break free. I was thrashing my arms, trying to stay afloat. But my body barely had any fight left in it, and I began to worry I might get pulled under, once and for all. The irony wasn't lost on me that, in my attempts to stay little, I developed a disorder that had grown unbearably big.

I was admitted to Boston Children's Hospital and brought by wheelchair to the 10-East unit, where a nurse gave me a blue medical gown and nonslip socks. I put on the gown and socks, settling into my new wardrobe. I felt a draft of cool air on my back, where my gown split open, and watched the hair on my arms lift upward. I had lost so much body fat that my arms and legs were covered in lanugo, the soft feathery hair that grows on people with anorexia as the body's way of keeping them warm. Lanugo is the hair that typically grows on human fetuses, signaling healthy development in the mother's womb. Here, it was a sign my body was trying to protect me from starvation. The attending physician ordered an EKG and described me in my records as "an emaciated girl with braces on her teeth who looks younger than her stated age and who has a bow in her hair." I was, by her assessment, "cooperative, seemingly honest, and pleasant, with complete answers to questions." My mood was "okay," and I had "some episodes of watery eyes, but no crying." I was trying so hard to be strong in the hospital, especially for my father. I wanted him to know that, even though my body was weak, I still had the strength to hold back my tears, just as I had after my mother died.

It was getting late, and my father needed to go home to get ready for work the next day. He had been staring at the floor, as though trying to avert his gaze from the painful sight before him: his little girl, sick with anorexia, in a hospital bed. I knew he hated seeing me there, but he came to the realization he could not save me on his own. If you bear that burden alone, the weight of the disease will crush you both.

"You're going to get better," my father told me, repeating the same words he had said to my mother when she was sick. "I just know it." He rubbed his nose as he spoke—a new nervous tick he developed—and he finally looked me in the eye. He reached for my hand and held it tight. Neither of us wanted to let go. My father had gotten used to saying goodbye to my mother and walking out of her hospital room with his hand in mine. But tonight, he would be going home alone. I watched him leave, and I sank into my hospital bed, feeling far away from my father but close to my mother. I didn't know my behaviors could land me in the hospital, but I liked knowing that they had. The hospital was familiar territory; it had been a fixture in my life during the three years Mom was sick. I had spent so much time with her on the cancer unit, curled up by her side. When she died, I lost the final places we had inhabited together and the people in these places: the hospital nurses who told me not to worry, the oncologist who gave me high fives, the techs who brought me orange sherbet. Now, from my spot in this new hospital bed, these pieces of the past had returned to me.

As sunlight streamed into my hospital room window the next morning, a nurse took my vitals and drew my blood. A dietitian came into my hospital room shortly after, handing me a sheet with several boxes printed on it. The boxes were divided into proteins, grains, vegetables, fruits, and fats. At the top of the sheet, there was a list of the number of foods I was required to choose from each box. The dietitian walked me through the sheet, placing check marks next to the foods I told her I felt safe enough to eat: cottage cheese, green beans, carrots, pita bread, hummus, a banana, a granola bar, and milk. I spotted orange sherbet on the list and felt a pang of longing, all the while knowing I could never bring myself to eat it. *Too much sugar*, I thought. *Too many calories. Too over the top.* The foods I used to love now filled me with so much fear I wondered if they'd ever feel safe again. Deep down, I wanted to eat them, but I worried that satisfying my own appetite would somehow starve my relationship with my mother.

When a nurse came back with my tray of food, she told me I had exactly thirty minutes to eat. If I didn't finish every bite, I would need to drink the caloric equivalent in Ensure within the space of fifteen minutes. If I didn't drink every last sip of Ensure, I would get a feeding tube. The thought of the tube scared me almost as much as the thought of eating the food. I stared at my tray with a mix of outward fear and inner desire. I wasn't "without appetite," as the origin of the word *anorexia* suggests; I was ravenous. After a year of slowly starving my skeletal self, I had come to view my perpetual hunger as a sign I was succeeding at anorexia. But in the hospital, I felt less pressure to succeed. My hospitalization felt like a permission slip to eat, an excused absence from anorexia. I now had a legitimate reason not to obsessively exercise—to lie flat and slow down my body under the weight of a white hospital comforter and a tray of carefully measured food.

I dipped my spoon into the mound of cottage cheese, eyeing the mini curds and wondering how many calories each contained. In the 1990s when I was sick, cottage cheese fit perfectly into the low-fat diet craze. Tasteless, but guilt-free. Now it seemed indulgent. The kind in the hospital was made with whole milk and was creamier than the fat-free variety I had been eating at home. I ate it all and scraped the bowl as I was instructed, earning nods of approval from the nurse who came in every so often to check on me and my progress. I took a sip of the pink drink that the nurse had placed on my tray. It was called Neutra-Phos—a concoction of electrolytes I would have to drink with every meal.

The Neutra-Phos looked like Crystal Light pink lemonade that hadn't been properly mixed, with tiny chunks of powder floating on the surface. I took a sip and swished it around my mouth, fearful of swallowing a mystery drink that might have hidden calories in it. But the flavor caught my taste buds by surprise. It was sweet and sour, and oddly familiar. It reminded me of the Ocean Spray Mauna La'i guava juice my mother and I used to drink together during summertime. I moved on to the pita bread, a lopsided circle containing exactly 180 calories. Then, the ¼ cup of hummus—140 calories. The steamed green beans were covered with water droplets. I reassured myself that the cup of green beans was only 35 calories and tried tuning out my fear that water had calories in it. My mind swelled with plus signs as I added up the grand totals of calories. I wanted to replace them with minus signs like I had done at home, cutting out 100 calories here, 50 calories there. But with the nurses hovering, there was no space for subtraction. I worked my way around the tray, wondering how much more I could fit inside of me. I ate everything as I was ordered to. By the time I was done, my stomach ached with expansion. The fullness felt unbearable. I started shaking my foot beneath the comforter, trying anything I could do to burn calories and rid myself of it.

My doctor later met with me to discuss my EKG results. Standing beside my bed, she handed me a page with four rows of squiggles that my heart had drawn. They looked like the lines I used to draw on my red Etch A Sketch—grainy gray and never as straight as I would have liked. I didn't know what the lines meant, but the doctor traced them with her finger and explained that the pauses between each peak were far longer than they should have been. She told me I had an ectopic rhythm, which explained why my heart often felt like it was skipping a beat. My heart had been vulnerable to anorexia's attack, and I had grown accustomed to feeling its prominent thump whenever I exercised or lay in bed at night. But I had no idea how much damage I was doing to it, and I never imagined it could fail me. Eating food, the doctor said, would make my heart happier. As she lifted off a stethoscope from her neck and placed it on my chest, she noted that one of the electrodes from the EKG was still on me. I liked seeing it there, a little pad of proof that my heart was getting help. She peeled it off, then asked me to take a few deep breaths. My lungs felt like they were shaking. A chest X-ray revealed that I had pneumonia, likely a side effect of my weakened body and waning immunity.

Despite all the medical complications I was facing, my bloodwork came back normal. I felt so inadequate when I heard the results. I didn't want anything about me to be "normal"; I wanted to be *special*—a child-like word I often used as a synonym for *perfect*. As a child, I had wanted nothing more than to feel special, perfect, in my mother's eyes. I knew my monster-like disorder was hurting my body, but I also saw it as a friend who was helping me feel special and closer to my mom. "The word *anorexia* kind of scares me," I journaled from the hospital. "But it also makes me think of a friend because, in a way, it is a very good friend to me."

My body was grateful to be in the hospital, where it could finally rest and be fed. But my mind wasn't. *You don't need rest*, it seemed to say. *You're so lazy, just lying there in bed, gaining weight. This year, you can't eat any Halloween candy. Not a single bite*. From my hospital bed, I thought about how Halloween was just two weeks away. My father told me he wanted to buy me a costume, hoping it might bring me some joy. He didn't know what size I wore because he hadn't needed to buy me any new clothes since my mom died; at thirteen, I still fit into outfits I wore when I was ten or eleven. So, he settled on a safe, one-size-fits-all costume: butterfly wings. They prompted unspoken remembrance of my mother, who loved the way butterflies fluttered their wings in a display of delicate freedom. She liked them so much she had asked my father to have one engraved on her tombstone. Now my father helped me put on my wings, then stood back to admire them. "They look beautiful on you," he said. It was an interesting turn of phrase, with an emphasis on the beauty of the wings and not my body. I liked wearing them because they reminded me of my mother. But they gave me no sense of freedom.

As my father and I watched *America's Funniest Home Videos* together that evening on the hospital TV, I thought of all the times we used to watch it as a family of three from my mother's hospital bedside. Dad kissed the top of my head before he left, then went downstairs to have dinner at Au Bon Pain. We had passed by it a few days earlier when I was admitted, and I had held my breath, afraid that simply inhaling the yeasty aroma of freshly baked bread would make me gain weight. My Italian American dad, meanwhile, has always found comfort in the smell and taste of bread. That night he stopped at Au Bon Pain for dinner, eating a sandwich by himself. Then he started his hour-long drive home.

My relatives and schoolteachers sent me flowers and get-well cards, and there was one in particular that stood out. My Spanish teacher, Ms. Meade, brought it to me during a visit to the hospital. The card was purple, and it featured a teddy bear with outstretched arms that embraced the words "Get well soon!" The inside was scribbled with get-well wishes from classmates who knew I was out sick but didn't know where I was or what ailed me. It's possible some guessed what was wrong. But I had not confided in any of them; it seemed better to surrender to silence than to explain something no one understood. As I read their sentiments, I focused on every detail: the hearts that dotted the *i*'s, the big smiley faces; the XOXO's punctuating most of the girls' messages. Reading them, I felt comforted but misunderstood. I knew, even then, what I had would not go away after a few days in the hospital. It had taken up residence, and I didn't see any easy exit signs where it could leave me. It would take me years to learn I would have to build those exit signs on my own, and that for the rest of my life they would be at risk of erasure.

While in the hospital, I was aware that my eating disorder had changed the way my body looked and felt. But I had no way of knowing the extent of these changes. In the years since, research has revealed that eating disorders cause both physical *and* neurobiological changes—so much so that some scientists in the field now refer to eating disorders as "brain disorders." Brain-based alterations have been shown to reinforce disordered behaviors—a connection that offers clues as to why it's difficult to shake these behaviors while you're acutely sick and why slips are common in the middle place.

As I've learned more about the physical and neurobiological side effects, I've become increasingly fascinated by the body's resilience. Because our ancestors frequently faced food shortages, our bodies evolved to endure famine. They respond to starvation by doing everything they can to conserve energy, primarily by slowing down the heart rate, digestion, and basal metabolic rate—the amount of energy a body needs to maintain basic life functions.

The physiologist Ancel Keys observed these bodily reactions and more in his seminal Minnesota Starvation Experiment. The 1944 study, which would likely never be replicated again because of modern-day ethical concerns, has been used widely in eating-disorder research. Keys recruited thirty-six young male volunteers for the experiment to better understand the psychological and physiological effects of starvation. At the time, people in Europe had limited access to food because of World War II, and there was very little scientific literature about how to treat starvation or manage one's recovery from it. After a three-month control period in which the men were fed 3,200 calories per day, Keys cut their calories in half over a six-month semi-starvation period and made them walk a few miles each day.

As the men starved, they experienced newfound psychological symptoms, including depression, irritability, and food-related preoccupations. They developed new habits of reading cookbooks and collecting recipes, and they fantasized about eating high-calorie foods. They became more isolated, but when they did talk among themselves, their conversations typically revolved around food, recipes, and agriculture. They became territorial over food and began cutting it into tiny pieces so they could spread out their meal consumption for hours—a food ritual that's common among people with eating disorders. One man reportedly engaged in psychotic behaviors. Another man would scour the trash in search of food. In between meals, some men chewed gum excessively to try to satiate their hunger, consuming as many as forty to sixty packs a day. In addition to losing about 25 percent of their body mass, the men experienced fatigue, swelling in the ankles and feet, and a reduced heart rate and basal metabolic rate—the same physical side effects that people with anorexia often face.

Once they began eating during a three-month rehabilitation period, the men regained the weight they had lost, and their physical ailments went away. But their relationships to food remained notable. One of the men went on to pursue a career in agriculture, and three became chefs. None were known to have developed eating disorders, but several reported having "abnormal" eating habits after the fact. One-third of the men said they engaged in binge-eating behaviors for a short period after the experiment, and half the men reported an inability to stop eating when they were full, saying they were unable to feel satiated.

When as an adult I read the results of this landmark study, I couldn't help but think about the damage starvation causes and the ways our bodies resist it. My starving body had endured so much leading up to my first hospitalization, even though my blood test results suggested otherwise. It turns out that it's common for people with anorexia who don't purge and who aren't experiencing organ dysfunction to have normal lab results. That's because when a body is repeatedly malnourished, it recognizes starvation as a threat and does all it can to balance out the electrolytes and keep us safe. At Boston Children's, I was fortunate to be in the care of providers who knew I still needed medical attention, even though my tests came back normal. But it's not common knowledge among medical and insurance providers. "Insurance companies, with their lack of eating disorder expertise, point to normal lab work as a reason not to authorize someone for a needed higher level of care," Dr. Jennifer Gaudiani writes in her book *Sick Enough: A Guide to the Medical Complications of Eating Dis-*

orders. As she explains, "Doctors' offices and staff members may believe they are being positive and reassuring in announcing the bloodwork is normal. Yet this may erroneously plant the message that the patient is therefore fine. Emergency department staff see normal labs and send patients home rather than admitting them medically."

Part of the issue comes back to the lack of eating-disorder training in medical schools, which no doubt affects emergency-room care. A 2021 study that examined emergency-medicine physicians' knowledge of eating disorders found that only 1.9 percent completed a rotation on eating disorders during residency. The majority were not aware of related resources for patients, including local treatment programs and online support groups. Emergency-room staff who aren't trained in eating disorders may also be unaware of what happens when people with anorexia start eating again in the hospital.

After that first meal in the hospital, for example, I thought my eating disorder had tricked me into believing I was full. But in fact, something medical was at play; my stomach couldn't physically accommodate large volumes of food. I had developed gastroparesis, a common condition among people with restrictive eating disorders, regardless of body size. In a healthy person, the stomach digests food with the help of muscles that move the food into the small intestine. In a starving person, whose body is trying to conserve as many calories as possible, these muscles don't function at their full strength. Food stays in the stomach for longer periods of time, which delays the digestive process. This causes bloating and upper stomach pain, and it leads people to feel uncomfortably full after even eating small amounts of food. The condition typically resolves with consistent food intake and with medication that helps the stomach speed up its emptying time.

My medical team zeroed in on my food intake and vital signs, knowing that the anorexic body must be stabilized before the mind can be mended. My low heart rate, low body temperature, low blood pressure, and blueish fingers all suggested my heart was unable to pump adequate oxygen and glucose throughout my body and to my brain. And since my heart was likely smaller and weaker from long-term malnutrition, I was at increased risk of cardiac arrest.

As I began eating in the hospital, my doctors also had to watch for refeeding syndrome—a matrix of complications involving the heart, energy, and electrolytes. It's a cause for concern among severely malnourished patients who begin consuming larger amounts of food in treatment. During the early stages of refeeding, the body's metabolism ramps up and begins burning energy faster than it can be replaced at the molecular level. Phosphorous, an important element in the production of these energy molecules, can become depleted. The depletion makes it harder for the heart to properly pump and, if unmonitored, can lead to cardiac arythmia or arrest. This explains why my doctors gave me Neutra-Phos—to increase my stores of phosphorous, an electrolyte that regulates the function of nerves and muscles, including the heart. It also explains why, instead of starting me off on a high-calorie diet, they increased my calorie intake gradually so they could monitor my body's response along the way.

In recent years, new research has suggested that this traditional "start low and go slow" approach to refeeding (which was common when I was in treatment) had an unintended effect: it led many malnourished patients to be underfed, resulting in poor weight gain and prolonged hospitalizations. In some cases this "underfeeding syndrome," as it's sometimes called, even led to death. Some doctors now recommend the approach be used only for severely malnourished patients and that higher-calorie refeeding approaches be used for "mildly" and "moderately" malnourished patients (descriptors partially determined by BMI). They point to evidence showing that patients who have greater weight gain in the hospital are more likely to still be weight-recovered six months and one year after hospitalization.

Most of the physical side effects of anorexia can be resolved with weight restoration. But some effects do carry scars. Among them is low bone density, which is of greatest concern for girls and boys undergoing puberty. When their bodies are undernourished, girls don't produce as much estrogen and boys don't produce as much testosterone—two key hormones needed for bone growth. The bone mass we're born with grows throughout childhood and then more rapidly during puberty. By the time men and women are twenty to twenty-five years old, their growth plateaus at what's called "peak bone mass"—the highest bone mass they'll have in their lifetime. Maximal increases in bone-mass accrual occur between the ages of thirteen and sixteen in boys, and between the ages of eleven and fourteen in girls—around the same age I was when I got sick.

"If you develop anorexia nervosa during those very critical years, there is increased risk of poor peak bone mass and therefore poor bone health for the future," said Madhusmita Misra, MD, an endocrinologist who chairs the Department of Pediatrics at the University of Virginia School of Medicine and is physician-in-chief at UVA Health Children's Hospital. There is, however, the possibility that bone growth can "catch up" if a person restores weight and keeps her body nourished before reaching peak bone mass. "This is not a lost cause," Dr. Misra told me. "It's important to know that there is hope, and there's a reason to try to get better because recovery has an important impact on your body." When people don't catch up during their teenage years and remain undernourished into adulthood, their bone health suffers, making them far more susceptible to fractures and breaks. One study found that roughly 40 percent of adult women with anorexia nervosa have bone density scores in the osteoporotic range, and more than 90 percent have scores in the osteopenia range, meaning their bone density is low. Dr. Misra recommends that everyone with anorexia—as well as those in recovery—receive a bone density scan to develop a better understanding of their overall bone health.

I can't recall anyone talking with me about bone health during that first hospitalization, and it wouldn't come up until a few years later. Even after being hospitalized, I still believed my disorder was helping my body, not hurting it. I was among the many people with eating disorders who develop *anosognosia*, a medical term to describe people who believe they're well even though they're sick. It's a common condition among people with schizophrenia or Alzheimer's disease and those who suffer brain damage from strokes. Several areas of the brain that are integral to developing a sense of one's body are commonly altered in anorexia nervosa, potentially contributing to difficulties in recognizing the severity of illness. Although anosognosia can correct itself as patients receive proper nutrition and restore weight, it can have devastating effects on patients' outlook and is a confounding barrier to treatment.

People with anorexia also tend to value their disorder, partly because they have cognitive distortions that are considered *egosyntonic*. The term refers to one's ego, or internal voice of reason that helps us do what we believe is right. Anorexia is considered an egosyntonic disorder because the cognitive distortions integral to the disorder (such as the desire to be thin and the act of restricting food intake) are consistent with longstanding societal messages that suggest it's "right" to be thin. This helps explain why, even after experiencing scary medical complications, many people with the disorder avoid treatment and continue to engage in destructive behaviors that put a strain on their bodies. It also explains why people with anorexia sometimes refer to the disorder the same way I did—as their "friend."

One young woman I spoke to, Molly, has been trying to stop referring to her eating disorder as a companion. She is in the early stages of recovery from anorexia and is beginning to recognize all that her disorder took from her when she was acutely sick. "I kept calling my eating disorder my friend, and my boyfriend was really hurt by that. He was like, 'This is my worst enemy. Why is this your friend?'" said Molly, a twenty-one-year-old from Spokane, Washington. "When I first went to treatment, I remember thinking, *I have to let go of this friend of mine, I need to let it go.*" She is beginning to realize that this so-called friend is actually a foe that carries hidden threats affecting both the body and the brain.

Neurobiological research has shown that brain reward processing, especially for food, is altered during anorexia nervosa. People normally find food more rewarding when they are hungry and less rewarding when they are satiated. But for those with anorexia, small amounts of food seem to cause elevated reward responses. Paradoxically, instead of motivating more food intake, small amounts of food may be experienced as an adequate reward. Personality trait differences may also be at play, as people with anorexia tend to have a low sensitivity to reward. If reward is not very important to decision-making, eating even a small amount of food may be enough, making it more feasible to maintain a very low intake of food.

Patients with anorexia and bulimia also are shown to have poor central coherence (meaning they fixate on details without seeing the bigger picture) and poor set-shifting (meaning they have difficulty shifting perspectives on, say, rules and rituals about food). These issues can persist even after a patient is weight restored, but the neuroscientists I talked to said it's difficult to know whether they are the result of predisposing traits or neurobiological alterations that don't resolve after starvation.

Other brain-based aspects of anorexia appear to be a direct result of starvation and can be reversed once a person is weight restored. I learned this when looking at the findings of a major 2022 study that analyzed structural magnetic resonance imaging scans of roughly 2,000 participants. Nearly 700 adolescents and adults with anorexia nervosa were included in the study, as well as healthy controls made up of people who never had the disorder. The study revealed that nearly every region of the brain thins during anorexia nervosa. Researchers observed significant reductions in brain size—most noticeably in three key areas that help make up gray matter in the brain: cortical thickness, subcortical volumes, and cortical surface area. The brain is made up of gray matter and white matter, but gray matter plays a more significant role in our daily functioning by helping us process information and control emotions, memory, and movement. Researchers concluded that the reductions were likely the result of low BMI, as they were most noticeable among participants who were underweight.

"The reductions were by far the biggest compared to other mental health disorders that are often studied," said Esther Walton, PhD, lead researcher of the study. "The very large effect sizes were much bigger than we expected." Specifically, the reductions were two to four times greater than those among people with obsessive-compulsive disorder and depression. Dr. Walton, a professor of biological psychology at the University of Bath in the United Kingdom, explained that the brain reductions suggest either a loss of brain cells or a loss of the connections between them. Such losses could make it harder for people to engage in complex thinking, which relies on connections between different regions of the brain. When these connections are lost, it's easier to get stuck in a "cognitive rut" regarding beliefs about food or body shape and size. Severely malnourished patients, for instance, may believe they are fat because there are no longer connections between their brain's sensory inputs about body size/shape and their ability to process these inputs.

For as scary as these findings sound, there's hope for restoration; size reductions appeared to normalize quickly among patients who had regained weight in treatment. "Cells can gain again, in shape and structure," Dr. Walton told me. "There's a fair amount of restorative potential in the brain, which is fantastic." She expects this will be the first of many large-scale studies aimed at showing how the brain changes during recovery not just from anorexia but other eating disorders as well.

Dr. Walton and a team of researchers conducted the study as members of the ENIGMA Consortium, a global effort to conduct wide-scale neuroimaging studies on how mental health disorders affect the brain's structure and function. "Whether you study anorexia nervosa, or depression or ADHD, the sample size is often very, very small," Dr. Walton said. "It's often ten or twenty participants, and that's not the right sample size you need to really disentangle what's going on in the brain and how the brain structure alterations relate to mental health disorders." ENIGMA has an Eating Disorders Working Group that's made up of researchers worldwide and dedicated specifically to studying structural brain changes in patients who are acutely sick with, or in recovery from, anorexia and bulimia. One of the group's main goals, Dr. Walton said, is to generate new research that can inform how we perceive, understand, and treat eating disorders.

This type of brain-based research is helpful not just for parents and medical providers but also for people like me, whose eating-disorder narratives have holes in their earlier chapters. These gaps are not born of storytelling deficiencies but of a field that years ago knew very little about how eating disorders affect the brain. My quest to further understand this topic led me to Guido Frank, MD, a leading expert on the brain biology of eating disorders. Dr. Frank is part of the ENIGMA working group and was among the researchers who contributed to the brain structure study. As a psychiatrist at the University of California, San Diego's Eating Disorders Center for Treatment and Research, he has witnessed a slew of triggers that may seem innocuous at the onset but can lead a person to restrict food intake: a desire to lose weight to run faster; an offhand comment about one's body; a choking incident that makes someone fearful of eating again; a health class. The list goes on. As people restrict their food intake in response to a trigger, there are unconscious biological adaptations that occur in the brain, including altered reward circuits that can reinforce food restriction. People can quickly find themselves trapped in what Dr. Frank calls a "psycho-biological conflict" between a person's conscious motivation to restrict food and the body's unconscious motivation to seek out food in response to caloric restriction and weight loss. These opposing motivations trigger anxiety, which maintains a vicious cycle of restriction and weight loss. Eventually, the fear of weight gain supersedes the bodily mechanisms that drive food intake.

I asked Dr. Frank to describe the parts of the brain involved in people's decisions to restrict food intake. He showed me a picture and pointed to the hypothalamus, saying it receives signals from the body and helps us make decisions that maintain the organism. The hypothalamus is involved in many metabolic processes that pertain to hunger, body temperature control, and fight-or-flight response, among others.

It's the part of the brain that tells us we should eat when we're hungry, and the same one that tells us we should run to safety if we see a tiger in a jungle. This type of response relies on a circuitry that travels from the hypothalamus to the ventral striatum, a part of the brain that helps process rewards. Curious to learn more about this circuitry, Dr. Frank conducted brain imaging scans on participants while they tasted sugar water. He found that in healthy controls, the circuitry activation traveled from the hypothalamus to the ventral striatum, which is the expected direction. However, among those with eating disorders, the circuitry traveled in the opposite direction, from the ventral striatum to the hypothalamus. This finding suggests that food becomes a conditioned fear stimulus that hijacks the circuitry meant for actual threats, like the tiger in the jungle.

"What we found is that the brain essentially learns to override hunger cues," said Dr. Frank, who has spent over a decade studying how the brain responds when people with eating disorders taste high-calorie food stimuli. "When you're in a threatening situation, you don't want to eat, so you respond with threat avoidance to food because the situation is perceived as dangerous. The conditioned fear of eating becomes so strong, the act of eating so threatening, that this overriding of appetite and eating will be triggered." Once altered, this circuitry can continue reinforcing eating-disorder behaviors.

Brain circuitry can normalize with changes in eating-disorder behaviors during the recovery process. But the mental health issues underlying the disorder can persist, sometimes requiring medication. "I really believe that medication can help to normalize brain circuits, facilitate psychotherapy, improve learning and cognitive flexibility, reduce distress, and reduce anxiety," said Dr. Frank, who draws upon neuroscience when prescribing medications. He typically prescribes his patients low-dose aripiprazole to improve cognitive flexibility and support eating, coupled with olanzapine for acute agitation and distress. Combinations of these drugs (which weren't used to treat eating disorders when I was sick) have proved to be moderately effective, particularly among younger patients and in the absence of better options. Still today, there is no FDA-approved drug shown to reliably treat people with anorexia. Early research into using psychedelics—including psilocybin, ketamine, and ayahuasca—shows promise for relieving symptoms in people with anorexia. Some clinicians I've spoken with say the eating-disorder treatment centers they work for have started using psychedelics to treat patients who are in their care. But it's hard to know how well these psychedelics work without randomized, controlled trials. Dr. Frank's colleagues at the University of California, San Diego recently conducted the first-ever clinical trial evaluating psilocybin among adults with anorexia. Though highly preliminary, the results found that 70% of participants "reported feeling a quality-of-life improvement and shift in personal identity" and 60% "reported a reduction in the importance of physical appearance."

Some experts I've talked to are optimistic that evolving neurobiological research will lead to advances in pharmacological treatments for eating disorders. Joanna Steinglass, MD, a psychiatry professor at Columbia University's Irving Medical Center, framed it well: "It's always been the case for the treatment of eating disorders that we've looked at something and said, 'Well that works for depression, so we're going to use it for our patients, who are also kind of sad,'" said Dr. Steinglass, who studies the neurobiology of anorexia nervosa. "Now it feels like we have a lot to say about what restrictive eating is all about and where in the brain that is and what kinds of things might be going on. Then we can decide what we should do for eating disorders and not just borrow from everybody else. It makes me hopeful for the future."

Chapter Four

The Treatment

I stayed on the medical unit for one week—just long enough to be physically stabilized. The day after I was discharged, I went back to school and faced questions from classmates who wondered where I'd been. I told them I had a weak heart. It seemed easier to talk about my heart than to try to explain anorexia.

I had always loved learning at school, but it was now a challenge to sit through my eighth-grade classes. While trying to calculate equations in algebra class, all I could think about was counting calories. In science class, when we learned about speed, velocity, and acceleration, I kept thinking about exercising. During a lesson about Isaac Newton, I fixated on his first Law of Motion: *An object will not change its motion unless a force acts on it.* I thought about anorexia's force over me and my every motion. "This disease is just so tough to fight," I wrote in a letter to my maternal grandma. "It's like a magnet trying to pull me closer and closer to it. It's pulling me one way, and my family and friends are pulling me the other way. I just don't know which way I should work on being pulled toward."

I had come up with so many words to describe my disorder—a friend, a foe, a magnet, a monster—but I still didn't really know how to define it.

I climbed the Japanese maple after school, admiring the strength of its trunk and the way its branches stretched toward the sky. The tree's auburn leaves surrounded me, their edges tickling my skin. From high above, I felt hidden from the world below. I stayed there for an hour or so, dreading dinner and longing to be back on the medical ward. I missed the floral smell of the pink hospital soap and the hospital gown that felt comfortably loose on my body. I missed the attention of nurses and doctors and dietitians who came in to check on me. The hospital was the one place where people seemed to understand my disorder and could adequately care for me. I pulled my shirt collar away from my neck and looked down at my chest to see if the sticky remains of the EKG electrode pads were still there. They were, and I didn't want them to go away.

At dusk I went inside. Dad had a printout of my meal plan, which laid out exact measurements of the food I was supposed to eat at each meal. He dusted off old measuring cups that we hadn't used since my mom was alive and carefully prepared my dinner. As I ate, he read from a new book he had bought for mealtimes, hoping it might serve as a welcome distraction from the food in front of me. The book, titled *Fathers and Daughters: In Their Own Words*, was filled with black-and-white photos of fathers and daughters from different walks of life, accompanied by brief quotes from each of them. I liked hearing my father read the quotes, and though I found it difficult to concentrate on most of them, one from a girl named Celestia resonated with me. Her quote was short and relatable: "I love my dad very much, and if anything ever happened to him, I would be sad. I wish that he would live forever."

I ate my entire meal, and my clean plate was met with praise. "I'm so proud of you, Mallary!" my father declared. "You did it!" I wanted to feel proud, too, but felt nothing of the sort. Shame and fear stirred inside me as I stared at the remaining crumbs on my plate. A tiny piece of pita bread. A green bean seed. *Now that I'm eating, does this mean I'm better?*

What happens if I am? Will people stop caring for me? Will I be less special? I worried what answers these questions would yield, and I didn't dare ask them out loud. I craved the attention I had gotten when I wasn't eating. So, I started skimping. My father continued measuring out my food, but I began leaving behind small bites, then bigger ones, then entire portions.

Dad was still dating Katie, but he never brought her to our house. He knew this would upset me, and he didn't want to risk doing anything that would provoke me. Instead, he would go out with her a couple evenings each week. I would stay home alone and exercise in my room, jumping my way through frustration and anger. My father suspected it wasn't good for me to be alone, so he asked Gramz to move in with us for extra support. She agreed to stay with us a few days a week. But even with her there, I kept slipping. Hard as she and my father tried, they couldn't catch my fall.

"Mallary has basically cut the meal plan in half," my Boston Children's outpatient doctor, Sara Forman, MD, wrote in my records, shortly after my discharge. "Although she is not allowed to exercise, her dad stated today in our meeting that she cannot sit still. . . . I am also concerned with the quality of life she is leading and that her father and grandmother are leading. Her father is concerned that the grandmother may be on the verge of a nervous breakdown because she cries heavily at every meal that she has with Mallary."

I had been engaging in mealtime rituals that often occur alongside anorexia: cutting my food into tiny pieces, eating my food as slowly as possible, chewing it incessantly before swallowing it. But my rituals manifested into something even more perplexing. I began punching myself, for instance, and I convinced myself I needed to do it in sets of threes. I would make a fist and hit my head nine times on each side, then get up and jump thirty-three times before I would allow myself to start eating. Three was my lucky number, and I thought if I doubled it by adding an extra three, it would be extra charmed. I found comfort in the idea that, if I were lucky, I could return to the hospital as I wished. After braving my first bite of food,

I would go to the sink and wash my hands for a few minutes. Then I would pour soap and water on a sponge without draining it and scrub the kitchen table as hard as I could. I constantly worried that calories had gotten onto my hands and the table, and I wanted to wash them all away. When I was done, I would hit myself in the head eighteen times and jump thirty-three more times. Eating made me feel like I was doing something wrong, as though I was disobeying my disorder. Punching was the punishment.

At first, these behaviors allayed my anxiety about eating, but they soon turned into grueling compulsions I couldn't ignore. Gramz watched on in horror. She tried to intervene, her dismay growing by the day. "Just scoot closer and hold my hand," she would plead, reaching an outstretched arm toward me. I wanted to sit down next to her, but I couldn't. Instead, I would jump beside her.

"I feel like my jumping and not eating are far beyond my control, and I can't help myself at all," I journaled. "My anorexia is so powerful that I don't seem to have the strength to overcome it and take control back over my life." I talked about this with my therapist and dietitian, both of whom I saw once a week as part of outpatient treatment. But, as my dietitian noted, I remained "very much entrenched in wanting to have the identity of an anorexic." Two decades later, I would read that line from my records and study the word *entrenched*, pausing to reflect on its weighty definition: firmly established and difficult or unlikely to change; ingrained. It was as though my dietitian recognized anorexia for what it was: a disorder that had worked its way into my core, ruling everything and giving nothing in return.

In November 1998, just two weeks after I was discharged from Boston Children's Hospital, I was readmitted. My weight and vital signs were stable enough that I didn't have to go to the medical unit this time. I was instead sent to the hospital's psychiatric ward. Between my food restriction and worsening behaviors, doctors thought that was the best option for longer-term, inpatient care. My father obliged, willing to try anything that might help. The ward was called Bader 5, named in honor of Mr. and

Mrs. L. F. S. Bader, who contributed the majority of construction funds for the six-story building that housed the psychiatric ward. The Bader building was one of the most modern hospital facilities in the country when it was built in 1930, on the corner of Blackfan and Shattuck streets in southwest Boston.

Bader 5 was an eighteen-bed ward on the fifth floor, a secure inpatient psychiatric unit for young children and adolescents up to age seventeen. It treated youth struggling with eating disorders, suicidal thoughts, schizophrenia, major depression, and more. Authorized visitors were patted down upon entry to keep out sharp objects—pocketknives, razors, glass picture frames. It was a place that both perpetuated and defied stereotypes, the halls echoing with the discordant sound of screams and slamming doors one hour and childhood laughter the next.

Behind those locked doors was where I needed to be. And a big part of me *wanted* to be there, at a place where a treatment team could help me in ways my family alone could not. I still didn't know if I could get better, but I started to hope. My second day there, I wrote a note to my maternal grandma: "Even though I hate traveling it, I think I am going to work my way toward the road to recovery. Hopefully this place will help me."

Bader 5 was the first place where I met other girls with eating disorders, and within a week, I had befriended many of them—Katie, Haniyah, Talia, Jessica, Tracy, Lily. Every morning at 6:30 a.m. sharp, we dutifully lined up in the hallway outside of the infirmary, wearing hospital gowns and looks of concern. Standing side by side, we whispered about the numbers we feared seeing on the scale. *I'm afraid to know my weight. . . . I better not have gained anything. . . . What if I somehow lost weight and need a calorie increase?* We'd stare at one another's bodies and silently envy the sight of protruding bones, too sick to realize we bore the same telltale marks.

In the dining hall, we scrutinized each other's plates, jealous of the new patients whose meals were smaller because they hadn't started receiving calorie increases. We fought about bananas, which spurred more drama than any other fruit. Half a banana counted as one serving of fruit;

a full banana counted as two. Many eating-disorder patients needed two fruit servings per meal and chose bananas with hopes they would get small ones. When we did get littler bananas, we didn't say a word. But when we were given especially large ones, we fumed. "Why is her banana so much smaller than mine?!" a patient asked one day as she eyed my plate. The staff member who was eating with us told her to stop making comparisons and referred her to the infamous banana-meter: a handmade sign featuring a drawing of a banana. The banana was drawn to scale, and it was nine inches—the size that constituted two servings of fruit. The banana-meter hung in the dining room to reassure us that large bananas were exactly what we needed. I grew accustomed to watching my fellow patients use the banana-meter at every meal, and I began using it too, barely giving thought to the absurdity of it all.

I also studied the other patients in a quest to be better than they were. But "better" wasn't about health; it was still about sickness. In pursuit of becoming "the perfect anorexic," I aimed to be the sickest of them all. My friendships with the other eating-disorder patients were rooted in a shared understanding of a lonely disorder that had landed us in a place far from home. Our interactions reflected a common but underdiscussed criticism of eating-disorder treatment facilities: social contagion and comparison. When I was with the other patients, I latched on to all the tricks they shared with me about how to lose weight. Once exposed to these tricks, I couldn't help but adopt them as my own. We compared ourselves to one another constantly and swapped stories about the origins of our disorders and the lengths we had taken to get to Bader 5. "I used to do 1,000 sit-ups a night," Talia once told me. I responded that same day in my journal: "I will beat her record. I'll do 1,033 sit-ups a day, or at night right before I go to bed." Being the perfect anorexic meant I needed to break the other girls' records. I attempted the self-imposed challenge that evening, but it was difficult to elude the watchful eyes of staffers, who made rounds through our rooms each night. I managed to sneak in only a few dozen sit-ups, but I fell asleep determined to try again the next day.

I journaled incessantly during that time, drafting pages of proof that anorexia consumed my every thought. "I don't want to get better because I like all the attention I get now," I wrote in one entry. "Also, it would be like giving up one of my best friends." I wrote about the "tips" the other girls shared with me, and I plotted how to weave them into my routine. I listed calories with a maddening level of dedication, and I wrote about what I feared those calories would do to me, unable to accept their worth. "The staff promised me that I won't get fat, only healthy," I journaled, not recognizing how much fatphobia was tangled up in that sentence. "They're definitely lying because I'm already so fat, and more food will only make me twenty times fatter than I already am." I liked that the staff were caring for me, but I also resented them for it. Being so young, it was hard for me to resolve this tension.

As a thirteen-year-old in a psychiatric ward, I felt far removed from the life I once knew. Dad and Gramz were the only ones who visited at first because I didn't want anyone else to see me. Whenever they came, they brought Boggle, a word-search game. I didn't want to discuss my disorder with them, and I wasn't up for talking about much of anything while on the ward. Instead of carrying on conversations, we silently searched for words in the game. I eventually agreed to see my maternal grandmother and a family friend named Eileen. Locked away from the world, I had begun missing them. But when they visited, I barely spoke or looked them in the eye; I was filled with both shame and pride that I was sick enough to be on a psychiatric ward.

"You looked like a ragamuffin," my grandmother told me years later. "I had never seen somebody look so devastated, so taken down. You kept looking at the ground. Your hair was a mess, your skin was pallid, and you were wearing sweatpants. You never wore sweatpants." When Eileen was leaving after our visit, the nurse who escorted her out said something she's never forgotten: "Mallary has the most severe case of anorexia I've ever seen in my career." Decades passed before I learned this, and I'm glad I didn't overhear it at the time; it likely would have validated my distorted desire to be the perfect anorexic.

The Bader 5 staffers were trained in eating-disorder care and knew that starvation distorts the mind and can lead to bizarre delusions about food and weight. They watched over me in ways I hoped my mother might if she were still alive—not with frustration or blame but with an understanding of what it means to struggle with a disorder that has overtaken you. They knew, for instance, that I couldn't stop my jumping cold turkey, so they tolerated it with limitations. Halfway through each meal, I could get up and jump ten times. I would sometimes sneak in one more jump, but I mostly stuck to this allowance out of appreciation that they didn't take an all-or-nothing approach. They let me scream into a pillow before and after each meal, with hopes that this would help me release the anxiety I felt. They knew how hard it was for me to try new foods, so rather than make me eat foods I considered "unsafe," they asked me to change the order in which I ate my foods. These small changes, they said, could lead to bigger ones. One of my favorite caregivers, a nurse named Elizabeth, wrote a list of facts to help counter my disordered thoughts. I carried the list to every meal and read the gentle reminders, hoping one day I would believe them: "I am safe. I can handle this. The pita bread is a regular size. The cottage cheese is not extra creamy. The kitchen didn't trick me."

Elizabeth and other staff members took care with the language they used with me. They knew I was afraid of getting better, so they talked to me about "normalizing" my behaviors instead of "improving" them, and they spoke about my past a lot more than my future. The more the staff got to know me, the more they tried to help me see that my aversion to food wasn't really about weight loss but, rather, about a maternal loss I hadn't yet grieved. In my medical records from that period, one provider noted that "Mallary simply stopped growing, emotionally and physically, when her mother died."

The staff came to know all this because they were near me, if not by my side, constantly. A staff member had to accompany me whenever I went to the bathroom, standing outside the door and listening as I counted out loud to prove I wasn't exercising or purging.

"One, two, three, four . . ."

"I can't hear you!" the staffers would nudge.

"One! Two! Three! Four!" I'd shout in frustration.

I often snuck in some jumps while counting, but I never made myself throw up. The thought of purging scared me in ways that starvation didn't; after years of holding back tears, I had mastered the art of bottling everything up inside and was too afraid to release it. I worried, too, that if I ever succeeded at purging, I would never be able to stop.

After a couple weeks on the ward, I was required to sleep on a mattress in the hallway—a result of having been placed on twenty-four-hour observation after being caught doing sit-ups in my bedroom late at night. My father thought the practice was demeaning. "I'll never forget walking through Bader 5 and seeing young girls lying in the fetal position in cots in the hallway," he later told me. "It bothered me a lot." The staff at Bader 5, who sat at a table down the hall from us, saw it as a necessary support for eating-disorder patients. Our vital signs were fragile, and we couldn't risk burning any extra calories in the confines of our bedrooms.

But those nights were hard. I slept under blinding lights and with a looming fear of what might happen once I closed my eyes. One time, a young boy whom I didn't know came out of his room and walked over to my mattress. I was awoken to the pain of him grabbing a chunk of my hair and pulling it as hard as he could. He yelled something incoherent as he pulled, and I screamed. Bader 5 staffers came running and pulled him off me. As they did, the boy spat on my teddy bear, leaving its soft white ears wet with his saliva. The staff lifted the boy by his arms and dragged him to the restraining room down the hall. The door slammed shut and I sat upright on my mattress, wishing I were home. The staff made sure I was okay, but I lay awake most of the night, alert and on guard.

The next morning, I wandered into the common room, a comfortable space decorated with upholstered chairs, a table with board games, and a TV that played the same old video on repeat day after day: *Be Somebody . . . or Be Somebody's Fool*, a 1984 motivational film featuring Mr. T. The movie was meant to convey positive messages to young audiences, including one about how kids our age should exercise regularly and avoid junk food. I tried my best to tune out that part of the video, frustrated that even from within the hospital I couldn't escape lessons about "bad" foods.

Next to the TV was a loveseat that the sole male anorexic patient would punch, as hard and as quickly as he could, to burn calories. I understood why he did that, in the same way that I understood why I jumped. It was a release, not just of calories but also of anger about what our disorders had done to us. One day, I was sitting at a corner table in the common room, settling into my usual spot next to another patient who was teaching me how to do origami. She always had a pleasant smile, and I don't recall ever hearing her talk. In the absence of words, she communicated with her hands, showing me how to turn colorful paper into cranes, turtles, and three-dimensional hearts. I soon learned how to make them myself and found that the art of folding paper quieted my mind in ways little else did. When I folded, my mental load lightened ever so slightly. I could focus on my moving hands instead of my racing thoughts about the calories I was eating and the weight I was gaining. Doing origami also made me feel closer to my mother, who had cross-stitched her way through cancer, turning tiny *X*-shaped stitches into intricate portraits and landscapes. She often made pieces for me, including a teddy bear picture that hung on my bedroom wall at home. While facing my own trauma in the hospital, I felt as though I could better understand why cross-stitching mattered so much to Mom during all her stays on the cancer ward. It was perhaps a way to temporarily escape her life-threatening disease, a chance to stay connected to whom she was before she got sick.

Through origami and other forms of art, I began to flirt with the happiness I once felt when doing arts and crafts with my mother. I painted pictures of happy people and butterflies and animals that came together in a collage of joy. In art therapy, I drew a picture of a black flower and surrounded it with a handwritten narrative that read, in part: "The flower represents the positive side of anorexia—looking thin, physically feeling better about yourself. The black represents the negative side of anorexia, such as dying, feeling unhappy and worthless, and putting such a terrible strain on your body." On the other side, I drew a colorful flower to represent recovery and wrote: "From what I have heard, full recovery is a flower in bloom. The anorexia is no longer a part of our life, and it no longer darkens our day or our personality." I shared the drawing with Elizabeth and another staffer named Glen. Recovery still seemed completely out of reach, but they considered it progress that I was even thinking about the prospect of it.

In the self-portraits I drew for art therapy, my mouth turned upward in a smile. One of my drawings, which still hangs on the wall in my father's house, has thirty-three smiley faces. It looks like artwork done by a girl who was as carefree and as happy as you'd hope a child would be. But it was from one of my darkest times. "Have you ever heard of the expression 'fake it till you make it'?" Glen asked me after seeing the drawing. I hadn't, but I guessed what it meant and hoped I would make it someday. Glen created a therapy workbook for me so we could interact through writing. He knew that although I was withdrawn in person, I was wordy on the page. "I want to be closer to my mother," I wrote in the workbook. "And I am afraid that the older and bigger I get, the farther away I will be from her." Glen responded with a related prompt: "Unscramble the following: NGOWRIG PU SI BVTILNEIAE." I studied the letters and filled in the blanks below them. *Growing up is inevitable.*

In another therapy workbook entry, I lamented: "I have two voices in my head, but the anorexia and OCD voice is louder than my rational voice." While on Bader 5, I was diagnosed with severe obsessive-compulsive disorder (OCD), anxiety, and depression, becoming one of the many people with anorexia who have comorbid mood and anxiety disorders. I had heard of OCD, from the occasional person who would conflate organization with obsession, making flippant remarks about how they were "OCD" about the way they stored Tupperware or folded their laundry. But my family and I didn't know much about the disorder, and we certainly weren't aware that people who are diagnosed with anorexia nervosa are up to 19 percent more likely to also develop OCD. I would later learn that researchers attribute this to the strong genetic overlap between the two disorders, as well as neurobiological and cognitive changes that can stem from prolonged periods of starvation.

I met with a Bader 5 psychiatrist every few days and was developing a deeper understanding of my disorder—exploring not only the destruction it caused but also the purposes it served: the false notion of control, the ability to stay little, the belief that it made me special. These things tethered me to anorexia, and my psychiatrist tried to help me break free from them—through a strict meal plan that nourished me, therapy that counseled me, and medication that numbed me.

I got discharged from Bader 5 after six weeks—a common length of stay at the time but far longer than the average seven- to ten-day stay nowadays. My family hoped my time on Bader 5 had healed me. But as soon as I got home, I began restricting my food intake again and falling back into my disordered behaviors. Over the next six months, I would get readmitted once more to the medical unit and twice more to Bader 5. During my three Bader 5 stays combined, I spent 113 dismal days on the ward. My psychiatrist prescribed me a cocktail of medications each time, with the hope that treating my anxiety, depression, and OCD would make it easier to treat my anorexia. With my father's approval, she first put me on the antidepressant Prozac, which had gained notoriety from the provocative memoir *Prozac Nation*, published four years earlier. The medication had been on the market for just over a decade at that point, and research has since shown that it's not effective for treating anorexia. At the time, I understood very little about the medication, and I was nervous to take it. Tangled in a complicated web of fears, I worried the medication might succeed in separating me from a disorder I wasn't ready to part with.

The Prozac didn't work as well as my psychiatrist had hoped, so she weaned me off it and put me on Zoloft. It seemed to help more than the Prozac, but marginally. During my last stay at Bader 5, I was taking Ativan (a benzodiazepine often used to treat anxiety) and Risperdal (an antipsychotic medication typically given to people with schizophrenia, bipolar disorder, or autism but that's shown to also work for OCD). I was also given vitamin E to help lower my chances of developing tardive dyskinesia—a condition that can emerge due to long-term use of some psychiatric drugs. The psychiatrist, who needed my father's consent for any change in medication, explained that tardive dyskinesia can cause patients to develop facial tics, such as lip-smacking, involuntary eye movements, and abnormal tongue movements. The thought that I could end up with such a condition haunted my father in that moment and in the days and weeks that followed. But he put his faith in the psychiatrist, hoping the medications would help me more than they would hurt me.

My anxiety about food and weight worsened on the ward, so my dosage of Ativan was upped. Even at a medically approved level, it was too much for my body, making me loopy and sleepy. In the Bader 5 classroom, where I tried to keep up with my eighth-grade schoolwork, I would fall asleep at my desk. At night, I started wetting the bed, too tired to be roused. I hid my soiled pajamas in a garbage bag in my closet, not knowing where else to put them. When Gramz came to visit me one day, she opened the closet door and seemed sickened by the stench. She took the bag home so she could wash all my clothes and bring me back new, freshly pressed ones. It was one of the few ways she could take care of me at the time. It made me feel loved, but also deeply ashamed.

The psychiatrist adjusted my medications, taking me off Ativan and putting me on Klonopin. But the Klonopin had the same side effect.

After repeated bouts of bed-wetting, I began wondering what these drugs were doing to my body. I didn't want to take them and had convinced myself there were calories hidden inside each pill. I decided to start "cheeking"—a term I learned from other patients on the unit to describe hiding pills in one's mouth. I got good at concealing the meds and then spitting them out when the staff wasn't looking. But after a week or two I felt so guilty I told my psychiatrist what I'd been doing. She switched me to all liquid medications, which made me regret my confession. The meds tasted foul, and the liquid multivitamin was even worse. The one I had to drink was a brown, mineral-filled sludge that looked like prune juice and tasted like dirt.

In June 1999, during my third and final Bader 5 stay, my psychiatrist used Rorschach tests, projective drawings, fill-in-the-blank sentence exercises, and other methods to assess my level of thought disorder. The results indicated I was "significantly depressed and anxious" and "vulnerable to thought disorganization and faulty logic secondary to situational stress." My coping skills were "significantly compromised," especially in the face of ambiguity, and my problem-solving strategies "often involved external powers and controls such as God or receiving signs from a higher being so that 'things will get better.'" According to the evaluation summary, "Mallary not only lacks adequate coping strategies, but the ways in which she perceives resolutions to problems involves wishful thinking and unrealistic, fantasy-like solutions which may exacerbate her ability to come to terms with and accept her reality." I was still holding on to all those fairy-tale-like storylines and endings my family and I had embraced when my mother was sick.

Oddly enough, just a few days later, I was told I would be going home soon. The thought scared me: Home was the place where coping seemed hardest and where my anorexia was always at its worst. I don't remember my treatment team ever explaining why or how they had decided to discharge me. I would later learn it was a combination of factors, including my own physical health, my ability to make progress in therapy and at meals, and a practical need to rotate patients in and out so children waiting for beds could get the care they needed.

"I don't know if I'm ever going to get better," I confessed to my father on the drive home. "It's just so hard."

"I know, Mal," he said, his eyes emptier than they used to be, his face creased with new wrinkles. "But I want you to remember—Mom fought so hard to survive. If you don't try to get better, then you're choosing to let yourself die."

Dad didn't draw words in the sand that night. He carved them in wet cement, where they stayed for decades. I felt so angry at the disorder that had given me control early on but now left me feeling as though I had none at all. My choices, it seemed, were no longer my own. "I'll try to get better, Dad," I said. "I promise I'll try."

For several weeks after that last Bader 5 stay I read my goodbye book— a file folder filled with three-hole-punched paper and bound with gold and red ribbons. It was my third goodbye book, and like the two others, it was adorned with aspiration. The front cover featured one of my signature collages—a rainbow, a butterfly, colorful birds, and smiley faces. Inside were dozens of handwritten goodbye messages from Bader 5 patients and staff. Most had an underlying message: I hope you get better and never have to come back to this place.

Some of the notes were from other eating-disorder patients I had befriended. "I was sitting one day and thinking about this whole disease. It has a death grip on both of us, but we can fight it!!" Tracy wrote. "I want you to win, not anorexia. Please promise me you'll keep on trying and won't give up. You have so much to live for. Don't let anorexia destroy your hopes and dreams." Next to her note, in big capital letters, was the word *SMILE*. Lily, another patient, wrote in part: "We haven't known each other for long, but I've seen enough of you to know that you will make it. . . . Please don't give up on your life, or on yourself. You are the only person who can truly change your life, for better or worse. Please use your will to make a difference, to survive."

Both girls shared their addresses with me. We exchanged a few letters in the months following my discharge but didn't stay in touch for long. Nearly twenty-five years later, I looked them up online in hopes of reconnecting. At the top of the search results, I saw obituaries. I knew, even before clicking on the links, that both girls had lost their lives to anorexia, joining the 5 percent of sufferers who die from the disorder. Tracy was thirty-seven. Lily was twenty-seven. The news of their deaths made my anger slowly rise, like a fire that crackles and then flares. I was angry not at them but at anorexia and its seductive ways. "I will be your best friend! I will help you stay little, be thin, look beautiful! I will make your pain go away!" the disorder teases, tricking you into thinking it'll help you get through life, never mentioning it might kill you in the process.

I was so deeply saddened by the news that I tracked down contact information for the girls' parents and mailed them handwritten letters to express my condolences. I explained how I came to know their daughters and why I wanted to mention them in the book—to honor their memories and to show that they were so much more than their disorder. In a follow-up phone call, Tracy's mom, Debby, got emotional as she told me how much she and her husband tried to help their daughter, who worked as a medical assistant and had dreams of one day becoming a nurse. "She cared about her patients, obviously, more than she did herself. And the patients just loved her," Debby told me. "She was a beautiful person inside and out, even though she didn't see that." Tracy was hospitalized numerous times for anorexia throughout her teenage and adult life, and she eventually went into hospice care. "The guilt we felt watching her slip a little each day is still with us today," Debby said. "We were supposed to take care of her, and there was not anything we could do to change the outcome."

I thought a lot about Tracy and Lily when I revisited Boston Children's Hospital while researching this book. As I walked down Longwood Avenue and approached the hospital, I hoped it would look the same as I remembered it. I wanted to go back in time and jot down all the details my memory has blurred—the exact layout, the particular colors, the subtle sounds. But it had been remodeled and looked completely different. When I was a patient there, the lobby had a mural with a rainforest motif—featuring colorful animals and a cascading waterfall—on one of the walls. I remember that it used to feel like I was walking into a science museum (except with a much more expensive admission fee). Now the rainforest mural was gone, replaced by heightened security and waiting areas that seemed sterile and cold. The hospital felt far less inviting than I remembered, perhaps because it's no longer a place I want to be. What had come to feel so familiar now seemed foreign, save for the one thing that hadn't changed: the Au Bon Pain, where my father ate many dinners alone. I inhaled the smell of bread as I walked by it, appreciating that I no longer felt compelled to hold my breath.

I tried to get permission from my former medical doctor to visit Bader 5, but I was told that outside visitors weren't allowed. I wandered around the Bader building instead, hoping to at least see the door to Bader 5—a portal that might spark some memories. But there wasn't an option for accessing the fifth floor from the public elevators, as though the ward didn't even exist. It always was, and still is, hidden away. I was steps away from the place where I had spent the sickest months of my life, from a place I will probably never see again firsthand. I felt let down but realized maybe it was a good thing I wasn't allowed in—a reminder that some parts of our life can inhabit our past without needing to invade our present.

Nowadays, there is a greater push to keep young people out of the hospital to begin with, in hopes that caregivers can help their children eat meals and manage slips at home instead of the hospital. As our collective understanding of eating disorders has evolved, so has inpatient treatment. It's now far less common for treatment centers to offer a smorgasbord of low-calorie foods like the ones I used to eat on Bader 5. Approaches vary according to treatment center and level of care. In hospital settings, the thirty-minute time limit for meals is still common, followed by the option to either drink Ensure or get a feeding tube. But rather than a long list of options from the five food groups, patients are typically given rotating options of balanced meals: a stir-fry with meat and veggies one day, pizza with sides the next.

To get a better sense of how things have changed, I spoke with Lisa Mancini, a dietitian who has worked at Boston Children's Hospital since 2012—on the medical unit and Bader 5, and now in an outpatient capacity. She said patients are asked to share five likes and five dislikes upon admission. From there, dietitians will select meals for each patient. "It's a rotation, so every Monday it's the same breakfast, and every Tuesday it's the same breakfast, with the hope that kids are not having to eat the same thing every day like you did," Mancini told me. I considered how much more effective this could be; it presents patients with greater variety, exposes them to new foods, and limits their eating disorder's ability to choose foods for them. "I always tell patients, 'I'm coming in,'" Mancini said. "The eating disorder can be really mad at me, and it can yell at me and despise me, but I am taking the choice away from the eating disorder until *you* can make the choice and not your eating disorder." Hearing Mancini talk about this made me think about how angry the other patients and I got whenever we were served larger-sized bananas. When I told her about the banana-meter, she laughed and said, "I never knew about that; thankfully, it's not there anymore."

Mancini and other eating-disorder dietitians say they avoid discussing calories with patients. "Many people who have an eating disorder are like walking calculators," said Allisyn Pletch, a clinical nurse specialist at Johns Hopkins Hospital's inpatient and day hospital eating-disorder program in Baltimore, Maryland. "I've talked with a number of patients who say that counting calories really drives them to more illness behaviors. If they know they have a certain number of calories left in their meal plan for the day and they want to have grapes, they're dicing a grape in half because they're trying to precisely meet that calorie goal." Instead of talking with patients about calories, Pletch discusses "exchanges," which are general categorizations of foods like grains, meats, dairy, fruits, and vegetables. Telling patients how many exchanges they need per meal helps them think more generally about nutrition in lieu of obsessing over calorie counts. "Everything in an exchange category is somewhat equivalent; something that's in a bread category is counted as the same regardless of the number of calories in it," Pletch said. That "allows patients to have more variety so that they're not just sticking with the white keto bread that has 80 calories and has become 'safe.'"

Dietitian Ryan Sobus said it can be helpful for patients to gradually work their way up to trying "fear foods." "When a patient logs on for treatment on their first day, our team is going to meet them with their safe foods or their preferred foods," said Sobus, clinical outreach representative for Within Health, a virtual eating-disorder treatment program. "It'd be really difficult if you hadn't had anything other than cottage cheese for three months to then be told you need to eat a cheeseburger. That doesn't feel fair." Instead, patients are encouraged to try different types of foods over time, starting off with small swaps. It could be swapping out cottage cheese, for instance, for a cheese stick or yogurt or peanut butter. They then work their way up to eating meals that Within ships them by mail.

In some treatment centers, patients cook their own food in independent kitchens, where they can practice handling and measuring food in healthier ways. When patients come in as vegetarians or vegans, the staff works with them to determine if the dietary restrictions are a result of an eating disorder or something else, like allergies, religion, or ethical concerns. According to one study, women with an eating-disorder history were four times more likely to be a vegetarian compared with control groups. I stopped eating meat when I was struggling with anorexia and wasn't encouraged to eat it during my hospital stays. So, I stayed loyal to my safe foods and shunned variety.

"Sometimes if you're being challenged to consume more, or being challenged to change your body size, you think, *Well, at least I can hang on to some control around the types of foods that I'm willing to eat*," Sobus said. "And at the end of the day, those food rules are still causing you to feel preoccupied by food and preoccupied by needing control over your body. Honestly, one of the biggest predictors of having less preoccupation with food and long-term recovery is going to be: What's the variety looking like?"

Research by Dr. Joanna Steinglass, the Columbia University psychiatrist mentioned earlier, supports this notion. One of her recent studies found that a person's ability to choose higher-fat foods by the end of hospital care is tied to better outcomes years later. Dr. Steinglass says it's critical to help patients venture beyond "safe" low-calorie food choices and toward higher-calorie ones to help them while they restore and stabilize weight. "It feels like what we've done so far in treatment is good and valuable," she told me. "But if we want to do better, this is where we need to focus our efforts."

In all these interviews, I found myself playing the "what if" game. What if my doctors had known this when I was hospitalized? What if I hadn't been allowed to choose all low-calorie foods? Would things have turned out differently for me? As I reported, I also remembered my family's consternation that I ate only low-calorie foods and even limited them. I can still picture their looks of dismay: *Why can't you just eat?!* I know now that this is a common and understandable response in the face of restrictive eating disorders. But it rarely yields productive answers and can be shaming. Less judgmental questions might be: *What can I do to help you eat?* and *What kind of support do you need right now?*

As a researcher, Dr. Steinglass often asks: Why are patients choosing this food over that food? "If you're trying to study why people *don't* eat, then you're trying to look at the absence of a behavior and that's hard," she said. "It's not exactly that people with anorexia are *not* eating; it's that they're making low-calorie, low-fat food choices—even when they're aiming for recovery. When we shift the focus, we can study choice and see exactly what's happening in the brain while people are making choices."

In one study, Dr. Steinglass and her colleagues found that when given a task designed to measure food choice, people with bulimia nervosa chose low-fat foods and avoided high-fat foods—a finding that aligns with other research showing that people with bulimia tend to make restrictive food choices outside of binge-eating episodes. The research is a reminder that restriction underlies not just anorexia but eating disorders of all kinds.

In another study, Dr. Steinglass and her fellow colleagues used functional MRI to explore what goes on in the brain when people with anorexia make choices about what to eat. Specifically, they examined the restrictive tendencies of anorexia nervosa (e.g., choosing the same foods over and over again, limiting portion sizes, or eating only low-calorie foods). The research, which was comprised of people with anorexia nervosa and healthy controls, found that those with anorexia used different brain circuits when deciding what to eat. Many regions in the brain were active when both patients and healthy controls made food-related choices. But a region called the dorsal striatum was engaged only among those with anorexia. This region is known to play a key role in the formation and expression of habits. The difference in brain activity for patients with anorexia suggests that this activity may relate to persistent food restriction.

"This research can help us think about why people get tripped up," Dr. Steinglass said. "Why is it that people who want very much to be done with this illness find themselves still doing stuff that serves the illness better than it serves them? This research is a clue to that."

Dr. Steinglass's research made me feel more empathy for people who can't seem to escape their disorder, and for people like Tracy and Lily, who lose their lives to it. The more we know about the neurobiology behind eating disorders, the more insights we'll have into the questions that keep patients and caretakers up at night: Why are eating disorders so overpowering? And why are they so difficult to break free from? New research is helping to dispel misconceptions about why people develop and remain stuck in anorexia. It also may help parents be better prepared for the reality that recovery is unpredictable and doesn't follow a timeline; it happens in a messy middle place and has no definitive end.

This was an important realization for a mother named Gabi, whose eighteen-year-old daughter Ana began struggling with anorexia nervosa during the Covid-19 pandemic. Ana's symptoms first manifested in March 2020, following a perfect storm of factors: anxiety about the pandemic, inability to keep up with competitive gymnastics during quarantine, exposure to TikTok accounts that promoted harmful weight-loss strategies, and a physical education class assignment to keep a diary of her daily food intake and exercise. Ana began keeping the diary and soon after insisted on making her own meals. Gabi, who works as a director at an environmental technology company, was glad to have help with meal prep. But as the weeks passed, she noticed that Ana was eating less and less and exercising more and more. Ana tracked this in her food diary, earning an A+.

"We assume that due to pandemic chaos, she was graded on completion, and her actual numbers were not checked," Gabi said. "But getting an A+ for displaying evident symptoms of restriction and overexercise reinforced her behaviors." In August 2020, Ana was diagnosed with anorexia nervosa and hospitalized. She was not alone; the pandemic sparked a 36 percent increase in symptoms among people with eating disorders and a 48 percent increase in hospital admissions. Gabi knew very little about eating disorders at the time, let alone the neurobiological factors that can contribute to them. She assumed her daughter would recover just as quickly as she got sick. "I thought we'd be done with it in a few months!" Gabi told me. Ana, who sat by her side during our Zoom chat, chimed in: "My mom told me that by Christmas I would be fully recovered."

While Ana was hospitalized, Gabi had weekly phone sessions with a treatment-center therapist. She learned that her daughter's disorder was far more complicated than she had imagined and that recovery was arduous. Gabi also joined parent support groups and realized she wasn't alone in her struggles to understand her daughter's disorder. "I had a lot of parents tell me, 'Even after the brain is nourished, it can take years for someone to recover.' I thought to myself, *Years? It's just been a few months and I'm exhausted!*" recalls Gabi, who lives in New York. "You have to prepare yourself for the long haul. If you understand this, you can be more effective in supporting your child in recovery instead of expecting perfection." She has also learned to be patient with setbacks in her daughter's recovery and to recognize that one slip doesn't have to undermine progress. "I learned so much as a parent—even though I still make a lot of mistakes," Gabi said. "It helped that Ana's treatment was so focused on families being part of recovery."

When we talked, Ana was getting ready to go off to college, with hopes of becoming a doctor. "I'm at a point where I can focus on other things more than my eating disorder, and I can go maybe a day without thinking about it at all," she told me. "I think there's still room to grow, and I don't think I'm at that perfectionistic 'full recovery.' But I'm in a much better place than I was a year ago, or even six months ago. I think the middle place is kind of an infinite space where you can keep going in one direction forever without reaching the perfect 'full recovery.' And I think my goal is just to keep going in the right direction."

Over the years, it has become increasingly common for medical providers to involve parents in their children's treatment and recovery process. But it wasn't always this way. Dating back to the mid-nineteenth century, the medical community long believed that children with eating disorders needed to be removed from the home to get better. William Withey Gull, the British physician who coined the term *anorexia nervosa* in 1873, once wrote that "relations and friends [are] generally the worst attendants."

He and his contemporaries, including French psychiatrist Jean-Martin Charcot, advocated for parentectomy—the removal of a child from her parents. Charcot went so far as to say that parents of young girls with anorexia "should go away or pretend to go away . . . as quickly as possible." Similar thinking persisted throughout the latter half of the twentieth century. Teens like me were sent away to treatment centers, far removed from home and family.

In 2001, three years after I was first hospitalized, new literature came out urging that parents be included in their children's care. Drawing upon a therapy developed at the Maudsley Hospital in London, psychologist Daniel Le Grange, PhD, and psychiatrist James Lock, MD, PhD, published a family-based treatment (FBT) manual that became a go-to guide for many eating-disorder clinicians and was used in clinical trials at universities. Instead of viewing parents as part of the problem, they saw them as part of the solution. At an eating-disorders conference, I had the chance to interview Dr. Lock, who listened intently as I outlined my rotations in and out of treatment. "That's why I started doing this work, because of your experience exactly," Dr. Lock told me. In his first job, in the 1990s, he worked as a psychiatrist at an inpatient eating-disorder unit. "I had kids in and out of the hospital over and over again," he said. "These were lovely young women who were thirteen, fourteen years old. We helped them and then we'd send them home. Their parents were told, 'Stay out of it, let her recover,' and most of them couldn't and they would come back. As a young doctor, I thought, 'This is unacceptable.'

"We were extremely well-meaning people," he continued, soft-spoken. "But there was nothing in the literature to tell us what to do as providers."

In the twenty-plus years since Dr. Lock and Dr. Le Grange published their manual, FBT has emerged as the gold standard for treating children and teens with anorexia. More recently, it has also been used to treat other eating disorders, as well as young adults. Unlike individual therapy, FBT focuses on treating symptoms first, *before* the underlying issues.

For instance, rather than exploring why a child started restricting, you first need to help the child receive adequate nutrition. In her book *When Your Teen Has an Eating Disorder*, psychologist Lauren Muhlheim, PsyD, of California offers a helpful analogy drawn from her colleague Tabitha Farrar: When a smoker is diagnosed with lung cancer, you don't start by examining what prompts them to smoke; you start by treating the cancer itself.

FBT ideally happens at home rather than a live-in facility. It is intended to treat children and educate their caregivers so they can be as supportive as possible. And it alleviates some of the blame and powerlessness that parents often feel when their children develop an eating disorder. Therapists coach them on how to react if, for instance, a child insists on preparing her own food or tries to purge after a meal.

There are some inherent challenges to the treatment. FBT providers aren't always easy to find, and caregivers need to have the bandwidth to take part and the willingness to engage in the treatment's three phases. Phase one, which typically takes the longest, focuses on renourishment. The child's caregivers have total control over what and how much food is served. Rather than follow prescribed meal plans, caregivers are encouraged to serve meals that their child enjoyed before the disorder's onset. Because food choices can create anxiety for children with eating disorders, FBT advocates eliminating those choices altogether. As children start making progress (e.g., eating all their meals and snacks, trying a wider variety of foods, gaining weight, etc.), they can begin to help with meal preparation. Now, in phase two, caregivers gradually hand over meal-prep responsibilities the child can handle. In phase three, caregivers begin to relax their oversight of meals and return some independence to the child—by letting them choose their own snacks, eat at friends' houses, or buy lunch at school. The goal is to help the child establish a healthy adolescent identity apart from the eating disorder.

Oakland-based psychologist Elizabeth Burns Kramer, PhD, told me that getting started is sometimes the hardest part. "If the child is frozen, the first intervention is going to be 'pick up your fork,' then 'put a bite on it'—no more than five-word directions to help the person start to engage with the meal," said Dr. Burns Kramer, who specializes in family-based treatment. In her private practice, she meets one-on-one with parents to be a sounding board and to review techniques. These include teaching parents how to establish ground rules for mealtimes and respond to their children in constructive ways. The "Why can't you just eat?!" question, for instance, would be reframed as less argumentative: "I know this is hard for you, but you're safe. I'm right here with you."

Dr. Burns Kramer is also deliberate about how she determines her patients' healthy goal weight. Rather than trying to get all patients to the "average" fiftieth percentile, she looks at each patient's growth patterns to help assess their individual needs. "If someone has come into this world as an eightieth percentile kid, I will not restore them to the fiftieth percentile because at fifty percent this person is still undernourished," Dr. Burns Kramer said. "For the brain to perceive that it's nourished and to remove the over-fixation on food and body, we need to get them back to their growth curve—if not higher—especially when they're adolescents and kids, who are supposed to be growing every year."

Lisa Mancini, the Boston Children's dietitian, takes the same approach. "If we have a thirteen-year-old in the seventy-fifth percentile who drops down, we're going to get them back to the seventy-fifth percentile, and we expect them to stay there right through puberty to regain their period (if it was lost) and to maintain good bone health," Mancini told me. "We have learned that if you're not fully weight restored, you're not going to cognitively recover."

When I've conveyed this approach to people outside of the eating-disorder field, they inevitably ask: "But what if the child's highest past weight fell into the 'overweight' or 'obese' categories?" This question doesn't yet have easy answers. In one paper, eating-disorder researchers looked at a case involving a patient who had been obese and then lost weight after developing atypical anorexia. The researchers cited the "clinical conundrum" of determining a goal weight for adolescents with eating disorders and prior obesity, citing "a lack of clear evidence or guidelines for weight management" in such cases and calling for more research and guidelines.

In general, the clinicians I spoke with said that weight suppression—which is the difference between people's highest past weight and their current weight—impedes recovery from eating disorders. Weight suppression can be simpler to detect among children, whose documented growth curves may be easier to access. It's trickier, though, among adults, who switch providers over time and may not keep track of their past medical records. Knowing that weight suppression and weight stigma can go hand in hand, some clinicians try to avoid making comments like the ones I received in treatment, when I was promised I wouldn't become fat. Comments like this are rooted in weight stigma and can be harmful to patients, particularly those who are already in larger bodies or those who recover into them. "They validate the patient's beliefs that being fat is bad, perpetuating the eating-disorder thoughts and making recovery more difficult," Mancini said. "An eating-disorder brain will see any weight gain as being 'fat.'"

For me, the "fat is bad" message has less to do with obesity's health effects and more to do with the inherent harm this blanket statement causes; it stigmatizes people in larger bodies and ascribes moral values to a person's weight, without any room for nuance.

As I think about the changes that have occurred since I was in treatment, the word *nuance* comes to mind a lot. There seems to be a growing understanding that people getting treated for eating disorders need help navigating the gray spaces between black-and-white thinking and behaviors. If we can help people move through these gray spaces—between "safe" foods and "unsafe" foods, between a wide variety of foods or none at all—they'll be better prepared for recovery.

Chapter Five

A Higher Level of Care

In September 1999, I should have been starting my freshman year of high school. Instead, I was headed to Germaine Lawrence, a residential treatment facility for troubled adolescent girls. It was three months since I was last discharged from Boston Children's Hospital. After faltering at home again, my family and medical providers decided I needed higher-level, live-in care. My doctor recommended Germaine Lawrence as a promising option, with hopes that going there would afford me the time and space I needed to get better. The average stay was a year—far longer than any of my hospital stays.

I knew that anorexia claimed lives, and I wanted Germaine to save mine. But I worried that even residential treatment wouldn't work. What if, after all this treatment, I remained sick? What if I never got better and died young, like my mother? The what-ifs felt insurmountable—not only for me but also for my father, who was worn down by three years of watching his wife succumb to cancer and two years of watching his daughter wrestle with anorexia. Both diseases had created a divide between the life we once lived and the one we now stumbled through. Anorexia had toughened my father's love; I still felt it, but the texture had changed. Once soft and smooth as sea glass, it now felt as rough and ragged as a barnacled rock. "I used to have a wife and a happy, healthy child. Then my wife died, and you got sick with anorexia," Dad said on the drive to Germaine Lawrence, his eyes fixed on the road ahead. "Now it's like I don't have a wife or a child anymore."

I felt crushed by the weight of his words and didn't know how to respond. "I'm sorry," I finally mumbled. "I'll always be your little girl." Dad told me he'd always love me, no matter how far away we were, and no matter for how long. He would be allowed to visit me, but I worried that all the time apart would further strain our relationship. I had always been the sturdiest line in our family triangle, the base that kept my mother and father connected in times of distress. But our triangle had collapsed, and now it was just me and Dad—two lost lines moving farther and farther apart.

Germaine Lawrence was just twenty-seven miles from our home in Holliston, but it seemed like we were driving to a distant land. The campus was in a neighborhood called Arlington Heights, known for low crime rates and hilly terrain, with views of the Boston skyline. The streets were lined with evergreen trees and Victorian-style homes that looked like colorful dollhouses. We turned down a quiet street that was divided into two incomparable halves: expensive single-family homes and Germaine Lawrence's buildings and dorms. Like many residential treatment programs, the campus was designed to have a homelike atmosphere. Each dorm was a house, and each was named after a famous female trailblazer. Among them were Harriet Tubman, Margaret Mead, Rosa Parks, Abigail Adams, and Elizabeth Garrett Anderson, the last a British physician and suffragist. Just a few miles away was McLean, the psychiatric hospital made famous by Susanna Kaysen's book *Girl, Interrupted* and the film adaptation, which was due out a few months later. Germaine Lawrence wasn't connected to McLean, but I always found their proximity striking.

The admissions director, a wavy-haired blonde woman named Jane, told my father that I had been assigned to the O'Keeffe dorm, named after the modernist painter Georgia O'Keeffe. It housed the youngest girls on campus, ages ten to fourteen. At fourteen and a half, I would be one of the oldest and the only one there specifically for an eating disorder. In the Anderson dorm across the street, there were a few older girls who had eating disorders. I was glad I wouldn't be housed with these girls; I worried I would look up to them and model their toxic behaviors, similar to what I did on Bader 5.

Jane showed us around the three-acre campus, much of which was tucked back from the road. We walked through the Germaine Lawrence admissions building, past some of the dorms, and inside the Chapel of St. Anne—an homage to the Order of St. Anne Convent, which was founded on the property. The St. Anne sisters, who were Episcopalian, ran a private all-girls boarding school on the grounds in the late 1920s; in the 1960s, the school partnered with the Department of Social Services to educate girls with behavioral and emotional issues. The school eventually separated from the order and, in 1978, Germaine Lawrence was established under new leadership and named after the head of the St. Anne Convent.

At the time, I didn't care about the history of Germaine Lawrence as much as I did its present, which I read about in the stapled packet of information mailed to my father. It included a September 1996 *Seventeen* magazine article featuring Germaine Lawrence and four of its residents. I liked knowing that my favorite magazine had written about it. There was one sentence in particular that stood out, and I read it over and over: "The Germaine Lawrence school is, for some girls, the home of last resort." Reading this, I got the sense that if I didn't do well there, I would be left with no other treatment options. Germaine Lawrence's executive director David Hirshberg told the *Seventeen* writer, "If many of these kids weren't here, they would be homeless or dead." The school had a reputation for admitting girls whose issues were so severe no one else would take them. The ninety-two girls on campus were there for a wide range of issues: eating disorders, sexual trauma, substance abuse, self-harm, suicide attempts, pyromania, truancy, physical or sexual aggression, and more. Many had been physically or sexually abused and were wards of the State of Massachusetts, having cycled in and out of foster-care homes for most of their lives. Germaine Lawrence provided them with stability and a predictable schedule: on-site school five days a week, group therapy four times a week, individual therapy once a week, and family therapy every other week (for the girls who had families).

At the end of our tour, Jane walked my father and me to the O'Keeffe dorm, where a staffer named Candice greeted us. It was time to say goodbye. My father stood in the foyer and hugged me, holding me tighter than usual. We'd had so many departures like this over the past year, but this one felt different. Beyond the tour and informational materials, Germaine Lawrence was a mystery to us. A spot had opened up the week before, and we hadn't had a chance to visit the campus until now. Parents weren't allowed to tour the dorms because of privacy reasons, so my father could only poke his head inside the dining room. He couldn't see my room, know who I would be living with, or meet the care staff. He just had to trust in this last resort, hoping it would be my last stop before recovery.

There was no Georgia O'Keeffe art on the walls of the O'Keeffe dorm. No signature red poppies or cow skulls or Southwestern landscapes. But there were some handmade posters, including one that said, "The key to good health lies within all of us," with prompts encouraging residents to "eat healthy food," exercise, sleep, shower, and socialize. The first floor had a living room, dining room, bathroom, staff lounge, and the classroom where I would attend school for a few hours a day. Upstairs were the bedrooms—mostly doubles, one triple, and one single. Every room smelled musty. I went to my room, a bare-bones space with a dresser and a bunk bed I would share with my roommate Jenny, who was singing an Eagles song. I exchanged a quiet hello with her, then had to start heading downstairs for dinner. As I walked around the dorm, I saw there was snot smeared on the wall of the downstairs bathroom and a bloody Band-Aid on the floor. In the dining room, there were crumbs on the picnic-style tables and a stray hamburger underneath one of the benches.

I sat down at a table covered with a pale yellow cloth. Candice set a tray of food in front of me. It was filled with the same foods I had gotten used to during my five Boston Children's Hospital stays. The other girls in the dorm, who joined me in the dining room shortly thereafter, typically were fed hearty casseroles, spaghetti, and other dishes easy for the staff to cook in bulk. My meals were personalized and came with an extra side of care and attention. They made me feel special, as though they were proof I was too sick to eat "normal" food.

Candice addressed me in a Boston accent: "If you don't eat all of your food within thirty minutes, you will need to drink Ensure." Despite the directive, she sounded hesitant and fidgeted with the stopwatch she would use to time me. I later learned she was only twenty and had no prior experience treating adolescents with eating disorders. Paperwork detailed what she was supposed to do and say. "If you don't drink the Ensure within fifteen minutes," she continued, "you'll need to go to the hospital to be tube-fed." This was the same routine I had followed at Children's Hospital, and I had heard it so many times I usually tuned it out. But on that first night at Germaine Lawrence, I fixated on the "if you don't eat" part. I sat and stared at that tray of food, unwilling to pick up my fork. *The girls who have eating disorders at Germaine Lawrence don't eat*, I thought to myself. *At this place, I'm sure girls drink the Ensure or get the tube.* I knew only the most troubled girls were admitted there, and I wanted to prove I belonged.

I ended up eating my first few meals at Germaine Lawrence, but I soon refused and started drinking the Ensure—something I'd never done in the hospital. I liked that it was predictable; it came directly from the can every time, with no margin for human error. The mere possibility of caloric error had always scared me, especially in a new place I hadn't yet come to trust. I would often picture the staff dishing out overflowing cups of cottage cheese and hummus instead of carefully leveling off each one with a butter knife that promised precision. With Ensure, I knew exactly what I was getting.

Every day, meal after meal, the staff would put my tray of food on the table in front of me, where it would sit untouched for the next thirty minutes. I spent most of the time glaring at my food, occasionally looking up at the other girls in the dining room. In those early days, I marveled at how easy it was for them to put their forks to their mouths, to clean their plates, to ask for more. They eyed me, wondering who the new girl was and why she got her own special food. When the thirty minutes passed and I hadn't touched my plate, the staff poured the caloric equivalent in Ensure Plus—about sixteen ounces' worth. It was thick and creamy, and before the metallic aftertaste kicked in, it reminded me of the vanilla milkshakes my mother and I used to drink together at Burger King.

Meal after meal, snack after snack, I bypassed food and drank the Ensure. My therapist Kerry, whom I met with weekly and liked, told my father what I'd been doing. He didn't understand why I seemed to be regressing in a place where I was supposed to be getting better. One month into my stay, he sent me a letter, worded in that barnacled kind of love: "I have done everything in my power to help you through these troubled times, but I have been a failure. I always think that I can make a difference, but unfortunately only you can, and you seem determined to fight any possible improvement. I miss you so much and feel like I don't even have a daughter anymore. You've got no incentive to eat? I'll give you one. I won't come visit you on weekends unless you eat your meals."

These turned out to be empty threats, as I knew all along they would be. My dad loved me too much to stay away, and I loved him for that. I flirted with the idea of eating my food, and a few times I did—out of hunger and a silent will to do better. But every time, I dreaded how brutal I would be to myself in the aftermath. One night, after eating my dinner, I crafted a solemn vow in my journal: "PLEDGE: I, Mallary Tenore, promise that I will not eat any food whatsoever, even if I'm hungry and even if a part of me wants to eat. I will only listen to my side that tells me not to eat. If I do not eat for one week exactly, then I will be awarded the Perfect Anorexia Award. That is my goal, to be a perfect anorexic, the sickest and skinniest anorexic in the entire world."

I was navigating a debilitating duality: a hidden desire to get better and a fear of showing any signs of improvement. I worried that if I ate, people would think I was fully recovered: *She can eat!* Then: *Let's see what else she will eat! A hamburger? A slice of pizza? Ice cream? She's better now!* My path to recovery was not a road but, rather, a tightrope stretched across a deep chasm. Everything about it seemed terrifying. I worried that if I walked across it and got better, I would lose the ecosystem of care that came with sickness. I would no longer need 24/7 supervision, wouldn't see my treatment team every week, wouldn't warrant stares of concern from family members and strangers who had become hypervigilant about my health and well-being. I equated recovery with an abandonment. It would be a different kind of loss, not of weight or a mother but of a supportive community that had scaffolded itself around me while I was sick. Who would I be if not the girl with anorexia? In one of my first therapy appointments with Kerry, I unpacked this question and explored my thoughts privately in a therapy journal: "If I were to get better," I wrote, "I would be expected to be the perfect, happy little girl again. And I don't know what my role in the family would be." I worried that I wouldn't fit into a life without my disorder and with my father and Katie together.

Anorexia had given me a way to rebel against their relationship. It was an escape from perfectionism, a way to show I wasn't the remarkable, resilient motherless daughter everyone had made me out to be. But the more deeply entrenched I became in my eating disorder, the more I fell for its lies. I continued to think that anorexia could help me not only feel closer to my mother but also *become* more like her. During my early days in residential treatment, I embodied my most accessible memories of her, which were also the most devastating ones: Mom sick with a disease, in the hospital, unable to eat, losing weight, without hair, barely recognizable. "I keep trying to pull out my hair so I'll be bald like Mom," I journaled. Woven throughout my entries was a constant refrain: "Mommy, please come back. I'm begging you. Please come back." At Germaine Lawrence—a place far removed from the life I had before my mom's passing—I longed for my mother's presence.

The more I gained, the more distant I felt from both my mother and my disorder. During daily weigh-ins, I saw the numbers on the scale climb into unfamiliar territory. Even though I wasn't eating solid foods, I was drinking enough Ensure to gain weight. As the weeks passed, I was growing unbearably uncomfortable in my new body. It felt like a scary Halloween costume I wanted to yank off, but it was stuck to me, part of me. I wanted to return to my shrunken body, the one that was smaller but still had never been small enough. "I'm so, so embarrassed to walk around the dorm or go anywhere in public for fear that kids will make fun of me for my weight and looks," I journaled. My clothes were starting to grow tighter, and I would stare in dismay at the "XL (14–16)" tag on my kid-sized shirts and pants. "The label even says 'XL' on it, and I'm still a kid," I wrote. "That means I'm an extra-large kid." In my journals, I tracked my weight gain and the total number of daily calories and grams of fat in the Ensure versus the food in my meal plan. All along I thought I was consuming less by drinking Ensure, but while recalculating the amounts one night, I realized I was wrong. Somehow, I had added the totals incorrectly. It was an infuriating rookie mistake for someone so experienced in counting calories. But it was motivation enough for me to begin eating food again.

As I started eating, I feared my treatment team would think I was all better and send me home before I was ready. Kerry assured me this wouldn't happen, but still, I felt compelled to compensate for eating by showing how sick I still was. I obsessively exercised late at night in bed, rebelling against my treatment plan; I'd lie on my back and circle my legs in the air, hoping to get caught. I would run up the stairs to my bedroom instead of walking, considering it a victory when the staff noticed and told me to stop. I would hide food in napkins or throw bits of it on the floor, with the goal of losing weight again and showing I needed to remain in treatment. One of the staffers, Jacqueline, learned to detect all my tricks. During meals, she would call me out on the clumps of hummus I hid behind the spoon in my bowl, or every bite of banana I'd try to spit into my napkin, or every piece of pita bread I purposely dropped on the floor. She and the other staff issued consequences for my behaviors, starting with a "timeout choice"—a phrase the other Germaine Lawrence girls and I got used to hearing a lot. It was intended to show us we were in control and had to take responsibility for our choices. If we were given a timeout choice, we could choose to stop the behavior or take the timeout. There were two timeout spots on the first floor: an empty room at the front of the house and a cramped space at the base of the stairs. The latter was often teeming with ants.

I frequently got timeout choices for shaking my leg, one of my many forms of exercise.

"Mallary, you have a timeout choice to stop shaking your leg," a staffer named Emma told me one day. After a minute or so, I hadn't stopped.

"Mallary, you now have a timeout for shaking your leg," she said, pointing to the space at the base of the stairs.

"I don't want to take a timeout there; look at all the ants!" I complained.

"Well, then," she said, "you should think about making a better choice next time."

Good choices led to privileges—the ability to play Nintendo, stay up late, and go on weekend outings to the local outlet mall or the FAO Schwartz toy store. Bad choices led to a slew of different consequences that each had a unique name. The highest consequence was called a

Shalom, which is the Hebrew word for "peace." It always seemed like an odd way to describe the worst of consequences, but it was aimed at helping us think about what we needed most during moments of unrest. A Shalom led to a long loss of privileges that could take days, sometimes weeks, to regain. I received a few Shaloms, usually for self-harm, which is common among people with eating disorders. My version: In the bathroom, I would turn the water on, let it get scalding hot, and watch it fall on my fingers. The pain made me feel as though anorexia was punishing me for eating dinner or gaining half a pound. In the dead of winter, I would forgo a coat when I went outside. I could recall my mother saying, "Mallary, put on your coat before going outside. It's cold out today! You're going to need gloves and earmuffs, too. . . . And boots!" The directives I once rolled my eyes at were now lost expressions of love. My heart mourned them.

While I acted out quietly, the other O'Keeffe girls acted out loudly, creating a din that heightened my anxiety. Almost every day, at least one girl would start screaming. Sometimes, the girls would run away from the residential grounds—a behavior that was relatively common among adolescents in residential care at the time. Unlike the locked Bader 5 psych ward, the doors of Germaine Lawrence opened onto the world. We weren't supposed to leave the building on our own. But there was a certain power that came with knowing we could run away at any point—and that we were worthy of being found. Many girls had gotten used to running away from foster homes, and some knew that access to drugs and other temptations awaited them off campus. They would sprint out the door, down the long set of stairs leading to Claremont Avenue, and flirt with that brand of freedom. Whenever girls ran off, two staff members would follow. Sometimes the girls would just walk around the perimeter of the O'Keeffe building as the staff coaxed them back inside. Other times, the girls would get all the way to Massachusetts Avenue, the main street a few blocks away. They would run past the Texaco gas station, the Blockbuster movie store, and the Walgreens, their final destinations unknown. The staff would follow on foot, walkie-talkies in hand, running along the city streets like a scene out of a crime show. They usually caught the girls, but sometimes they'd lose track of them. The girls in my dorm would be gone for a day or even two days. But they always came back.

It would be easy to dismiss Germaine Lawrence as a "loony bin." But we girls were far more complex than the harmful and simplistic stereotypes ascribed to people in psychiatric wards and residential treatment facilities. Though we each had different issues and behaviors, we all harbored inner demons we didn't know how to tame. Over time, we became friends. Every week we had "Friday spa night," which was the only time we were allowed physical contact. Under staff supervision, we would paint one another's nails and braid one another's hair or adorn it with rows of butterfly clips. Throughout the week, we decorated the stairs leading up to O'Keeffe with sidewalk chalk, and we did art projects together, turning to clay and oil pastels when we needed to express feelings we couldn't verbalize. I taught the other girls how to do origami, passing on the techniques I had learned while in the hospital.

With hairbrush microphones in hand, we sang along to our favorites: Destiny's Child's "Say My Name," Christina Aguilera's "Genie in a Bottle," NSYNC's "Bye Bye Bye." And with rolling eyes, I learned to tolerate my roommates' favorite songs. There was Jenny, who played the Eagles song "Hotel California" on repeat, and Carla, a later roommate who had a six-foot-high poster of The Rock on our bedroom wall and a World Wrestling Federation music album she played every day. The O'Keeffe girls and I compared notes about what we did and didn't like about the staff members, and we complained about the consequences they doled out. We talked about the troubles that had led us to Germaine Lawrence and discovered how our stories differed and dovetailed.

At one point, two girls who had substance-abuse issues told me they wished they could be like me because I had never done drugs. "All you have is an eating disorder," one of them said. "*And* you have a father." It felt like they were minimizing my disorder, completely unaware of all the torture that accompanied it. I was hurt by the comment—but also understood I was luckier than most. Of all the girls at Germaine Lawrence, I was one of the few who had a stable and loving family I could someday return to. Very few of the girls knew what genuine love felt like—or even that it was attainable. Decades later, when I was interviewing people for this book, a former O'Keeffe staffer told me: "It was easier to care for you because you were willing to accept care; we could all tell that you had known what it meant to be loved."

As hard as it was to be at Germaine Lawrence, I can look back and know that I received the best care available to me at the time. In the twenty-five years since, eating-disorder care has evolved considerably.

There is still hospital-based inpatient treatment for patients who need medical and weight stabilization and/or psychiatric treatment, similar to the care I received at Boston Children's Hospital. And there are still residential treatment centers, though the typical stay now averages just thirty days. Unlike when I was in treatment, there are now more levels of care available to patients at various stages of sickness and recovery. These include partial hospitalization programs (PHPs), intensive outpatient programs (IOPs), and fully virtual options. With PHPs, patients generally spend their waking hours in a treatment center, five to seven days a week, and return home at night. With IOPs, patients receive a few hours of care per day from home, three to four times per week.

It used to be the norm for patients like me to go from the hospital to the home, without any transitional treatment options. Treatment centers with PHPs and IOPs offer this in-between step, helping to ease the change and advance care. Some eating-disorder treatment programs offer several or all these options, creating a continuum of care that enables patients to move from one level to another as their conditions improve or worsen. In healthcare circles this is known as "stepped care," meaning patients can "step down" or "step up" the intensity of treatment depending on their needs. The stepped-care model recognizes that eating-disorder recovery is an up-and-down process, a middle place where progress and slips often coexist.

For all the advances in treatment, there is still a lot of room for improvement—especially with regard to accessibility, affordability, and transparency. I thought about this when meeting with leaders of eating-disorder programs during the International Conference on Eating Disorders and the International Association of Eating Disorders Professionals Symposium—two annual gatherings that attract researchers and clinicians. The leaders were stationed at sponsor booths, eager to explain their programs and offerings. They handed me glossy brochures and pamphlets that were a far cry from the stapled packet of informational materials Germaine Lawrence had sent my father all those years ago. Some of the marketing materials painted alluring images of residential treatment centers: serene, spa-like centers complete with lush meadows, waterfalls, and bridges, tucked away in forests. There were photos of colonial-style homes with wraparound porches and rocking chairs on the outside, and brightly lit dining rooms and bedrooms on the inside. I chuckled when I saw them, remembering Germaine Lawrence's ant-infested timeout space and snot-covered walls. The people in the photos showed no signs of crisis; they wore wide smiles and looked to be enjoying their meals. And they showed no signs of the comorbidities that often accompany anorexia: depression, anxiety, obsessive-compulsive disorder, and post-traumatic stress disorder.

The marketing materials raised issues of representation, too: Except for a few brochures that featured people with larger bodies, most of those pictured in the marketing materials were thin. I couldn't help but think about how the materials perpetuated one of the biggest stereotypes about eating disorders: that only thin, white, rich females are afflicted. When treatment centers disseminate these marketing materials to clinicians, they reinforce the same misconceptions that have made it so hard for people in larger bodies to seek out and be referred for treatment in the first place.

Angela Guarda, MD, director of the eating-disorders program at Johns Hopkins Hospital, has been vocal about the need for improved marketing. In a 2016 report, Dr. Guarda and her colleagues encouraged clinicians to consider how marketing materials can impact patient referrals. They noted that some residential treatment centers lure patients with offerings like dance classes or equine therapy—activities that may have therapeutic qualities but are not evidence-based treatments. They also urged reporting policies to disclose financial relationships between treatment programs and referring clinicians. Many eating-disorder centers offer meals, travel reimbursements, promotional gifts, and continuing-education credits to clinicians—practices without much oversight. "Legislation and policy changes have limited these types of activities when conducted by the pharmaceutical industry, and awareness of conflicts of interest associated with clinician-targeted advertising of drugs and devices has increased," the report read. "However, similar practices by the behavioral healthcare industry have evolved without oversight." *The New York Times* wrote about the report, quoting clinicians who said they didn't think they were swayed by treatment centers' incentives. But studies of the pharmaceutical industry have shown that even small gifts could influence doctors' prescription preferences, suggesting the same could be true for other industries.

Some treatment-center leaders are trying to address these issues through a group called the Residential Eating Disorders Consortium, which has served as a professional association of eating-disorder treatment providers since 2011. Though it started off for residential treatment providers, it has since expanded to include PHP and IOP providers and now goes by the acronym REDC. About 85 percent of the nation's eating-disorder programs are part of the consortium, according to REDC president and co-founder Jillian Lampert, PhD. In response to criticism in the field, REDC created marketing best practices, calling for messaging that is truthful, fair, and nondeceptive. The guidelines encourage members to consider specific questions when crafting marketing materials, including "Are we careful not to exaggerate services or promise unrealistic outcomes?" and "Do we avoid terms such as 'cure,' 'full/permanent recovery' and 'miraculous'?"

"We need to be really transparent with people that it's probably going to take a while to get better; eating disorders don't happen overnight, and they don't get better overnight," Dr. Lampert said. "You have to be really clear with individuals that once they leave, that's not it; the parts that follow after treatment are going to be key to their recovery."

Dr. Lampert told me that a big part of the challenge is getting people access to care in the first place. She cited four main barriers: insurance, stigma, lack of awareness concerning eating disorders, and lack of geographic accessibility. "Accessibility has improved so much, but it's still not where it needs to be," said Dr. Lampert, who is also vice president of communication and brand at Accanto Health, the parent company of Gather Behavioral Health and The Emily Program. "Some states have almost zero eating-disorder treatment resources. It's a real problem if you don't have care near home." This is especially true in rural areas.

One woman I interviewed, Charlotte, said it's been challenging to find care for her daughter Belle, who has anorexia. They live in a tiny, rural town in the heart of the Appalachian Mountains. Because there aren't any eating-disorder treatment centers nearby, Belle needed to travel five and a half hours to receive inpatient care. When she was discharged to outpatient treatment back home, she had to drive two hours just to see a dietitian. "There's no one here where we live who has any experience with eating disorders," said Charlotte, who grappled with anorexia nervosa herself as a teenager and young adult. She recalled one time when she took Belle to a local cardiologist to get her heart checked, concerned about anorexia's effects on it. "The medical staff told me, 'Oh, she's fine. Her heart rate looks good; she must be a runner,'" Charlotte said. "And I'm thinking,

No, no, you can't tell her she's fine." Their family doctor, meanwhile, has told Charlotte: "You know more about eating disorders than I know."

Charlotte and I talked about how specialized eating-disorder care isn't just hard to come by; it's also hard to pay for. The two types of treatment I received as a child—inpatient and residential care—remain the most expensive of treatment options outside of emergency-room visits. At the time of my research, residential and inpatient care was roughly $2,000 a day for an average thirty-day stay, meaning one round of treatment could cost upwards of $60,000.

When I was at Germaine Lawrence, from September 1999 to January 2001, the program cost $259.37 a day for its residential and day school services. That's more than $92,000 a year—nearly two times what my father was making as a director of housekeeping. There's no way he could afford such care at the time, and our insurance didn't cover residential treatment for eating disorders. The only reason I was able to go to Germaine Lawrence was because my father didn't have to pay for it. Instead, my school district shared the costs with the Massachusetts Department of Mental Health.

At the time, Massachusetts's special-education standards exceeded those of the federal law. The federal standard was "free and appropriate publication education," while the Massachusetts standard was "maximum feasible benefit." Passed in 1972, the Massachusetts standard directed districts to consider providing services to ensure the maximum benefit possible to students eligible for special-education services. Eventually, the state's more generous regulations were criticized for spiraling costs as well as vague categorical eligibility criteria, which caused Massachusetts to identify a higher proportion of special-education students compared to other states. But it meant I had access to the care I needed.

In 2002, a state-commissioned report estimated that adherence to federal standards could save Massachusetts $37 million annually and would allow greater oversight of who was being serviced. "Our definitions and prototypes have been so broad that kids who are not necessarily disabled are being serviced," the then state commissioner told a local news outlet. Just one year after I left Germaine Lawrence, the state dropped the maximum feasible benefit and adopted the less generous federal standards.

I realize how lucky I was to have had my residential treatment paid for in full. And I shudder when I reflect on how many others were struggling during that same period, in the late 1990s, without adequate access to care. While researching this book, I learned about a young woman named Anna Westin from Minnesota. She developed anorexia at age sixteen and struggled for five years before dying of suicide in 2000. Anna's parents were told they had to wait for their insurance company to "certify" their daughter's treatment. This delayed and limited Anna's access to the care she needed. Following Anna's death, her mother, Kitty Westin, began working with lawmakers on what eventually became known as the Anna Westin Act. Passed in 2016, the act aimed to provide more training for medical providers and better treatment coverage for those affected by eating disorders.

The question of who pays for residential care has become increasingly complicated. Some diligent school districts still help cover the cost for young people. But too often, families nationwide who are desperate to provide their children with a level of care that's too expensive to pay on their own have taken legal action against school districts for failing to help with those costs. In response, the districts cite a lack of funding. A school district's community culture has a lot to do with it, too, says special-education expert Margaret Reed, EdD. She was the special-education director of my school district in Massachusetts, and she was the Individualized Education Plan team member who advocated that the district help pay for my treatment. "Schools reflect a town's investment in itself as a community of people who care about each other. In other towns, with different cultures from your hometown's, the minute something like that is asked for, they will say no," Dr. Reed told me. "They will just cite regulatory interpretation to create barriers and make the family jump through every single hoop. And then, finally, when it gets to the point of the family saying, 'Forget about it, we'll remortgage the house or we'll hire a lawyer to go to a hearing,' then the district will say, 'Alright fine, we'll pay for it.' This happens all the time."

Insurance can also help, but coverage is complicated. Patients' decisions to enter treatment, and at which level, often depend on whether insurance will help cover the cost. In some cases, patients need to attempt treatment at lower levels of care multiple times before their insurance companies will cover the higher levels of care their clinicians recommend. It's an unfortunate reality, and one that shows the flaws still existing in our healthcare system, despite improvements throughout the years. Unlike when I was in treatment, private insurance companies are now required to cover mental health care, thanks to the Affordable Care Act of 2010 and the Mental Health Parity and Addiction Equity Act of 2008.

With greater insurance coverage available for mental health services, private equity firms saw a lucrative opportunity. They soon began buying and expanding longtime residential treatment facilities for eating disorders, such as Monte Nido and the Eating Recovery Center. But while those expansions led to a greater number of treatment facilities, they also widened the gap between those with private insurance and those without it. Most clinics owned by private equity firms take only private insurance, effectively disqualifying the roughly 41 percent of Americans with public insurance and the 7 percent who don't have any insurance at all. According to a 2023 study in the *Journal of Eating Disorders*, patients with public health insurance are one-third as likely to receive treatment compared to those with private insurance.

When those with public insurance do receive treatment, it is almost always in an academic setting because the funding to educate and train physicians and researchers comes from the government—not only through reimbursement for care of patients with public insurance but also through grants and subsidies supporting the education of clinicians and researchers. In contrast, private insurers typically provide a higher reimbursement for delivering care but do not directly fund education or research. As privately owned, profit-driven treatment programs for eating disorders have expanded over the past fifteen years, academic eating-disorder programs have lost patients, and many have closed.

Carrie McAdams, MD, an associate professor of psychiatry at the University of Texas Southwestern Medical Center, has experienced this firsthand. Her university had an eating-disorder program that was shuttered in 2018, twelve years after she had started working there. "Now our psychiatry residents have little if any exposure to eating disorders," Dr. McAdams told me. "Academic treatment programs for eating disorders are a necessity to both advance our understanding of eating disorders and to ensure that clinicians treating eating disorders know the standards for evidence-based care." It's yet another reason why so few doctors know how to adequately treat eating disorders and why so many of the afflicted are left untreated.

Most of the people I interviewed had been treated in private treatment centers, and many encountered issues with insurance. Among them is Laura, who developed anorexia nervosa when she was thirteen and struggled for eight years before getting help. When we spoke, she was thirty-five and had been in a dozen different treatment centers during her adult life. She has stepped up and down the ladder of care multiple times, moving from inpatient treatment to residential, to PHP, to IOP, and back again. She has spent up to nine months in treatment during a single stay—enough time to restore her weight but not enough to adequately address the psychological underpinnings of her disorder. "Every single treatment stay I've had has ended before I've felt ready because of not being able to pay out of pocket," Laura told me one evening from her home in Denver. As soon as she reaches a healthy BMI, her insurance typically stops coverage. This has become a painfully predictable reality—so much so that it has prevented Laura from ever wanting to go back into treatment: "It validates the eating-disorder thoughts—that

I won't receive help and care if I'm not in a smaller body, or that people won't see that I'm struggling if I'm in a more 'normal'-sized body. When insurance is saying—'Oh, you reached a certain weight, now you're good, go live your life'—it validates that the only way to show I'm in pain, or that I'm hurting, or that I'm struggling, is through my body."

Not long after Laura and I spoke, Colorado passed a new law that limits the use of BMI in determining treatment for the state's residents. Laura said she hopes this will lead to higher levels of care than insurance companies—and even eating-disorder treatment centers—have previously allowed. "I will say it's frustrating that laws are finally being passed to eradicate BMI B.S. from insurance language, yet some eating-disorder treatment centers are still determining access and level of care based on BMI," Laura said. "So many places now claim to have 'individualized care,' and they base admission on a holistic picture of a person's behaviors, medical information, societal background, and support. However, I don't know how many centers have turned me down once they learn my BMI. Every other box was checked and deemed appropriate for lower levels of care, but as soon as 'the number' comes up, I'm denied."

Clinical social worker Rebecca Lester, PhD, told me that people with eating disorders are "the wrong kind of patients" for insurance companies. "They want people who are easy to diagnose, with a clear treatment pathway that has time-limited intervention that can be tracked and then ended, and they want to have a successful outcome. For insurance companies, that's the 'right kind of sick,'" said Dr. Lester, who struggled with anorexia nervosa as a child and young adult and is now an anthropology professor at Washington University in St. Louis, Missouri. "With eating disorders, it's not like that at all. It's difficult to diagnose them; people go back and forth in terms of recovery and how they're doing with their treatment, and you might not know if treatment was successful for quite a while." Just as people with eating disorders tend to have restrictive mindsets, so do insurance companies. "There's this kind of ethos that less is better—the less care you use, the less you consume of our product, the better," said Dr. Lester, who wrote the book *Famished: Eating Disorders and Failed Care in America.*

Insurance companies tend to claim that eating disorders are expensive to treat because acutely sick patients often require a multidisciplinary team of providers, including a primary care physician, a psychiatrist, and a dietitian. This is true, and it's complicated by the fact that people with eating disorders often need multiple rounds of treatment, just as Dr. Lester and I both did. Dr. Lester has since recovered from her eating-disorder behaviors but says she is "continuously working on the underlying issues." In her psychotherapy practice, she has encountered many patients who received insurance coverage for their first round of inpatient treatment but then relapsed at home and couldn't get insurance to cover a second round. Insurance companies determined that the patients had "failed" treatment the first time and wouldn't authorize further coverage. This is at odds with the "revolving door phenomenon" of eating disorders, in which people rotate in and out of treatment in a short amount of time—typically due to high relapse rates and/or the limits of insurance coverage. In one study, researchers looked at 170 patients with anorexia who were hospitalized for the first time. Over a three-year period, nearly 40 percent of those patients needed to be readmitted at least once.

Many sufferers get stuck in the revolving door, spinning at a pace so dizzying they can barely stand upright. As I would come to learn, there is no instruction manual for getting out; the steps and tools that work for one person may not work for another. The key to getting unstuck is figuring out which steps are going to work for *you.*

Chapter Six

The Possibility of Recovery

Six months into my time at Germaine Lawrence, I had finally begun grieving my mother's passing with help from my therapist Kerry. I was making new connections between Mom's death and my disorder, and I was beginning to realize that grief didn't have a fixed end. But for all the progress I was making in grief work, I was still stuck in sickness.

I was eating all my meals and restoring weight, but I was no less intent on being anorexic. I still felt disoriented and disconnected from the happy little girl I once was. And I was still very much guided by an enigmatic disorder that made me feel special and stripped away all at once. Anorexia had depleted my self-worth to the point where I didn't think I mattered. In my dorm room, I would sometimes turn off the lights and write journal entries in the dark of night. It was a self-imposed punishment, a quiet deprivation. "I don't deserve the light," I wrote in one of the entries, straining to see the words in front of me.

I began talking about this with Kerry, who considered ways we could try letting the light back in.

"Let's trace your body," Kerry said during one of our sessions.

"Trace my body?" I asked, on edge.

"We'll trace it, then you can draw your reactions to different parts of your body," Kerry said. She explained that it was an exercise to help me feel more comfortable seeing my body from a different perspective. I placed myself on a large sheet of butcher paper on her office floor, feeling uncomfortable and exposed. The 36-inch-wide butcher paper didn't seem big enough to fit me. I drew my arms and legs as close to my body as I could, trying to minimize space. With a black marker in hand, Kerry asked me to spread out a bit so she could trace my body's outline with a marker. Lying there, my arms and legs now outstretched, I thought back to wintertime as a child, when Mom and I would make snow angels in our front yard. We'd fan our arms and legs out as wide as we could to make the imprint of our wings bigger in the snow. But those days had long since melted away; now it felt like I was left with nothing but a cold recognition of all I had lost.

"All done," Kerry said, motioning me to stand up. I stared at my traced body, ashamed of how unbearably big it seemed. Kerry encouraged me to think about the different parts of my body and the functions they serve. She wanted me to see my body not for its size but for its strengths—the way my legs helped me walk, the way my hands helped me hold a pen to write. I wanted to appreciate these strengths, but I couldn't. Kerry handed me some markers, and I started filling in the finer details. I drew a smile, an awkward-looking nose, almond-shaped eyes, and a single tear running down my cheek. The smile was like all the other ones I had drawn in my happy hospital collages, but the tear was something new, a breakthrough; I didn't want to keep burying sadness behind smiles. I drew a long shirt and pants on my body, then added dangly earrings, bracelets, and a necklace, trying to beautify the body they hung on. But beneath all those sketched accessories, my outlined body was a topography of loss. Skinny arms. Shrunken legs. Stunted height. A child's body that, in the absence of my mother and in the presence of anorexia, felt both empty and full of loss. I was laser-focused on my body and disconnected from it all at once; I had mastered the art of scrutinizing it, but I had lost the ability to listen to it.

"Anything else you want to add?" Kerry asked.

I looked at the drawing again. It was missing one thing: a heart. I drew one on my chest and wrote "Mom" inside it.

Kerry then laid out a smaller piece of paper, next to the tracing, and asked me to sketch what I *wanted* my body to look like. I drew a stick figure, struck by a new thought: *We all start by drawing bodies that look anorexic.* I attempted to color knobby knees on my straight-lined legs, but in my mind they looked like rolls of fat. My body did not feel like artwork worthy of display; it was merely a sketch I wanted to throw away.

Kerry and I had been talking a lot about my mother in recent months; sometimes it seemed we talked more about her than about my disorder. Ever since my mother died, I had arranged my memories of her into a portrait of perfection. I airbrushed it to conceal the painful memories of her yelling at me, questioning her beauty, and sick in bed; remembering those parts hurt too much. Once they were gone, I placed the portrait on a pedestal. When I talked about my mother, I framed the portrait with phrases I had used in my eulogy: "a wonderful, loving, and sincere person," "a mighty strong fighter," "a pure angel." I never once spoke ill of her. I didn't think you were allowed to say anything bad about people who had died.

In therapy, I would come to realize this wasn't true. I learned that death changes the way we see the world and the way we remember. It blurs and bends memories, prompting us to recall things not necessarily as they were but as we hoped they would be. The grandmother who succumbed to old age becomes wiser. The once-estranged brother who passed away seems ever more present. The hard-edged mother who died of cancer becomes softer. Kerry was the first person who told me it was okay to remember my mom realistically. In one session, she had me write what I loved about my mom—and what I wish I could have changed. I wrote a long narrative about everything I adored, then finished by saying: "I wish she would have prepared me for her death. Maybe then things wouldn't be so bad for me now. Like, if she made a video or if she had told me that she might *not* make it. If only she had said those words to me. . . ."

In another session, Kerry had me describe the similarities and differences between my mother and my anorexia. The differences were hard to come up with, and I could only think of two: "Mom and Mallary liked to eat together; anorexia is about not eating" and "Mom is real, but the things anorexia tells me are fake." The similarities came to me with greater ease, reflecting devastating symmetries:

— Both are related to a disease
— Both are controlling
— Both give me negative attention
— Both give me positive attention
— Both are related to dying
— Both can be used to punish
— Both are related to body image (Mom focusing on her body in the mirror)
— Both I don't want to let go of

By revealing the similarities, I began to see that my disorder was reflective of my worst memories of my mother: her controlling temper, her sickness, her death. All along, I clung to only the best memories, but in reality I was living out the most terrible ones of all. These two things were at odds with one another, Kerry said, because I had never dealt with the loss of my mother. To get better—to start separating myself from both the perfection and the disorder—I had to learn to grieve and to recognize my mother for who she was: beautiful but flawed. By acknowledging my mother's imperfections, I could more easily accept my own. And by letting myself feel angry about some of the choices she made as a mother, I could recognize that her flaws were not my fault. I could see beyond the picture of perfection I had crafted for myself and my mom. I could begin accepting the blemishes that made her who she was and me who I came to be.

At times, I remained hungry for answers from my mom. *Why didn't you prepare me for your death? Why did you leave me? Why did you expect so much of me?* I knew there were no easy answers, but I liked asking the questions and exploring the emotions they sparked. Kerry encouraged these questions and gave me what I had needed all along: Permission to feel anger. To grieve. To recognize that my mother wasn't perfect, and neither could I be. It had taken five hospitalizations and six months of residential treatment to get to this place. It wasn't a turning point that changed everything, but it was a meaningful pivot.

As I spoke more honestly about my mother in therapy and in the pages of my journals, my mental load lightened. I still calculated calories and critiqued my body multiple times a day, but I was no longer utterly consumed by thoughts of food and weight. With support from Kerry and Dr. Sara Forman (my Boston Children's Hospital outpatient doctor), I made incremental changes to my meal plan and grew comfortable with more variety. I tried carrots instead of green beans, peanut butter instead of hummus, Chex instead of Rice Krispies. These changes, small though they were, felt momentous. To the staff and the other girls in the dorm, I claimed I was disgusted by these new foods. But to my journal, my greatest confidante, I confessed my desire: "I'm about to share a secret with you. Part of me is actually excited about trying the new foods because I really want to. I'm so tired of the same old foods." That private admission felt like change.

About nine months into my stay at Germaine Lawrence, I began to read books again—*The Scarlet Letter*, *Mrs. Dalloway*, *A Tree Grows in Brooklyn*, *Harry Potter and the Prisoner of Azkaban.* I found I could focus on the stories with that lightened mental load. I could retain character names and plotlines, and I looked up new words I came across: *languid*, *reverie*, *loquacious*, *evanescent*, *irrevocable.* I felt like I was reuniting with the girl I used to be before my eating disorder—the one who found joy in reading and writing, who loved learning in school, who played freely, who could smile at her reflection. I wanted to be more like her. "Shhh, I have a huge secret to tell you," I wrote around that time, addressing my journal like I would a best friend. "I looked in the mirror today and I thought I looked pretty! It must be because I wore makeup. . . ."

Not long after I wrote this latest secret, my father revealed one of his own. As we sat in Kerry's office for a family therapy session, I could tell something was off. Dad wouldn't look me in the eye.

"Mal, I have some news to share," he said, bouncing his leg up and down and rubbing his nose. He paused. The seconds felt like hours. "Katie and I are getting married."

Before my father could finish, I stormed out of the room and raced down the hall, trying to get as far away from him as possible. My dad and Katie had been dating for about a year, but I barely saw them together when I was at Germaine Lawrence, and I didn't know how close they'd become. Hearing about their marriage came as a shock. *How dare he?* I thought to myself, my anger bone-deep. *Doesn't he understand how hard this is for me?* At fourteen, I was too young to consider how hard it must have been for *him* to break the news to me.

Kerry followed me out the door and told me to go to the timeout room down the hall. It was a big room with white padded walls, staffed around the clock. That evening, a woman named Virginia was on duty. I'd never been to that particular room before, but I had been to enough other timeout rooms to know they were safe havens for feelings that couldn't be easily tamed. As soon as I entered, I started screaming and kicking the padded walls as hard as I could. When my legs got tired, I started punching the walls. Virginia intervened, holding up a large red mat in front of me. "Hit this instead," she told me. I pounded the mat until my hands felt numb, all the while yelling: "Mommy, Mommy, Mommy, please come back. . . . Erase this from my mind, erase this from my mind. . . ."

I looked down at my hands, which had never before hit anything so hard. My anger—all that rage—stunned me. Virginia left for a minute, then came back with a Yellow Pages telephone book. "Focus on this, not your hands," she encouraged. "Rip out all the pages you want." I was in awe of her readiness—and her plentiful stash of telephone books. I tore out every page until I was surrounded by mounds of paper covered with business names and phone numbers. In the confines of the timeout room, I felt so alone in my grief. I couldn't fathom how my father could move on with his life, and I didn't want to believe he could spend the rest of it with someone other than my mother. My heart longed for what was and what would never again be: me, Mom, and Dad, living together as a tight-knit trinity.

Virginia handed me another phone book, and the pile of torn pages grew. I crumpled them into yellow balls that I threw at the padded wall. My fingers, legs, shirt, shoes, and hands were smeared with black ink. The scene in that timeout room would have seemed overly dramatic or downright peculiar to an onlooker. But at that point in my treatment, the piles of Yellow Pages were signs I was regaining a sense of self. They were proof I could let myself feel intense emotions without quashing them through food restriction, obsessive exercise, or self-injurious behaviors. "You got out about three years of crying," Kerry told me later that night, alluding to the time that had passed since my mother's death and my dry eyes at her funeral. She told me my father returned home while I was in the timeout room. He and I didn't talk for several days.

In the months that followed, Katie joined some family therapy sessions, and I went on a few home visits so I could practice spending time with her and my father together. I still felt anxious every time I was around them, but I could at least be in their presence without melting down. Being well enough to go on home visits made me feel more distant from the O'Keeffe girls, many of whom were without a home. The better I got, the more empathetic I became. No longer completely absorbed by my disorder, it now pained me more than ever to watch the other girls go into crisis.

They would repeatedly slam doors, scream in the middle of the night, hurt themselves or the staff, destroy property. Girls would try to steal or wreck one another's belongings—until it got to the point where the staff gave timeouts if we so much as touched what was not ours. The destruction, it seemed, had less to do with the person who owned the property and more with the rush that came from ruining what you could not have.

One evening when I was downstairs in the common room, my two roommates barricaded our bedroom door with a bunk bed. Trapping themselves in our room, they tore Backstreet Boys and 98 Degrees posters off our bedroom walls. They pulled the clothes out of our dresser drawers, threw all my jewelry across the room, and crinkled up several rolls of scented stickers I had been collecting. They knocked over our dressers and nightstands and somehow smashed the window next to my bunk. I didn't know what was happening until I heard the glass break. Three staffers eventually pushed the bedroom door open, and my two roommates were escorted to the Yellow Pages timeout room. The cocoa-colored carpet in our dorm room glistened with shattered glass that was no longer capable of reflection or protection. It took two hours to vacuum up the glass and put things back into a shaky semblance of order. I never knew why my roommates tore our room apart that night; that crisis, like so many others, remained inexplicable.

In need of comfort, I called Gramz. I missed her and my father, whose weekly visits never seemed long enough. I missed my friends, most of whom no longer reached out, too busy buying dresses for semi-formal dances, going on first dates, learning how to drive. They were out there, and I was in here, in a treatment facility where day-to-day life unfolded in a way they could never truly understand—and I could never truly explain.

"I don't want to be here anymore," I told Gramz for the first time. "I wish I could come home."

"I know, Mal, I know," she said, an echo of that wish in her voice. "Soon enough."

Fifteen months into my time at Germaine Lawrence, I was beginning to realize how much anorexia had taken away from me and how much more I could do now that my body was stronger. I was deemed healthy enough to go for walks, participate in gym class, and play basketball with the other girls. I could take part in these activities without feeling exhausted or thinking nonstop about how many calories I was burning. But my body still carried the scars of anorexia and wounds that eating in and of itself couldn't erase. My bone density remained low; a scan showed ominous black spots that looked like ink blots on my spinal cord and hip bone. I was fifteen by that point and hadn't started menstruating. And my mind was still in need of critical care. I had freed up some mental space, but I couldn't rid myself of the belief that my eating disorder made me special. "You'll always be special, and nobody can change that," Germaine Lawrence's head nurse, Maureen, often told me. But I worried what would happen if I started to reject the disorder that had been so integral to my identity during the past three years. Would the separation be too much to bear? Would it feel like a loss of self?

Kerry suggested I try to distinguish myself from my anorexia. We began talking about "the fake Mallary" (the girl who believed she needed anorexia in order to live) versus "the real Mallary" (the girl who knew anorexia almost caused her to die). I responded well to the exercise, driven by a desire to hear my own voice more clearly than that of my disorder's. I started writing poems about the real Mallary, yearning to reconnect with an estranged self. In my journal, I replaced calorie counts and self-loathing sentiments with a new refrain: "I am beautiful, and I'm built nicely. I am beautiful, and I'm built nicely." I wrote it repeatedly, hoping one day I would believe it. I also began separating "myths" and "facts"—the lies my eating disorder told me and the rational truths that exposed them. I hoped that committing the differences to paper would help me commit them to memory.

MYTH: I'll get fatter if I eat a bite of food.

FACTS:

1. It's impossible to get fatter after just one bite or snack or meal.
2. I'll have more energy, but I won't get fatter.
3. Food is fuel for the body.
4. Food is important and healthy to eat.

MYTH: You have to eat the same thing every day in order to "be safe."

FACTS:

1. I choose to eat the same thing every day and I don't *have* to.
2. Eating the same foods every day does not make me safe.
3. There are ways I can be safe other than revolving my safety around food.
4. Eating a variety of foods is more fun, and it's actually healthier.

MYTH: Spilling something on my shirt means I'm a pig.

FACTS:

1. Everybody spills on themselves at one point or another; it's normal.
2. A pig and spilling something on yourself are not related to one another.
3. When sauce spilled onto your shirt the other day, it's not as though you were literally pouring the sauce on yourself.
4. Pigs are not known for spilling on themselves.

As I sorted through more myths and facts, I thought about the origins of my eating disorder. For so long I had believed that by staying small, I could make my mother's presence bigger. But the truth is, distancing myself from my disorder was in fact what drew me closer to my mother. I had fallen for anorexia because I thought it would give me a sense of control after my mother died; instead, it stole what little control I had left. To reclaim what was mine, I had to widen the distance with slow crawls that eventually turned into tiny steps. I widened the distance whenever I tried new foods and whenever I remembered me and my mother having fun together with food—times when we found joy in our tiny kitchen, a place where there were no food rules, where eating could be playful, where the smell of fresh-baked chocolate cookies filled the air. Our kitchen was even a place where lobsters could race.

Whenever our local grocery store advertised deals on lobsters, Mom would let me know it was time. "Alright, let's go! Lobsters are $4.99 a pound this week. Can't beat that!" We would drive to the store and head straight to the seafood section, where we would peer into the lobster tank and ooh and ahh over the biggest ones. We'd bring our selections home and Mom would set a big pot of water to boil. Then she'd take the lobsters out of the bag and put them on the kitchen floor next to the washing machine—a.k.a., the starting line. Whichever lobster made it to the kitchen table first won the race. Sometimes, they charged forward in a squiggly line. Other times, they just sat there, as if stunned by a sudden freedom, feigned though it was. After a few minutes, whichever lobster was farthest from the kitchen table went into the pot first. The winner went last. Mom would put the lid on the pot, and I would wave goodbye.

I found myself longing for memories like this and craving the foods my mother and I used to enjoy together: Cape Cod lobsters, American chop suey, roasted chicken drizzled with cranberry sauce, homemade macaroni and cheese topped with a mound of Ritz crackers, mocha-almond chip ice cream with chocolate sprinkles. I so badly wanted to eat ice cream again, but anorexia told me I should be ashamed for that wanting. I listened to my disorder, thinking the craving would go away, but it subsisted to the point where I confided in Kerry. Admitting my desires felt like a betrayal of anorexia but a victory for recovery, and I needed all the small victories I could get. Kerry suggested we take a therapy field trip to Ben & Jerry's. Part of me felt ready to make the step. Instead of letting my fears fester, I shared what I was thinking.

"It's been three years since I've eaten ice cream," I told Kerry. "Not many people can go that long without eating ice cream, and I like knowing that I can. I'm afraid that if I eat it now, I won't be special anymore."

Kerry didn't give much of a reaction to my comment. She knew I was far enough along in my treatment to see how ridiculous that line of thinking was, even though part of me still believed it. I summoned my courage and accompanied her to Ben & Jerry's, where I ordered a kiddie-sized cup of Vanilla Chocolate Chunk. I hesitated, then dug my spoon into the scoop. As I took a bite, I was transported back in time to the days when my mother and I would cuddle up and eat ice cream together on the green-quilted couch. I chewed the chocolate chunks and swirled the soft vanilla ice cream in my mouth. It felt like my taste buds were awakening after a long, restless slumber.

This reunion with sweet treats prompted several others. Each was accompanied by a desire for something else—something that had been emerging in small bits and pieces and was now taking shape: recovery. In the moments when I turned down the volume on anorexia, I began asking myself a question that deserved answers: What would it take to not just leave Germaine Lawrence but also to stay better after I left and returned home?

When I first sat down to write this book, I had trouble pinpointing what helped me get better. Throughout most of my young adult life, I attributed my recovery to one thing: residential treatment. But as I look back on all the hard work I did at Germaine Lawrence, I'm struck by how much better I got once I started releasing my long-held fears about food and reconnecting with my desire for it. So many of us with eating disorders get accustomed to suppressing our desires. To fulfill them is an exercise in letting go—of the eating disorder and the misguided belief that we will never be safe or special without it.

I spoke about this with Kerry, whom I reconnected with when researching this book. Twenty-one years had passed since Kerry and I last interacted, but she said she thinks of me often. On her bedroom desk is a small wooden angel I painted for her when I was at Germaine Lawrence. "I saved the angel because you gave it to me, and you were and still are special," she told me. "You were dear, open-hearted, feisty, sweet, smart. A fighter."

In a series of conversations, Kerry and I recounted the grief work we did together and the exercises she had me do: the body tracing, the myths-versus-facts lists, the real-versus-fake Mallary lists. "Eating disorders take so much work, and my goal was to get you to instead put all that work into being a warrior for self-acceptance, for body acceptance, for grief and loss," Kerry said. We talked, too, about how much has changed since I was at Germaine Lawrence, including the different therapies that clinicians now use to treat eating disorders and to help people move through the middle place. The standard forms of therapy that have been used for decades remain, including the two that Kerry used with me: cognitive behavioral therapy (CBT) and dialectical behavioral therapy (DBT). CBT is one of the most widely used therapies for eating disorders, largely because eating disorders are both cognitive and behavioral disorders, and CBT is designed to produce both cognitive and behavioral changes.

A newer version of the treatment—known as enhanced cognitive behavioral therapy (CBT-E)—has emerged in the past two decades as a leading form of treatment for eating disorders. Originally developed for people with bulimia nervosa, CBT-E was modified in the early 2000s to become transdiagnostic, meaning it's now used to treat a range of eating disorders. It focuses not just on current symptoms but also on maintenance factors that keep people tethered to their disorder, such as dietary restraint and obsessive exercising. Patients are encouraged to monitor thoughts and feelings about food and body image in real time so they can be more aware of what's happening in the moment and begin to make changes to behaviors that seem automatic or out of their control. In the process, patients learn problem-solving skills for handling triggers and for identifying and modifying the eating-disorder mindset. Many providers use CBT-E, as well as other therapies that augment the more traditional ones, including temperament-based treatment, perfectionism therapy, and targeted exposure therapies for fears around food, weight gain, and body image.

In researching different therapies and therapeutic exercises that have come about since I was acutely sick, I find myself drawn to those that recognize an undeniable reality: eating disorders stem from a complicated matrix of factors that can't be easily untangled. For a long time, full recovery seemed unavailable to me, partly because some of my treatment providers described it as the *absence* of the eating disorder and all the distorted thoughts that came with it. I came to equate full recovery not just with the disappearance of my disorder but also with the abandonment of temperament, a loss of self. If I didn't have anorexia, would I still be me?

Many recovery narratives are rooted in this idea of removal: the tumor is excised; the stitches are taken out; the mediport is extracted. But for people struggling with eating disorders, there is no easy removal, no easy remedy or redress. It's why so many of us live our lives in the middle place, recovering but not completely removed from our eating disorder. As I've unpacked the word *recovery* and explored its multitude of meanings in the eating-disorder space, I've found that it's less about the eradication of one's disorder and more about the elucidation of it. It's about developing a clearer understanding of the parts of ourselves that may have contributed to the disorder and turning them into strengths rather than dismissing them as weaknesses. Instead of diminishing who we are, we learn to *expand* our sense of self.

In their book *8 Keys to Recovery from an Eating Disorder*, therapists Carolyn Costin and Gwen Grabb explain that everyone with an eating disorder has a "healthy self" and an "eating-disorder self"—two internal forces at odds with each other. The eating-disorder self may tell you to skip dinner, for instance, while the healthy self understands this is not okay. The two are always battling and vying for your attention. Costin, a renowned clinician who is fully recovered from anorexia, says the goal isn't to get rid of the disorder self but, rather, to learn from it. You have to acknowledge what the disorder is doing for you and then strengthen the healthy self to take over its job.

The "healthy self" versus "eating-disorder self" concept is similar to the "real Mallary" versus "fake Mallary" exercise I did at Germaine Lawrence. But rather than referring to the eating disorder as "fake," it recognizes that it's real. "I don't like the term 'fake Mallary' and 'real Mallary' because my point is, both of those are you," Costin told me from her home in Malibu, California. "That's why when I treat people I talk about integration. I never say, 'We're going to get rid of that part of you.' I say, 'What we're going to do is get rid of the behaviors that it carries . . . and make your healthy self so strong that you don't need those behaviors anymore.'" As the healthy self gets stronger in recovery, the eating-disorder self becomes an internal alarm of sorts, flagging feelings that need your attention. Costin teaches that you need to listen to this part of yourself, determine what's happening, and respond with your healthy self instead of engaging in eating-disorder behaviors. Without this internal shift, Costin says, behavior changes are harder to make and sustain.

It can sometimes feel safer to hold on to the eating disorder than to risk losing it altogether. However, in realizing that the part of oneself that engaged in eating-disorder behaviors remains as an alert system but the behaviors it used to engage in are gone, recovery becomes less about loss and more about letting go. This is why Costin uses the term *integration*. "When you are recovered, you no longer have two split selves," she told me. "Your two parts are integrated, you are again whole."

In her chapter on the two selves, Costin encourages readers to write a thank-you note to their eating-disorder self and acknowledge what it has done for them. Maybe, for instance, it helped you deal with trauma, cope with anger, or numb your pain. Whatever the case, "write everything you can think of. Let your eating-disorder self know what you think might have happened or might happen without it being there for you." Then, write alternatives for how these hardships could have been handled without the eating disorder—an exercise meant to give voice to the healthy self. By acknowledging the eating-disorder self and the purposes it serves, Costin says, you can empower your healthy self to serve these purposes and take back control, putting the eating-disorder self out of a job. Recognizing what the eating disorder gave you at one point in time (or what it continues to give you) can help you more easily identify all that it threatens to take away. Maybe, for instance, you started restricting your food intake to cope with emotional pain, only to find that you're constantly hurting. Or, you started binge eating because you wanted an escape, only to find that you feel more trapped than ever. When you unearth these ironies, feelings of anger, resentment, and frustration can more easily rise to the surface—the very feelings that those of us with eating disorders tend to hide.

Costin also encourages people to write a goodbye letter to their eating-disorder self, even if they don't yet feel ready to do so. "Use your healthy self to tell your eating-disorder self what it has done for you but also the price you have had to pay," Costin writes. "Let it know you will not be following its directives anymore."

Costin now carries out these teachings in a new program she developed to train people (many of whom are recovered from an eating disorder) to become recovery coaches. The coaches aren't clinicians, so they can't make diagnoses or treat conditions. Instead, they help people tackle day-to-day behavioral challenges. Some coaches, for instance, accompany patients on trips to the grocery store or temporarily live with patients as they transition from the hospital to a home setting.

One of my survey respondents named Rose, who has struggled with anorexia on and off for nearly thirty years, said she has made notable progress with the help of one of Costin's coaches. She doesn't consider herself to be in recovery but says she's "striving toward" it. With her coach's support, Rose engages in daily writing exercises that capture the dialogue (or, more accurately, the diatribe) between her healthy self and her eating-disorder self. At first, she was skeptical about whether the exercises would help. But she told me it's been revelatory to seek out both selves and to witness them at odds with each other. She's found that it's especially helpful to do these exercises before dinner, which is her hardest meal of the day. One of her recent dialogues went like this:

> EATING-DISORDER SELF (EDS): Ugh, I can't believe it's dinner now. I just don't feel like pushing myself.
>
> HEALTHY SELF (HS): I have done everything I can to make this as easy as possible [listed all the things you did during the day like spreading out meals, etc.].
>
> EDS: I've eaten so much today. This is the meal that's going to lead to weight gain. You've already followed your plan all day, so if you can restrict a little bit at dinner then you won't gain.
>
> HS: I'm not afraid of weight gain. I am committed to healing my relationship with my body and food.
>
> EDS: You're not hungry and you are going to feel so full.
>
> HS: I have felt full before and it will pass.

Rose, who shares these dialogues with her recovery coach, said she likes the act of writing them—partly because it's different from anything she's ever done with previous treatment providers. It has also given her a new sense of self. "I think the main benefit is knowing there is a part of me that wants to make pro-recovery choices, and that's empowering," said Rose, a mother of four. "Even though I still struggle with letting my eating-disorder self create a lot of noise, I now know my healthy self is there, too."

This idea of two selves may seem like new age jargon to some. Or, it might raise questions along the lines of: Why even bother trying if there's no guarantee that my eating-disorder self and healthy self will become integrated? This feeling of futility comes up, too, in discussions about genetics. I surveyed many people who believe they "inherited" their eating disorder from their parents. But the truth is, we don't inherit eating disorders; we inherit a vulnerability to them. Others I surveyed fear that their eating disorder has caused irreparable damage to their brain. "I honestly don't think I will ever get better," one person wrote in response to my survey. "The only way I see myself without any sort of eating disorder is if I have a brain transplant, at which point, am I still really me?"

There again is the belief that recovery requires a removal, an erasure. It's easy to feel like we will never get better because of our brains, our genes, or our temperament traits. But a growing body of research shows that our brains have a remarkable capacity to be rewired through repeated behavior changes. And we're learning that we don't need to try to get rid of our traits (like perfectionism) in order to achieve and sustain recovery.

One woman I spoke with, KC, is a perfectionist in recovery from orthorexia—a pattern of disordered eating in which people develop an unsafe obsession with healthy food, driving them to eat "perfectly." KC's eating disorder developed when she was twenty-three, after her mom died of colon cancer. Growing up in a conservative Christian household, KC was told that praying would keep her mother alive. When it didn't, she was tortured by a question with no easy answers: "Why did my mom have to get cancer and die so young?" She craved something to blame so she could make better sense of the loss. Food became an easy scapegoat. KC remembered the times her mother would eat at Dairy Queen or drink root beer floats. "I thought, *Oh, my mom died because she was eating Peanut Buster Parfaits and chocolate, and she had too much fun.* She didn't adhere to these really rigid diet rules; that must have been why she died," KC told me.

Determined not to get cancer herself, KC started looking for ways to keep herself healthy. She hunted for stories about so-called cancer-causing food, losing herself down a Google rabbit hole of fear, combing through thousands of search results to build a list of foods to avoid. Soda (or "liquid cancer," as she started calling it) and red meat were at the top, then the list grew to include refined sugar and carbs, fried foods, and all meat except salmon. She had read that salmon and broccoli could help prevent cancer, so she based the bulk of her diet on them.

At the time, she was working for an environmental magazine, where lunchroom chatter sometimes lauded the benefits of vegetarianism: It was good for the environment; it could help save the planet; it could, possibly, prevent cancer. These remarks fueled KC's obsession even more, and she found herself ascribing moral values to food. She was "good" if she ate a quinoa salad for lunch, but "bad" when she went out for pizza with friends. "It really mirrored religion in the sense of trying not to sin and trying to do everything right and appear holy," KC said. She took pride in being uber-healthy and never assumed she had a problem. But as the years passed, her body told her otherwise. On a few occasions she woke up in the middle of the night with panic attacks. "I think it was my body's way of saying: 'You need to eat something. Your blood sugar is too low. We have to do something or we're going to shut down . . .'" KC told me, fighting back tears.

It wasn't until a friend began treatment for an eating disorder that KC realized she might have one, too. She sought help from a specialist who told her she had orthorexia. The term, first coined in 1997, describes people who rigidly avoid "unhealthy" foods. Though it has been gaining attention from eating-disorder specialists, orthorexia is not yet recognized as a psychiatric or eating disorder in the *DSM-5*. Some clinicians argue that it's not really a distinct psychiatric disorder but rather a cultural manifestation of anorexia nervosa, or a food-specific manifestation of obsessive-compulsive disorder. KC felt torn when she received the diagnosis; she was relieved that someone had recognized and named what she was dealing with, but she felt inadequate for not meeting the criteria for more common eating disorders. "Being in this weird 'other' category made me think that my eating disorder was kind of fake and that my therapist was just out to placate me," KC said. "I still have trouble accepting that this is a serious problem."

After her diagnosis, KC started working with a dietitian who helped expand her diet, adding foods she had long considered "forbidden." She dared occasional fast foods, followed by Sour Patch Kids, soda, fried chicken, and chocolate. She started eating Pop-Tarts, which her mother had refused to let her have as a child, and she tried out every flavor. (The Frosted Boston Creme Donut ones were her favorite.) KC met weekly with a therapist to work through the emotions that came with eating more and gaining weight. She came to realize she had oversimplified the story of her mother's death by convincing herself that food alone was the culprit. "Black-and-white thinking was just such a huge part of my religious experience growing up—right and wrong, good or bad, A+ or F, broccoli or Coca-Cola," KC said. By exploring the nuances in her mother's illness narrative—including the multitude of factors that could have contributed to her mom's cancer—KC began to see that food wasn't a villain.

KC, who's in her late thirties, considers herself to be in recovery from her eating disorder. She is learning to embrace other parts of her identity—she is queer, she's a caring friend, she has a good sense of humor—with the goal of elevating her healthy self. She still has days when she fixates on food and her body more than she'd like. But instead of viewing her slip-ups as unforgivable failures, she tries to accept them. "When I have those slips, I'm ashamed," she said. "I don't want to tell my therapist about them because I feel this self-induced pressure to present a linear path through recovery, where every day I'm getting better and then someday I'll be fully healed. And at the end, my therapist will pat me on the head and give me an A+ and I'll be done. . . . I'm a perfectionist, so it's hard for me to acknowledge that there are ups and downs."

In recent years, some clinicians have begun targeting traits such as perfectionism with specific treatment approaches in hopes of helping patients like KC. Cheri Levinson, PhD, founder of the Louisville Center for Eating Disorders, conducts perfectionism therapy aimed at helping people with eating disorders relax their unrealistic standards and lessen their anxiety over mistakes. The treatment helps patients identify the ways in which they're perfectionistic, challenge their perfectionistic thoughts, and make mistakes in a safe environment. In a study on perfectionism group treatment, Dr. Levinson found that the therapy was effective at decreasing unrealistically high standards. "There's perfectionism and there's healthy striving for excellence, and we're not trying to get rid of striving for excellence. What we're trying to do is reduce problematic perfectionism," Dr. Levinson told me over coffee in Washington, D.C., where we met at an eating-disorders conference. "I also think our society has suggested that it's good to be perfectionistic when it's actually not. Perfection is an illusion." This is an important reality to convey in treatment so that patients can be better prepared for the imperfect, slippery nature of recovery.

Dr. Levinson's work dovetails with another form of treatment called temperament-based therapy with support (TBT-S). Temperament is the biological basis of our personality—the neurobiological and genetic underpinnings that influence our feelings, behaviors, and thoughts over a lifetime. TBT-S, which is informed by research on the neurobiology of eating disorders, suggests the same temperament traits that exacerbate these disorders can also be useful during the recovery process. I learned more about this during a conference session led by two TBT-S founders, Laura Hill, PhD, and Christina Wierenga, PhD, both University of California San Diego psychiatry professors who study the neurobiology of eating disorders. Hill told attendees to picture a tree, with the branches symbolizing a patient's symptoms. She said many treatment models—including cognitive behavioral therapy, dialectical behavioral therapy, and family-based treatment—focus on symptoms, or the parts of the tree we can see. But TBT-S augments this approach by focusing on the tree's roots, or the underlying neurobiological factors that contribute to a patient's eating disorder. The field knew little about these factors until the early 2000s, when research began to uncover the neural circuits associated with eating disorders. Thus, TBT-S draws upon this ever-evolving research to help patients understand the brain-based aspects of their disorders, including their traits.

Dr. Wierenga explained that people with anorexia tend to share a lot of the same traits, including perfectionism, rigidity, persistence, risk aversion, sensitivity to criticism, the ability to delay gratification, preference for routine/structure, and attention to detail. Traits develop from brain circuits, which are structured by genes and influenced by the environment. People with anorexia have alterations in the wiring of these circuits, which can lead their traits to be expressed destructively instead of productively. Take attention to detail. I interviewed many people who said their attention to detail was a productive trait that helped them succeed academically and professionally. But this trait turned destructive when they got sick and then began trying to carefully count every calorie they consumed. The same was true for me.

At the heart of TBT-S is a simple call to action: "Treat to the trait." In other words, identify how people can use their traits as strengths that help them reduce their eating-disorder symptoms. During TBT-S sessions, patients are asked to list positive and negative expressions of their traits so they can begin to harness the positive facets for good. Rather than pathologizing their traits, patients learn how to take a strength-based approach to appreciating them. The underlying message is that getting better isn't about getting rid of those traits; it's about shifting their expression in service of recovery. "I've heard a lot of patients tell me over the years that they felt very invalidated by their treatments because they felt that they needed to change who they intrinsically were in order to recover. And that's just not the case," Dr. Wierenga told me. "These traits can be expressed in very positive, productive, healthy ways, and they can also be expressed in ways that are destructive and unhealthy."

Rose, the mother of four, said this framing helps her recognize how her traits express themselves differently in her eating-disorder self versus her healthy self. When we spoke, she highlighted two specific traits: perfectionism and her preference for routine. Perfectionism exacerbates Rose's eating disorder, leading her to feel shame and guilt whenever she strays from her strict meal plan. But her healthy self reminds her that perfectionism and rigidity aren't all bad. "My healthy self would express these traits as determination, persistence, and dependability, which are wonderful and feel like who I was before my eating disorder," said Rose, who has learned TBT-S techniques from her recovery coach. "I don't want to change who I am. I still value routine and structure, and I'd like to consciously work on being more spontaneous. I think that will naturally evolve as I continue to heal my body and mind through nutrition, coaching, etc."

TBT-S patients work closely with "supports" (parents, partners, friends, etc.) who help them pinpoint when a particular temperament trait may be taking over. Patients receive educational resources alongside their supports, including handouts about different brain systems related to traits, appetite regulation, and eating behaviors. They learn, for instance, that "neurons that fire together wire together," meaning the brain can be rewired through the repeated practice of healthy behaviors. Molly, from Spokane, Washington, recently attended a five-day TBT-S program along with her parents, partner, and friends. "It was the first time we learned that eating disorders are brain disorders," said Molly, who's twenty-one. "And it was the first time I felt like people understood what I was going through—that my eating disorder wasn't a choice, and it has never been a choice." A year earlier, Molly was getting progressively worse and went to a residential treatment facility 1,400 miles from her home. It was the only option available, due to limited beds, and Molly was so desperate she decided to give it a try. She found the treatment to be ineffective, though, partly because it felt isolating; the treatment didn't involve her family, making her feel even more disconnected.

Molly liked the TBT-S focus on involving supports, which can be especially effective for young adults who may feel too old for family-based treatment but too young to be without parental support. "For so many years I thought, *No one else can know about my eating disorder, and I'm going to need to heal and recover on my own,*" Molly told me. "But I realized after the first day of this treatment that there was just no way I could do it alone. Now everything is out in the open, and I can't hide anymore." Molly appreciated the TBT-S approach to "treating to the trait" because it made her recognize how traits like anxiety and impulsivity contributed to her eating disorder. Rather than ignoring or demonizing these traits, she acknowledged and faced them.

Molly and her supports received a four-page contract explaining how she can remain true to herself while making behavioral changes that support recovery. The contract acknowledges that recovery isn't perfect, and it even has a section asking patients to fill out questions about how they'll make "repairs" after the inevitable breaks in momentum. For Molly, this means acknowledging her slips and sharing them with someone in her support circle within twelve hours. Molly's father, Shane, said this has emboldened him to be more involved in his daughter's recovery process. "We had to forget the secret crap because secrets are part of the disease. If the truth isn't in front of us, then we're losing," he told me. "I knew she was going to have slips, but as long as we have the truth, we're still fighting, we're still in the game, we're still winning."

Dr. Wierenga, the psychiatry professor who helped shape TBT-S, said it's important for people be honest with loved ones about setbacks; doing so alleviates the shame. "Slips will happen. But they're not going to negate all the progress that has been made, and they're not the definition of recovery; they're just part of the process," Dr. Wierenga said. "It's not at all a sign of failure; it's actually a sign of recovery when you can admit that you've had a slip."

This type of messaging is so important to convey to people with eating disorders, who may view every falter as a failure. As new treatments emerge, I'm hopeful that (like TBT-S) they'll be informed by science and will challenge conventional thinking on full recovery by acknowledging the vast middle place that lies before it.

Chapter Seven

Slips

"You ready?" my dad asked.

"I'm ready," I said, hoping it was true.

It was my last day at Germaine Lawrence. I had finished my teary-eyed goodbyes to the staff and girls in the O'Keeffe dorm, where I had lived for seventeen months. And now, on a bleak winter morning in January 2001, I was headed home. My father rolled my suitcases down the tree-lined avenue toward our car. Temperatures were in the twenties, and Dad marched ahead as I trailed behind. I wasn't sure if he was rushing because he sought the car's warmth or because he couldn't wait to get away from Germaine Lawrence.

Over the past three years, Dad and I had spent more days apart than together. My medical records testified to that separation: 134 total days in the medical unit and psychiatric ward of Boston Children's Hospital, and 489 days at Germaine Lawrence, totaling eighty-nine weeks of treatment. Anorexia had sentenced me to an institutionalized life, with the blinds and doors closed to the outside world. Now the blinds were lifted. The door was opened. And I stepped outside, feeling as though I was entering a new phase of life that was both familiar and unknown. What would it be like, I wondered, to return home to my family, but in the absence of *both* my mother and my eating disorder?

"I missed you, Dad," I said, leaning over and giving him a kiss on the cheek as we drove along neighborhood roads, leaving Germaine Lawrence in our rearview mirror.

"I'm so happy to have you back," he gushed in response, as though referring to both my return home and a return from the disorder that held me hostage for so long. "I'm proud of you."

I was proud of myself, too. I had been eating all my meals, trying a variety of foods, and listening to my body's wants and needs instead of heeding anorexia's demands. I had lessened my grip on the eating disorder and no longer wanted to hold on to it with a white-knuckled refusal to let go. The journal pages I once filled with calorie counts and self-disparaging remarks were now replete with a desire to make up for lost time. At fifteen, I wanted to return to school and reconnect with old friends. I wanted to work toward my goal of one day becoming a journalist. I wanted, above all else, to be back with my family.

The first few meals at home felt celebratory. My father and I were finally able to eat together without anorexia crowding its way onto a seat at the table. Our conversations no longer revolved around food-related arguments or pleas to "just eat!" And gone were the days when I would get up every few minutes to jump. I reunited with foods I loved, and Gramz delighted in making them for me. One of my favorites was her cranberry-walnut bread. Not long after I came home, we made it together. Gramz stood over the gray granite countertop as she measured out a cup of flour, then carefully leveled it with a butter knife. "When baking, Mal, you always need to be precise," she told me, as she had done many times in the past. Standing next to her, I felt like I was watching her not with the wide eyes of a child but with the open heart of a teenager who wanted to reconnect. Once we measured out all the ingredients, I mixed them into a chunky batter studded with cranberries and walnuts. I handed the spatula to Gramz, who stirred the batter a few more times to incorporate the last streaks of flour. I discovered comfort in the rhythm of her stirring, with her right hand moving in a swift, circular motion while her steady left hand kept the mixing bowl in place.

When I was sick, I had looked away from that motion, not willing to see food being made. Eventually, I had left the kitchen altogether, trying to be as far away from food as possible. Gramz stopped making the cranberry-walnut bread, knowing I wouldn't go near it, let alone eat a bite of it. But now we could stand side by side in the kitchen, where food brought us together instead of tearing us apart. When the bread was done baking, Gramz and I shared a thick slice together, just like old times. I was happy—to feel my grandmother's love instead of her angst, to feed my desires instead of depriving them, to eat and enjoy.

I eased back into my studies at school. During my time away, I had received credit for classes, so I didn't have any gaps in my transcripts. But the schoolwork in treatment was rudimentary—and secondary to therapy. I got an education in mental health, but I had learned very little about biology, U.S. history, or world geography. My school district and treatment team at Germaine Lawrence arranged for me to finish out my sophomore year at an alternative school, where I took classes with teens who had dropped out or been kicked out of traditional public schools. While at the alternative school, I did everything I could to not only catch up but also get ahead. I worked diligently in class, did homework and readings every afternoon before dinner, and signed up for additional evening classes at a local vocational school—the same one my mother had graduated from.

When I returned to my public high school in my junior year, some of my peers knew where I had been. But hardly anyone asked me about it, and I didn't divulge any details. No longer intent on being the girl with anorexia, I wanted to just be Mallary. I was healthy enough to exercise, so I tried out for varsity cross-country and landed a spot on the team. Instead of isolating myself like I had when I was sick, I befriended my teammates. We went out for pizza and hung out at the local Dairy Queen, where we'd indulge in late-night Oreo Blizzards. Eating was so much easier, even pleasurable. My eating disorder had faded into the background, out of sight, and I began to wonder if it was gone for good.

By the second half of my junior year, I let myself be tugged into the familiarity of overachievement. I was elected president of the National Honor Society, and I signed up for an exhaustive list of volunteer opportunities. I got a job in the customer service booth at a local grocery store, joined the high school newspaper staff, and landed an internship at my hometown paper, *The Holliston Tab*, where I wrote so many stories that I began to think of myself as a journalist. Family and friends weren't surprised when they saw my byline, a reinforcement of my well-known love for the written word. "Mallary is an excellent writer," my mother had noted in a scrapbook of milestones when I was just eight years old. "She's going to go places with her writing."

By the start of my senior year, though, I found myself grappling with an unsettling question: What if I could no longer live up to that "excellent writer" description? I began to dread turning in stories and essays, fearing that one bad grade or one too many edits would convince people I didn't deserve such status. In recovery, I already had lost a big part of my identity: anorexia. I didn't want to risk losing my identity as a writer, too. I tried my hardest to hold on to that part of myself, hoping I could perfect it into permanence.

One night, while I worked on an essay about the Albert Camus book *The Stranger*, my father reminded me it was time for bed. "I'm not done yet, but I'll finish up soon," I fibbed, giving Dad a kiss goodnight. It was the first time I had ever stayed up late to work on an assignment, and it was the start of what would become a new habit: sacrificing sleep to succeed academically—and later, professionally. In the lonely quiet, I wrestled with words that warred with me. I cursed the Delete button and struck it with my middle finger every few seconds. Every sentence felt like a battle, every period a hard-fought victory.

Around 1:30 a.m., I heard my dad's bedroom door open. "Mallary! What are you still doing up? You have to be awake for school in less than five hours!"

"I'm almost done, Dad," I lied. "I promise."

I wrote for another hour and went to bed, tossing into the lightest of slumbers. When my essay came back with an A, I felt the late night had been worth it.

As senior year unfolded, the perfectionism that began with my writing trickled into my recovery. No longer intent on being "the perfect anorexic," I channeled my energy into becoming the poster child for eating-disorder recovery. I gave an inspirational talk to girls at Germaine Lawrence and was regarded as real-life proof of a girl who had gotten better. I was doing so well that I stopped going to therapy and was weaned off antidepressants. I had occasional follow-up appointments at Boston Children's Hospital, where I was praised for my progress. "I went to see Dr. Forman today, and she said that I'm one of the reasons why she keeps working. She's so incredibly proud of me," I journaled. "We were talking about how cool it is now that my weight has found a place where it wants to be, and how I don't have to be on a meal plan and add calories to maintain my weight. Way to go, Mallary!" I still didn't love my body, but I loved knowing it made people proud.

I graduated fourth in my class. Classmates voted me "Most Likely to Succeed" and "Most Likely to Change the World"—worthy accomplishments for my imagined recovery report card. Keen on excelling, I couldn't help but keep score. *If this is what full recovery looks like,* I thought, *then I'm getting an* A+! And by all accounts and standards, it *seemed* like I was thriving. But the truth is, I didn't know exactly what "full recovery" meant, and I couldn't recall anyone ever defining it for me. In my mind, it was the ultimate measure of success: a life completely free from anorexia. My black-and-white views of sickness and recovery came with protective barriers: If you master the art of full recovery, I reasoned, then you won't get sick again. If you don't make any mistakes, you'll be safe.

Living in those extremes was exhausting, and at times I wondered if it was hurting me more than protecting me. But I didn't trust that there was a space in between; it seemed too unknown, too precarious. I worried that if I made just one wrong move—by skipping a meal or sneaking in some jumps—I would fall into dangerous territory. If sickness was a dark dungeon, full recovery was a pristine house with floor-to-ceiling windows: Everyone was watching me, willing me to keep the house free from messes. And so, I made sure to keep it as tidy and as sanitized as I could. I was afraid that if I didn't, I would get kicked out, proving I never really belonged there in the first place.

I wrote about my eating-disorder journey in my college application essays, with hopes of showing how much I had overcome. I had applied to nine competitive schools in the Northeast, including some Ivy Leagues. With a 4.12 grade point average, all those extracurriculars, and a moving personal essay, I assumed I would be accepted into every school. Instead, I was rejected by four and waitlisted at one. I mostly blamed the rejections on my SAT scores, which were mediocre at best. But I also wondered if my essay—with its descriptions of the treatment I received and all the school I had missed—made me seem too vulnerable for college. I stopped sharing my eating-disorder story, not wanting it to be misconstrued.

In the fall of 2003, I packed my bags for the best school I had gotten into: Providence College. It was a small liberal arts school in Rhode Island, about an hour from home, run by the Dominican Order of priests. In treatment, I didn't have access to the Catholic church and hadn't attended Mass in years—not since the days when I dreaded the calories in the Communion wafer. But on campus, with a chapel that was open 24/7, priests who taught classes, and homilies tailored to college students, it was easy to follow my faith. I joined the liturgical choir, went on religious retreats, and attended the popular "Last Chance Mass" on Sunday nights, where I found a sense of community among other students. Yet as my faith deepened, I also came to question parts of it, realizing I didn't agree with all the church's teachings. I never admitted this to the priests, assuming they wouldn't approve, but I remembered what Gramz told me years earlier. "It's okay to be a 'Cafeteria Catholic,' Mal," she said, encouraging me to pick and choose what I wanted to believe.

Like a respectable Catholic, I prayed for my family and those in need. And like a typical teenager, I prayed for what I wanted: Good grades. A caring boyfriend. A boost of confidence. And an end to my father's dating.

Dad had ended his engagement to Katie a year earlier because she wanted children and he didn't—not at his age, not after what he had been through with me. He soon started dating new women, but he didn't click with any of them until he met Gina, a medical records clerk who worked in the same office my mother had many years earlier. This struck me as both an odd coincidence and a reminder that life after loss has a way of hauling us back to familiar territory. I hoped my father's relationship with Gina was just another fling, but he seemed smitten.

When I came home for Thanksgiving and saw them together, it was clear that no amount of prayer was going to break them apart. I was easily annoyed by Gina. She sniffled nervously when she was around me and seemed to stomp with every step, making our old floorboards creak. Whenever I saw her in our home, I rolled my eyes and let out dramatic sighs in a show of defiance. I was eighteen—old enough to know better but young enough to want to rebel against my father and his love interests. I likely would have found fault with whomever he was dating because no one could have ever measured up to my mother.

I sensed that Gina, who didn't have any children, was uncomfortable in my presence. She would look away whenever she passed by and wouldn't stay in the same room with me unless my father was there, too. Instead of trying to get to know each other, Gina and I both stayed where we felt safest: apart. Like two strangers on an elevator, we stuck with small talk or avoided conversations altogether. I side-eyed her, choosing to see only part of who she was. Had either of us looked past the eye rolls and sniffles, had we listened for something more than sighs and stomps, she would have seen I was afraid of her replacing my mother, and I would have seen that she was a good person who had no intentions of doing so. It would take years for me to truly see and hear her.

During the Thanksgiving break, it was evident Gina took up more space in our house and in my father's life than she had before I left for college. She hadn't moved in yet, but many of her belongings had. I made note of each one: the toiletries, the corduroy jackets in the hall closet, the Mickey Mouse figurines that had found their way onto our mantle. I scowled at them all. When Gina headed home after Thanksgiving dinner, I plopped on the couch next to Gramz and caught her up on college life. My dad strummed his guitar downstairs. He often played when he needed a creative outlet or when he was nervous. Then I heard him come back upstairs.

"I have something I want to tell both of you," Dad said, his voice quivering as he addressed us. "Please hear me out." He held two letters in his hands, and I assumed they held hard truths he couldn't say out loud. The written word has always been my father's armor.

"What is it, Andy?" Gramz asked. "Is everything okay?" Dad nodded, handing each of us a copy. "Please read the whole letter before saying anything." Then he went back downstairs.

The letter, which was about 800 words long, carried life-altering news that I was not prepared to hear or accept: My dad had decided to marry Gina. "I love you both and don't want to do anything that upsets you, but I have to think of myself also," he had written. "I am doing what I believe in my heart is the right thing to do." I was furious that my father had asked Gina to marry him just eight months into their relationship, without even hinting at the possibility of a proposal. I ran down the hall to my bedroom and slammed the door shut. My first reaction was, *How could he?* Then I turned this question on myself. *How could I not have seen this coming?* In my mind, the engagement signified an erasure—of my mother, and of my father's relationship with her. In that moment, I felt a world apart from my mother, further away than ever before. Anorexia stepped in after my mother died, and at least temporarily, it had made me feel closer to her. Now, six years later, I found myself wondering if it could serve that same purpose again. My disorder knocked on that closed bedroom door, promising to unlock connections to the past. *Let me in*, it beckoned. *Let . . . me . . . in.*

In the weeks that followed, that eating-disorder voice tantalized me with false promises. *I will give you a way to be special. I will make you feel closer to your mother. I will give you a way to maintain self-control.* I hadn't deliberately turned up the volume, but now it was all I could hear. After every bite, I berated myself for eating. In between meals, I thought about what I would eat at my next meal, when I would eat it, and how much I would allow myself to eat. I critiqued my body, disparaging every part. In a bid to rescue myself, I revisited the myth-versus-fact exercises I had done in residential treatment, counteracting distorted thoughts with reactions from "the real Mallary"—the part of me that knew my eating disorder was lying. *The sense of control it promised is false*, I reminded myself. *I am special on my own, apart from anorexia.* But these truths were weak whispers compared to the roar of anorexia.

My recovery didn't come with any "fragile" labels, but I sometimes wish it had. Maybe then I would have learned how to handle it with care. Maybe then I would have realized that recovery isn't ironclad; it's more like glass—beautiful to behold but breakable.

As a child, I had let anorexia speak for me. Rather than saying I was having a hard time with my mother's death, I let my body get so small and weak that no one could deny I needed help. But as a freshman in college, after years of treatment, I didn't think it was acceptable to seek support. *You're fully recovered*, I told myself. *You shouldn't need help anymore.* I had enough self-awareness to recognize I needed help but not enough self-compassion to ask for it. I knew I had a healthy self within me, but it wasn't strong enough yet to overpower the eating-disorder self. I was sucked back into a war between my two selves—one healthy, one sick—battling for my attention. I prayed someone would notice I was struggling, but there were no visible signs, no weight loss or spurned meals to signal that something was wrong. Internal and infernal, my thoughts went unnoticed by everyone but me.

I've since learned that many people with eating disorders struggle with distorted thoughts even after years in recovery. This is especially true for people in the middle place, who may be far along in their recovery but who still grapple with distorted thoughts that cause them to slip more often than they'd like. While I was reporting on this issue, some key questions guided my interviews: If people are at a "healthy" weight and have stopped engaging in eating-disorder behaviors but are still consumed by debilitating thoughts, are they fully recovered? How can clinicians better prepare patients to deal with these thoughts? And how do we reduce the stigma of asking for help when these thoughts creep back in?

Dr. Jennifer Gaudiani, the aforementioned Colorado-based internist specializing in eating-disorder care, said perfectionism often adds to people's belief that they shouldn't ask for help in recovery. With this in mind, she works with patients to help them do the following: (1) identify what they need; (2) accept that they have needs; and (3) learn how to meet those needs. "I think part of the recovery relationship involves helping individuals get back to those three core tenets, which really allows them to have confidence that if they think something's wrong, then it's wrong—even if their labs are normal, or their vitals are normal, or their weight is normal. If they have a sense that they're suffering, then it is real, and it deserves attention and care," Dr. Gaudiani told me. "Things don't have to descend to the point of a relapse to show that there's really something wrong here."

This type of messaging is especially important for patients to hear in the early stages of recovery, when they may have stopped engaging in disordered behaviors but are still experiencing distorted thoughts about food and body image. Having space to verbalize these thoughts is critical to maintaining recovery. It turns out it can also be helpful for those in recovery to consider other people's perception of them. University of Texas Southwestern's Dr. Carrie McAdams has observed this while researching brain activity and self-perception among women with eating disorders and those in recovery. When the women in both groups were asked to think about themselves, their reward circuits were not engaged. But when the recovered women were asked to think about themselves from someone else's perspective (an activity known as *perspective-taking*), they engaged the same brain regions that are observed among healthy controls who engage in positive self-talk. "These results changed my clinical treatment, as I began to prioritize teaching patients to reframe their ideas about themselves by building perspective-taking skills," said Dr. McAdams, who has developed a group-therapy intervention aimed at helping patients use those skills to reduce self-blame. Participants learn the basics of how eating disorders affect the brain, and they engage in group art therapy projects designed to produce imperfect results. Participants then share their reactions to the projects, observing any tendencies to blame themselves for the imperfections or overthink others' perceptions of their contributions. Since all participants contribute to the art projects and then hear one another's reactions, the tendency to blame oneself for the imperfections gets challenged.

New therapies like this could help to reduce distorted thoughts and ruminations (sometimes referred to as *cognitive factors*), which are often the last symptoms to wane and are known to contribute to relapse. When you're constantly bombarded with preoccupations about your body, it's easy to resort to eating-disorder behaviors. You hope the behaviors will quiet the thoughts, but they end up amplifying them instead. Eventually, it becomes hard not to wonder whether those thoughts will forever be the soundtrack of your life.

Olivia, who developed anorexia nervosa as a teenager, lives with this soundtrack. She attributes her eating disorder to societal pressures to be thin. Originally from Korea, Olivia was adopted into a white American family and said she developed a keen awareness of how the United States values and valorizes thinness. She has had anorexia for more than fifteen years and said her persistent fear of weight gain prevents her from recovering. "I feel like the last thing to fall with my eating disorder is going to be changing the standard that I hold my body to," explained Olivia, now in her thirties. "Maybe this is something that will never go away, but it seems like it's something that I need to work at."

Olivia said she'll go for stretches when she doesn't engage in eating-disorder behaviors and, for a brief period, the distorted thoughts will subside. But every time that happens, she begins to feel removed from her disorder and worries that a prolonged distance will make her lose control over her body. "All these thoughts flood my brain. *Am I getting fatter? Do I need to start exercising more?*" she told me. "It's really tough to resist those thoughts from coming into my head, and they definitely end up changing my behaviors." Olivia doesn't want her eating disorder to take up her whole life, but she isn't yet ready to let go of it. "I don't think there's ever been a moment when I've one hundred percent wanted recovery with every fiber of my being," she said. "Sometimes I wonder, *Can I just have a little bit of my eating disorder, to cope with my life?*" Her question speaks to an important aspect of recovery: the ability to see the eating disorder as the problem rather than the solution.

Another young woman I spoke to, twenty-five-year-old Fatima, shared similar sentiments. She was diagnosed with atypical anorexia in her teens, and she struggled with it for many years. While in college, she was admitted to an outpatient treatment program, where she stopped restricting her food intake and restored her weight. But as Fatima transitioned out of treatment and into recovery, her eating-disorder thoughts remained loud and insistent. "All of my suffering is cognitive," she told me, estimating that 95 percent of her thoughts center on her food intake and body image. They flood her mind with punitive refrains: *You're wrong for wanting to eat. You shouldn't eat. If you gain weight, you will be a failure.* Fatima said it takes all her energy to resist the temptation to act on those messages. She also wrestles with other invasive thoughts, including fear of weight gain, dissatisfaction with her body, guilt about wanting food, and more.

"I can't seem to move beyond this thing, even though in many ways I'm better. I have so much more of my life back. I can eat, I can socialize, I have friends, and I'm not hurting my family," said Fatima, who's from Canada. "But this place in my recovery hurts, too, because no one knows what's going on inside my head. I eat, but I hate myself for eating and for wanting to eat, and I am still constantly afraid of weight gain. This fear is the fuel that keeps the cognitive aspect burning." Fatima prefers not to use the term "full recovery," which she sees as an unrealistic ideal. "Life isn't like that; there's no finish line," she said. "For me, it's less about full recovery and more about being able to develop a different relationship to the cognitive aspect of the eating disorder."

Some in the field believe treatment providers should put more focus on that cognitive aspect, especially with regard to *fatphobia*—a pervasive form of oppression that demonizes weight gain and people in larger bodies. People with eating disorders often experience an internalized fatphobia, driven by distorted thoughts about their bodies and fear of weight gain. "Body image is an umbrella; it includes all kinds of things like skin color and even whether you have tattoos," says Chevese Turner, CEO of the Body Equity Alliance, a consulting and education organization that promotes health equity and weight inclusivity. "But when you are specifically talking about body image as it pertains to shape and size, you cannot talk about it effectively without talking about weight stigma." And yet, many people I've spoken to said weight stigma never came up while they were in treatment. It didn't come up in mine, either. Turner says part of the problem has to do with providers who haven't addressed their own fatphobia and therefore don't feel comfortable talking about the issue with patients, or don't recognize it's an issue in the first place.

Fatphobia "shows up across the spectrum of size—whether it's promising someone they won't get fat or promising someone that once they're in recovery, they can pursue weight loss," said Turner, who founded the Binge Eating Disorder Association, which is now part of the National Eating Disorders Association.

Fifty-six-year-old Turner, who considers herself to be fat, oscillated between atypical anorexia and binge-eating disorder throughout her childhood and into her adulthood. Whenever she tried seeking help, medical providers would discredit her eating disorder by recommending weight-management programs. She eventually went to an eating-disorder treatment program when in her twenties, but she was put on a weight-management track. It wasn't until years later that Turner began her recovery—after finding a therapist who validated that she had an eating disorder and that weight loss wasn't the way to treat it. Turner's experiences have shaped the work she now does as a health advocate and have prompted her to recognize and reduce her own internalized weight bias. At least once a year she takes Harvard University's implicit bias test for weight to gauge how she's doing. "I've seen it get lower over the years, but it's still there," she said. "How could it not be?"

Psychologist Tara Deliberto, PhD, says acknowledging our biases and challenging our distorted thoughts—rather than ignoring them—is integral to recovery. "My goal as a therapist is to really target fear of gaining weight and what will happen if one gains weight," Dr. Deliberto said, reminding me of Fatima's and Olivia's experiences. "To me, recovery means addressing those fears, processing them, and having them decrease, in addition to the behaviors being under control." Dr. Deliberto relies on body acceptance and exposure therapy to help patients address weight-related fears.

Body acceptance, she told me, involves a three-step process: (1) helping people abandon attempts to "fix" their body; (2) tolerating negative emotions about their body; and (3) working to appreciate their body. Patients begin by writing mini narratives describing scenarios that would make them feel poorly about their body (such as wearing a bathing suit in public or stepping on a scale and seeing they have gained weight). Patients read their narratives aloud to Dr. Deliberto and rate their distress on a scale of 1 to 10. Dr. Deliberto asks them to recognize their thoughts, emotions, physical sensations, and any urges they may have to engage in eating-disorder behaviors. She then helps patients develop a personalized "real-life body exposure" plan for handling these urges so they can better cope with them in real-life situations. Dr. Deliberto's work is related to research showing that imaginal exposure therapy—in which people write about and imagine their fears—helps decrease these fears and related symptoms. Mirror exposure therapy—in which people stand in front of a mirror and learn how to describe and view their body objectively—has also been shown to effectively treat body dissatisfaction among those with eating disorders.

In learning to address our own weight-related fears, we can become more aware of how they influence us and those around us. "I tend to think about recovery from an interconnected perspective," said Dr. Deliberto, co-author of the book *Treating Eating Disorders in Adolescents.* "No one person with internalized fatphobia is to blame for the massive, interconnected problem that is fatphobia, but if you're walking around with this fear, it's going to trickle out. Uprooting fatphobia for yourself and others paves the way for personal recovery and for healing on a more societal level." Dr. Deliberto's perspective on recovery is different from others I've heard, but truthfully, they are all different.

In the eating-disorder field, there seem to be as many definitions of "full recovery" as there are studies about it. Medically, it's often defined by physical indicators (such as BMI) and behavioral indicators (the absence, for instance, of restriction, binge eating, or purging). But these indicators alone can be limiting. If we want to arrive at a more comprehensive definition of full recovery, we need to consider a wider range of factors, including cognition. Historically, the multiple definitions of recovery have made it difficult to assess illness duration and treatment outcomes, leading to wildly different research results. Recovery rates, for instance, are shown to be anywhere from 57 to 94 percent for anorexia and 13 to 74 percent for bulimia. (Yes, you read that right.) The ranges are so wide as to be meaningless, and they reflect a lack of consensus on how to define "weight restoration"—a key indicator of physical recovery. Some studies define it as someone reaching 85 percent of the median BMI, while others define it as 100 percent of the median BMI.

Additionally, when it comes to patients' body preoccupations, there is significant variability in how research differentiates "normal" versus "abnormal" weight and shape concerns. And the duration of illness studied in research varies widely, with some studies monitoring recovery over a period as short as six months and others for as long as twenty-two years. "Our field is devoted to a concept we have not yet defined," says Kansas-based psychologist Beth McGilley, PhD. "And not only have we not defined it; it is so rapidly defined in different ways that you can't compare the research. If you look at all the recovery and outcome literature, and compare it based on all these definitions, either everybody gets well or nobody gets well." Metaphorically, she said, that makes recovery either a "cakewalk" or a "death march." Dr. McGilley, sixty-four, had anorexia in her college years and is now recovered. To get better, she had to choose her life over her eating disorder. "Getting well was about being willing to sign back up to life, knowing I was just going to be ricocheted one thousand times, and brokenhearted, and still come back to it again and again," Dr. McGilley told me. Full recovery is when "your relationship to body and weight and food is inherent to health and well-being and not a source of coping."

For much of her career, Dr. McGilley has advocated for a change in language that could expand our understanding of what recovery means. The word *integrity* (the state of being whole and undivided) "seems to better capture what we've been referring to as recovery," she wrote in a book chapter on the topic.

Renowned eating-disorder researcher Cynthia Bulik, PhD, has

shared similar sentiments. "A gaping omission in the eating disorders field is consensus definitions of remission, relapse, and recovery in anorexia nervosa," she wrote in an *American Journal of Psychiatry* editorial. "In fact, we are not even clear on whether we should consider anorexia nervosa to be episodic, remitting and relapsing, or, if once afflicted, one remains at elevated risk of recurrence throughout life."

Some researchers and clinicians argue that clearer definitions of recovery need to include the views of patients and caregivers. A study of nearly 400 caregivers of children with eating disorders found they held a multifaceted view of recovery—one that focuses not just on weight restoration and symptom reduction but also on engagement in social activities, emotional well-being, and cognitive flexibility (the ability to think less rigidly about food and exercise, for instance). Of those surveyed, 72 percent of caregivers reported that their child had achieved a state of partial or full recovery at some point, but only 20 percent said their child had sustained full recovery. Nearly one third said they were not confident that their child would ever recover.

The study broke down "full recovery" by considering a multitude of factors, including physical and behavioral recovery, social and emotional recovery, and cognitive recovery. The rates of cognitive recovery were notably lower than all the rest, with just 12 percent of caregivers saying their children had reached full recovery in this area. The study concluded that "the desire for a holistic approach to recovery is in contrast to current evidence-based treatments that focus more narrowly on weight restoration and/or behavioral symptom reduction. As a field, we cannot assume that treatments are effective if we fail to incorporate outcomes that caregivers believe to be important or fail to follow participants across their recovery trajectory."

I'm grateful for studies like this, which are helping the field arrive at a more comprehensive definition of recovery. I felt similarly when reading a study co-authored by my former Boston Children's Hospital doctor Sara Forman. In it, she and her colleagues looked at the ways that patients, parents, and clinicians define recovery. They concluded that recovery cannot simply be defined by physical markers; it needs to also account for three other factors: psychological well-being, eating-related behaviors/attitudes, and self-acceptance of body image.

Researcher Anna Bardone-Cone, PhD, also has spent years advocating for clearer definitions of recovery. In a 2010 paper, she raised a provocative question: Can people with eating disorders every truly recover? "To begin to answer that question, we need to have a clear sense of what 'true recovery' looks like, yet this is precisely what the field is lacking," wrote Dr. Bardone-Cone, a professor in the Department of Psychology and Neuroscience at the University of North Carolina at Chapel Hill. "Adopting a consensus definition of recovery is necessary for comparison of findings as well as for the combination of data across studies." The paper concluded that definitions of recovery need to account for cognitive aspects, noting that this is "critical for identifying a more meaningfully recovered group that should be at low risk for relapse in what are often seen as chronic disorders."

In the years since that paper was published, Dr. Bardone-Cone has begun using a more comprehensive definition of "full recovery" in her research—one that accounts for cognition, as well as physical and behavioral indicators. Doing so has helped her differentiate between people who are fully recovered and those who are partially recovered. By Dr. Bardone-Cone's definition, individuals who are still consumed by eating-disorder thoughts, despite improvements in physical and behavioral aspects, fall into the partially recovered category. To measure the cognitive aspects, Dr. Bardone-Cone uses a self-reporting tool called the Eating Disorder Examination Questionnaire, which asks research participants questions such as: "Have you had a definite fear that you might gain weight?" and: "Has thinking about food, eating, or calories made it very difficult to concentrate on things you are interested in (for example, working, following a conversation, or reading)?" She said it's relatively easy to test for cognition and admits that it's "mystifying" why more researchers don't account for it when defining full recovery. "I think eating disorders are so rooted in a medical model," she told me. "I don't want to throw the medical model under the bus here, but I wonder if there's a little bit of that medicalized thinking that just doesn't consider cognition as much."

Dr. Bardone-Cone's work has also led to new and revelatory findings in her research, some of which have changed her own views on topics such as perfectionism. In a comprehensive review, Dr. Bardone-Cone and her colleagues analyzed fifty-five studies on perfectionism that had been published between 1990 and 2005. Based on a comprehensive review of that research, they found that high levels of perfectionism were associated with poor prognosis for those with anorexia nervosa, suggesting that perfectionism is a risk factor for relapse. The research also found that even people who were considered fully recovered had elevated levels of perfectionism. "The possibility that it remains a long-term 'scar' of the eating disorder must be considered," the review concluded.

Two years later, Dr. Bardone-Cone conducted a follow-up study on perfectionism and used a more comprehensive definition of "full recovery" that accounted for cognition. She predictably found that people who were partially recovered still had elevated levels of perfectionism. But to her surprise, people who were fully recovered had lower levels of perfectionism—comparable to levels among people who had never experienced an eating disorder. These new findings contradicted the perfectionism-related studies she had analyzed just a couple years earlier. Dr. Bardone-Cone attributes this contradiction to the way she defined full recovery, and to her evolving views on perfectionism. "I think my colleagues would still see perfectionism as a risk factor, and it still is a maintenance factor," she told me. "But I would not see it as a scar anymore."

Dr. Bardone-Cone's work is a reminder that we need to define eating-disorder recovery in ways that account for distorted thoughts and better align with people's lived experience. My own experiences and reporting have taught me that recovery's size and shape varies, depending on whether you're in the middle place or beyond it. Everyone has a slightly different view on what recovery means, how it plays out, and whether it's possible, let alone sustainable. Acknowledging this seems key to advancing discussions of what it means to get better—and stay better.

Chapter Eight

Relapse

I entered college wanting recovery to be the foundation of my life. But by the spring semester of my freshman year, recovery began to feel more feeble than foundational, more precarious than possible. I became increasingly intent on avoiding the "Freshman Fifteen"—the cliché describing the supposed number of pounds students gain during their first year of college. I wouldn't learn until years later that the Freshman Fifteen is a myth debunked by research. The average weight gain for first-year students is only two to three pounds. (Far more concerning is the fact that the median age of onset for eating disorders in the United States coincides with the typical age of college enrollment.) Along with my fear of weight gain, I struggled with a mountain of schoolwork, the belief I would never be attractive enough to find a boyfriend, and the unsettling reality that my father had gotten engaged to a woman whom I felt I barely knew. I could have sought counseling or talked to my father, but I was determined to figure it all out on my own. Everything felt like an emergency, and in the absence of any other help, anorexia was my first responder.

During this time, my disordered thoughts persisted, becoming more and more invasive. Like black watercolors, they spread into every mental nook and cranny, staining my sense of self-worth. I tried holding them off by counteracting every negative thought with a positive one, and I revived the refrain I had learned at Germaine Lawrence: *I am beautiful, and I'm built nicely. I am beautiful, and I'm built nicely.* But the eating disorder said otherwise, insisting I *could be* beautiful if only I lost some weight. After a few months of unsuccessful attempts at silencing the thoughts, I surrendered to them. I once again critiqued my body in front of the mirror, rekindling a twisted admiration for protruding bones. I squeezed pockets of fat on my thighs and tummy, unable to appreciate my body's protective padding. In a warped way, it seemed easier to slide back into an abusive relationship with anorexia than to accept that my father was in a loving relationship. I started restricting food again, and my eating-disorder thoughts intensified.

The thoughts were especially loud one night when I was alone in my room toward the end of freshman year. I lived on the eighth floor of McVinney Hall, a ten-story dorm known on campus as "The Virgin Vault"—home to 300 female freshmen at a strict Catholic college that preached abstinence. My roommate had gone home for the weekend, and my friends were at a nearby party. I wanted to join them, but I had stayed back to work on an essay about the Catholic novelist and short story writer Flannery O'Connor. I wrote a few words and then deleted them, falling into a familiar pattern of perfection. I finally plodded my way through the first paragraph of the essay—then stared at the blinking cursor on my laptop screen with a rush of anxiety and hunger. I reached for a coffee cake muffin that I had grabbed at the all-you-can-eat campus cafeteria and took a bite. It tasted like relief.

I kept breaking off small pieces, thinking about my essay but keeping my hands busy with the muffin. I sank my teeth into the muffin as sugar crystals fell off the top of it. I picked up and ate each crystal, finishing every last bit like I did in treatment. Still wanting more, I eyed the cranberry-walnut bread that my dad and Gramz had dropped off that morning during their monthly visit. The nut bread had become my ultimate comfort food—the one most linked to home. I walked over to the loaf, picked it up with both hands, and brought it to my desk. I freed it from the cling wrap and made a jagged cut with a butter knife. With a slice by my side, I typed a sentence, then ate a bite. Typed, then ate. Typed, then ate. By the time I finished the slice, I had several new sentences to show for it. I cut myself another one, this time slightly bigger, and wrote a few more sentences in between bites. I could feel my heart thumping as I grabbed the knife again, cut another slice, and stuffed half in my mouth at once. Barely chewing, I swallowed, then shoved the other half inside. My throat throbbed. I cut myself yet another slice, realizing I had eaten more than half the loaf in one sitting. Anorexia soon intervened. *You are going to regret this in the morning. Who do you think you are, eating like this?*

I stepped away from the bread, worried I would eat my way through the whole loaf if I didn't create some separation. I peered inside the mini fridge, where I had a 24-ounce container of Hood cottage cheese. I scooped out a small bite, hoping to balance out the muffin and cranberry-walnut bread with something healthier. I ate it while standing, with the refrigerator door open, thinking maybe I wouldn't eat as much that way. I scooped up the little curds one by one, resurfacing a behavior from earlier days. The cottage cheese did little to satisfy my appetite, so I closed the lid after a few minutes and hunted in the fridge again. I grabbed a packaged ham-and-cheese wrap that Gramz brought me and took big bites, paying no mind to calories or taste. I brought the wrap back to my desk and tried to write, but all I could think about was whether to have another bite. Maybe if I ate the whole wrap, I wouldn't think about it anymore. I stuffed it inside of myself, staring in shame at the empty package on my desk. I had been tempted by food before and at times would indulge in a bigger-than-usual meal or snack. But I had never felt out of control when eating. My mind rushed ahead of me; *What if every time I started eating, I wouldn't be able to stop?*

Loud music pulsed from down the hall, and girls laughed as they passed my door. I longed to be one of those girls—carefree and able to go out, get drunk, and be okay with it. I still hadn't tried alcohol, and I wouldn't until the night of my twenty-first birthday. I was a rule follower, yes, but I also worried that if I took even one sip, I would become an alcoholic. I had dealt with anorexia long enough and wasn't willing to expose myself to another affliction, let alone one that involved extra calories. Whenever my friends drank, I would calculate the calories in my head and watch in silent stupefaction as they drank can after can of beer and ate Golden Crust pizza slices straight from the box. Beer never really appealed to me, but in recovery I had reacquainted with my love for pizza. My consumption of it came with rules, though, and I wouldn't allow myself to eat it outside of mealtimes.

If I had Golden Crust pizza in front of me that night in my dorm room, I would have devoured it.

We were in the middle of mid-terms and Lent—the solemn season during which Catholics commemorate the forty days that Jesus fasted in the desert. Even when tempted by Satan, who implored him to turn stones into loaves of bread, Jesus abstained. Traditional Catholics are taught to honor Christ's sacrifice with their own, by giving something up during Lent. Most often, that something involves food. "Discipline your body," Saint Benedict had advised. "Do not pamper yourself, but love fasting." The more I thought about Lent in college, the more I understood it as a demand for deprivation, even a celebration of starvation. Most of my classmates' abstinence involved taking a temporary break from eating meat, cookies, frozen yogurt, chocolate, or even any and all sweets. When I was sick, it was easy for me to do the same. But after leaving Germaine Lawrence, I had chosen to avoid Lenten sacrifices, knowing that rejecting any sort of food would be a self-imposed trap—a diet in disguise. I worried it would put me in an even more vulnerable spot. I didn't like the idea of that, just as I didn't like that Eve was blamed for the original sin because she ate forbidden fruit. Binging that night made me feel like a modern-day Eve, gluttonous in the eyes of God and disobedient to the disorder I had so long worshipped. I felt like a bad Catholic and a bad anorexic, which unnerved my always-eager-to-please self.

Years later, I learned that many prominent female Catholics from the Middle Ages abstained from food to avoid "the vice of gluttony." They believed they could survive solely on the Eucharist—the body and blood of Christ. Physicians referred to this extreme religious fasting as *inedia prodigiosa* ("a great starvation"), and *anorexia mirabilis* ("miraculously inspired loss of appetite"). In his book *Holy Anorexia*, the late historian Rudolph Bell, PhD, studied the behaviors of 170 female religious figures from the Middle Ages and found that more than half of them engaged in starvation. Among them was Saint Veronica, who ate little to nothing for days at a time, allowing herself only to chew five orange seeds on Fridays in honor of the five wounds Jesus endured during his crucifixion. Saint Catherine of Siena (a Dominican sister who has a building and a scholarship named after her at Providence College) purported to eat just a few handfuls of herbs a day and used twigs to induce vomiting before receiving the Eucharist. "There is nothing we can desire or want that we do not find in God," she once wrote. Catherine died when she was thirty-three from heart-related complications caused by starvation. Similarly, the Dominican sister Columba of Rieti subsisted on very little food and is thought to have died from starvation at age thirty-four. In catechism classes I had learned that gluttony is one of the seven deadly sins—never realizing the deadly lengths these women took to avoid it. It was hard for me to reckon with the idea that starvation was once considered saintly, having for so long been under its demonic grip.

Now it was midnight back in that lonely dorm room. I was surrounded by food wrappings and had little to show for my Flannery O'Connor essay. I was so full that it felt uncomfortable to sit, so I moved my laptop to my bed and stretched out on my belly; lying flat made my stomach feel less round. I typed a bit more, unable to stop thinking about the remaining half-loaf of cranberry-walnut bread on the desk. I told myself there was no way I could eat it. I didn't need it. I was already full. But I still craved more. I brought the loaf over to my bed, just to be closer to it. I plucked a tangy cranberry from the center of the bread and swirled it around on my tongue. Then I picked out a softened walnut and sank my teeth into a food I had long labeled "unsafe" because of the fat it contained. I tore apart the bread and picked out all the cranberries and walnuts I could find, separating the calories. I knew how many calories were in one whole slice of cranberry-walnut bread, but I wasn't sure how many were in all the cranberries and walnuts and sugary crumbs I had consumed while picking the loaf apart. Had I eaten the caloric equivalent of one big slice? Two and a half slices? Not much at all? For once, I had found a way to render my calorie calculator dysfunctional.

My shirt and lap were dotted with crumbs—pieces of evidence I was frantic to hide. I brushed them off and watched them fall onto the blue quilted comforter on my bed. That crumb-covered quilt looked so different from my mother's spotless, neatly aligned green quilt, and I couldn't help but feel ashamed by what I had done to it. I pictured sugar ants dotting my room days later and wondered what I'd tell my roommate when she asked about it. I tried to clean the crime scene, scooping the bread remnants into a grocery bag and taking it to the communal bathroom down the hall. I stuffed it into the trash, happy that no one else was in the bathroom to see me. I considered purging but couldn't take that risk. I had been in treatment with girls who had bulimia, and I'd heard them talk about how much it tormented them.

I hurried back to my room, where I locked the door and tried to finish my essay. But I was too distracted by what I had just done and what others would think if they found out. I pictured my mother watching over me. *If she had been there in the flesh and witnessed what had happened, would she be disappointed in me? Would she forgive me for making such a mess? Would she sit beside me on the bed so that I wouldn't have to be alone?* In my mother's absence, loneliness had always loomed large, lurking in the empty house I came home to every day from school, in the library cubicles where I studied, and in my college dormitory late at night. If Gramz had seen me that night, she would have been devastated by the possibility I had found a new way to engage in disordered eating. She thought I was better, and so did I. But there I was, trapped by something I couldn't name. Maybe it was a form of rebellion against anorexia, or a horrifying lapse in judgment, or an irreversible mistake—or something else entirely. The words to describe it didn't just elude me; they were completely inaccessible to me.

I retreated to bed, wide awake and painfully full. As I lie on my side, I stared at my bloated stomach in disgrace. Hoping to flatten it, I turned onto my back and started moving my legs in a circular motion as if riding an imaginary bike—a behavior I hadn't engaged in for many years. In that post-binge state, stillness was inexcusable. I kept pedaling for hours, then finally fell asleep. The next morning, I threw out the rest of the food from the mini fridge, ran six miles, and skipped all my meals. *It was just a bump in the road*, I thought. *I can get back on track.* But later that night, starving and lightheaded, I brought home snacks from the campus cafeteria and binged again. A new ruthless cycle emerged: late-night binges followed by day-long restrictions. I would try to eat dinner most nights with friends so they wouldn't suspect anything, but I wasn't fooling myself. I felt—I *knew*—that I was slipping further away from all I had accomplished in treatment.

Locked in that binge-and-restrict cycle, I believed I was failing at both anorexia and recovery. I was no longer acutely sick, but I was far from better. I was so deeply ashamed of my binges that I never spoke a word about them to family or friends. I was fully recovered in their eyes, and I could not bear the thought of shattering that image. The cycle continued through the rest of the semester and into the summer. I scheduled lunch dates with different friends, hoping this might help me stave off binges. But so often, I would binge the night before and then cancel the lunches out of obligation to my day-long restrictions. It seemed that no one suspected anything; and if they did, they didn't say anything. Starting my sophomore year, I confided in a Dominican priest who worked as a psychologist at the college counseling center. He didn't specialize in eating disorders, but he agreed to meet with me a few times a month and acted as a helpful sounding board. I never told anyone else about my behaviors, and I was even afraid to research them online. I didn't want to be diagnosed with a new illness, let alone one that seemed to be the antithesis of anorexia. But the cycle had closed in on me so quickly and with such force that by my senior year I was convinced I could never escape.

I now know, all these years later, that I was in the midst of a relapse. I didn't realize this at the time, partly because my behaviors were different from the ones I had engaged in when acutely sick with anorexia. I've since learned that relapses are common and that eating-disorder behaviors can, and often do, change shape during the recovery process. At times, these behaviors can even begin to feel like an addiction. Living in the middle place is an acknowledgment that recovery isn't a smooth ride; it's lined with roadblocks you have to learn to navigate around, sometimes indefinitely.

As surprising as it sounds, I can't recall anyone ever talking much about these roadblocks when I was in treatment. Other patients from that time confirmed my memory. We weren't prepared for the possibility of relapse at all, much less that the risk was high. On average, relapse rates are 40 to 50 percent for anorexia nervosa, 41 percent for OSFED (other specified feeding and eating disorder), and around 30 percent for bulimia and binge-eating disorder. The greatest risk for relapse from anorexia occurs within the first couple of months after discharge from acute care, but relapses can occur at any point in the recovery process. To prepare patients, many treatment centers now offer relapse-prevention plans for patients at various levels of care.

"Acknowledging and understanding that challenges will exist—and that the process of recovery is not linear—is essential," says Allison Chase, PhD, senior clinical advisor for the Eating Recovery Center (ERC), a national eating-disorder treatment program that offers various levels of care and a relapse prevention program. "Eating-disorder behaviors show up to help patients manage the uncomfortable underlying emotions that they are experiencing," said Dr. Chase, who's based in Austin, Texas. "As a patient moves through treatment, complicated by the external challenges of life, it would make sense that some of the unhealthy coping behaviors would show back up." As part of ERC's prevention planning, patients learn to brace for common triggers, such as starting or ending college, moving, becoming pregnant, and aging. They also develop an awareness of warning signs that could lead to relapse, such as reducing the size of meals or snacks, making excuses for not eating, and brushing off concerns with a dismissive "I'm fine." Additionally, patients are coached on how to react to slips, with a focus on self-compassion. A recovery-focused response might sound something like this: "I'm disappointed that I used a behavior when I felt angry, and I wish I had been better prepared for that situation. I see what I need to do differently next time. Slips are bound to happen in recovery, but overall, I am doing much better than before treatment and that feels hopeful."

In learning these strategies, ERC's patients and their caregivers develop a shared language for talking about slips. They learn the differences among a *slip* (an unplanned, one-time deviation from the treatment plan); a *lapse* (a more significant engagement in eating disorder thoughts and behaviors over a period of time); and a *relapse* (a repetitive pattern of eating disorder thoughts and behaviors with an inability to get back on track). Some treatment centers also use the term *collapse* (a worsening relapse that requires higher levels of care). Learning about the possibility of setbacks helps patients realize that recovery isn't perfect, nor should they expect it to be.

These setbacks can throw people off guard, especially when they involve new behaviors. It wasn't until I started writing this book that I realized how common my binge-and-restrict behaviors were. I was experiencing what the dietitian Christy Harrison calls "the restriction pendulum"—the body's natural reaction to deprivation. "When the pendulum swings over to the side of restriction—which diet culture frames as 'success' and 'being good'—inevitably there's going to be a swing back in the other direction because your body perceives restriction as dangerous," says Harrison, author of *The Wellness Trap*. This pendulum swing is not *always* inevitable; some people who develop anorexia nervosa will never develop binge-eating or purging behaviors, but the ultimate development of these behaviors is common. The swinging motion is also prevalent among people dealing with food insecurity, who may experience fluctuations in their food availability, leading to a feast-or-famine cycle. Research shows that restriction during times of scarcity can lead to binges once food is available, and there is sufficient evidence to suggest that food insecurity contributes to weight stigma and binge-eating disorder in adults.

My own binge-and-restrict cycle reflected something called "diagnostic crossover"—a term describing what happens when people move between eating-disorder subtypes or diagnoses over time. According to a study in the *Encyclopedia of Feeding and Eating Disorders*, an estimated 50 percent of people with anorexia will develop binge-eating and/or purging behaviors. This crossover can occur repeatedly, frequently, and bidirectionally (moving from restricting to binging, for instance, then from binging to restricting). It's a phenomenon specific to eating disorders, and it most often happens during periods of partial recovery, when individuals have stopped or lessened their old behaviors only to adopt new destructive ones in their place.

One obvious challenge in recovery is that you can't overcome an eating disorder through abstinence; you have to face the substance (food) multiple times a day, every day. Naturally, as you do this, the disorder may change shape and take on characteristics of other eating disorders.

Almost half of the 719 people I surveyed characterized themselves as having had multiple eating disorders at some point in their lifetime. Roughly 28 percent said they had struggled with two eating disorders, and 20 percent with three or more. Some had been officially diagnosed with more than one eating disorder over a span of time, while others had diagnosed themselves. The data made me ponder a question that lacks a unified answer in the eating-disorder field: Is the crossover simply a continuation of the original disorder, or a new one entirely?

Kamryn Eddy, PhD, who studies diagnostic crossover, said she believes it's more of a continuation. "Eating disorders are hard illnesses. Symptoms change over time, and they can change in all different directions. It's the natural course of these illnesses," said Dr. Eddy, who is co-director of the Eating Disorders Clinical and Research Program at Massachusetts General Hospital and an associate psychology professor at Harvard Medical School. She told me that when patients with anorexia develop binge eating (or other compensatory behaviors such as purging, over-exercise, or laxative abuse), they usually maintain some restrictive behaviors. The underlying symptoms of anorexia are still there; they have just morphed over time. To diagnose such patients with anorexia, bulimia, and binge-eating disorder can be "artificial" and "confusing," Dr. Eddy said. Rather than using different diagnostic labels, some clinicians prefer subtypes. Had I sought specialized care in college, for instance, I may have been diagnosed with binge-eating/purging–type anorexia (with obsessive exercise being my form of purging).

People with anorexia may think that consuming large amounts of food is a shameful, out-of-control behavior, without recognizing that their body needs those large amounts following prolonged starvation. "It's hard to know if 'overeating' is pathological because it's part of what's going to help people with anorexia get better physically and mentally, since their body and brain really need to be nourished," Dr. Eddy said. She talks with her patients about the possibility of diagnostic crossover so they're not caught off guard. It can be "terrifying," she said, for people with anorexia to hear that it's possible they may develop binge-eating behaviors. But this kind of transparency supports the recovery process; if patients know what to expect and have a plan for seeking help, they may be less inclined to shroud their new behaviors in secrecy, as I did. They may also be better equipped to recognize that their view of "overeating" could be distorted, and that a desire for a large amount of food doesn't have to devolve into a binge. In the *DSM-5*, a binge-eating episode is defined by eating a lot of food and experiencing a loss of control, along with additional symptoms: eating rapidly, alone, or past the point of fullness—or feeling ashamed, depressed, or disgusted about the episode. Dr. Eddy said if patients learn that the desire to eat large amounts of food is an expected and normal part of recovery, they may feel more in control of their eating, thereby reducing or eliminating the loss-of-control feeling that defines binge eating.

A longstanding body of literature has since shown that binge eating isn't just a physical reaction to restriction; as with anorexia, there are emotional, behavioral, and neurobiological factors at play. I've found validation in much of the research, including Ancel Keys's Minnesota Starvation Experiment, in which many of the men who had endured the 24-week semi-starvation period ended up binge eating during the refeeding process. One man even went to the hospital to get his stomach pumped because, in his words, he "just simply overdid it." In another study, the social psychologist Roy Baumeister posited that people binge as "an escape" from the belief that they're "failing to live up to high standards and expectations."

The book *Treatment of Eating Disorders: Bridging the Research Practice Gap* offers up three other reasons why people with anorexia may develop binge-eating behaviors. First, life difficulties and associated mood changes increase the chances that people will break their restrictive rules. Second, binge eating can temporarily improve mood and provide relief to the point where it becomes a new coping mechanism. And third, if people take laxatives or purge (through vomiting, exercising, or restricting), they can more easily justify their binge-eating behaviors and stay stuck in a binge-and-purge cycle.

There may also be neurobiological factors at play. Psychologist Laura Berner, PhD, is working on new research aimed at understanding what happens inside the brain when a person engages in restrictive and binge-eating behaviors. "For people who have never had any eating pathology, being fasted feels dysregulating. Some of our data suggest that the opposite might be true for folks who find themselves stuck in oscillating extremes of either restricting rigidly or binge eating and purging," said Dr. Berner, an associate professor of psychiatry in the Icahn School of Medicine at Mount Sinai Hospital in New York. "The prolonged fasting might feel relatively easy to maintain. But once the streak is broken and eating starts—and the body moves into a new metabolic state, which affects the brain—decision-making and cognitive control circuits cannot come online in the same way, and that could make it feel hard to stop."

This is a feeling I once knew well. Many people I've interviewed have also described it, and some said it led them to think of their eating disorder as an addiction. Researchers throughout the years have drawn parallels between anorexia and substance-abuse disorders, saying that both tend to develop in adolescence and both are used to modulate anxiety. When people with anorexia eat, they feel increased anxiety; when those suffering from substance-abuse disorders try to abstain, they feel a similar sense of anxiety. Compulsions are also common in both. One study found that people with anorexia experience many of the same symptoms as those outlined in the *DSM-5* criteria for substance-abuse disorders, including escalating compulsions, impaired control, and continual use of detrimental behaviors.

The experts I interviewed acknowledge these parallels but hesitate to classify anorexia as an *actual* addiction—in part because there's no conclusive evidence to prove this is the case. There's even disagreement among researchers about whether people can become "addicted" to food. Some top researchers have urged that food addiction be officially recognized in the *DSM-5*. A recent University of Michigan poll found that one in eight American adults over the age of fifty show signs of food addiction. And research suggests that ultra-processed foods can trigger neurobiological and behavioral responses (such as cravings and lack of control over consumption) similar to addictive substances. But some doctors I spoke with say that binge relationships with food emerge as a bodily response to restriction and are by no means an addiction. They point to research showing that food addiction is an "unnecessary medicalization" and worry that it's "another example of modern-day pseudoscience." Rather than getting hung up on dueling studies and viewpoints, I defer to the many people with eating disorders who have told me they *feel* like they're addicted to food or to starvation.

"Food is my drug of choice," says Mary, who has had binge-eating disorder for twenty years and equates it with an addiction that can't end with simple abstinence. "With recovery for addiction, you can choose not to drink, and you can choose not to do certain drugs or refrain from them. But you can't *not* have a relationship with food." Mary's eating disorder started when she was a freshman at Providence College, after failed attempts to get help for depression. She was just a year ahead of me, and though we were acquainted, neither of us knew that the other was struggling. "Food became my antidepressant; it made me feel better and it made me feel less dead inside," Mary, now forty-one, told me. "It served a purpose for me, and I would say it still does."

Mary said she always feels better during and after a binge, a sentiment I've heard others share. Interestingly, some research has found that many people with binge-eating disorder report a persistent belief that eating makes them feel better. But recent data collected from people who responded to their binge-eating behaviors in real time suggests that binge eating actually makes them feel worse. "That persistent belief, despite these experiences to the contrary, might mean there is an altered learning process that could maintain binge eating, or that there are just different time scales of the experience for different people and it's hard to capture them," says Mount Sinai's Dr. Berner, who is studying this complicated topic.

While in the throes of my own binge-and-restrict cycle, I always felt ashamed. My inability to stop made my eating disorder seem like its own kind of addiction. In my reporting, I learned that a high percentage of people have both substance-use disorders and eating disorders, often simultaneously. A major study conducted by the National Center on Addiction and Substance Abuse found that up to 50 percent of people with eating disorders abuse drugs or alcohol, compared with 9 percent of the general population. Substance abuse appeared to be highest among people who experience binge eating during their eating disorder. Medical experts point to likely reasons for the high comorbidity: Some people use drugs or alcohol to self-medicate and temporarily escape the agony of their eating disorder; others intentionally use substances that suppress appetite, setting a maladaptive cycle in motion. In the latter case, food restriction increases one's vulnerability to taking the drug, and the drug in turn decreases appetite, resulting in greater food restriction and weight loss.

In her perceptive memoir, *The Recovering: Intoxication and its Aftermath*, author Leslie Jamison writes about the overlap between her own history with anorexia and alcoholism. "For a long time, I'd thought of my drinking as the opposite of anorexia, as abandon rather than restriction. Starving myself meant resisting an endless longing, and drinking meant submitting to it," Jamison writes. "When I restricted my eating, I was ashamed that there was nothing I wanted more than to eat—endlessly, recklessly—and when I drank, I was ashamed that there was nothing I wanted more than to drink. Trying to control my drinking only illuminated how deep that wanting went, like tossing a stone down a well and never hearing it hit bottom."

Jamison's story reminded me of one of my survey respondents named Danielle, who is in her late thirties and has grappled with anorexia nervosa, bulimia, and alcoholism. Her eating disorder began when she was just nine, after a family member sexually abused her. In the weeks following the abuse, she began restricting her food intake—not to get thinner but to stay small and take up the least amount of space possible. The closer she was to invisibility, she reasoned, the less chance she would have of getting hurt again. As she restricted, Danielle's body and sense of self began to shrink. Family members and friends watched on in silence, unsure how to help. Her handwriting grew smaller, too, becoming so tiny it was barely legible.

Danielle got good grades, never caused any trouble, and rarely asked for help. She told me that when she confided in her parents about the sexual abuse, they didn't do anything about it. And when she told her mother about her disorder, around age twelve, her mother simply replied: "Pull yourself together." All these years later, I could still hear the longing in Danielle's voice: "Every time I remember having gone through the agony of thinking, *Should I put myself out there and ask for help*? I didn't get the help."

The longer Danielle spent in the grip of anorexia, the more her body rebelled. She felt enervated, and her bones were brittle. She would later be diagnosed with osteopenia—a condition that occurs from loss of bone mass and is a typical precursor to osteoporosis. Danielle wanted to get better, but she worried that once she started allowing herself to eat more, she would not be able to stop.

After a few years, Danielle began binge eating, too, becoming one of the many people who experience diagnostic crossover. She quickly fell into a binge-and-purge cycle that became all-consuming and wreaked havoc on her body in different ways than anorexia had. She developed sores on her knuckles, as well as gum recession (both side effects of vomiting). She also developed sepsis, a life-threatening infection that enters the bloodstream and can lead to organ failure. Danielle said her doctors never determined a cause, but she blames her out-of-control eating: consuming moldy food or uncooked meat during a binge, for instance, or throwing away food in hopes of staving off a binge, only to eat it straight from the trash soon thereafter. "For years, my only thought was, *What am I eating next and when am I throwing up?*" said Danielle, who is from England. She lost all sense of how much food her body needed. And she worried that if she didn't binge, she would restrict and sink back into anorexia again.

In the throes of this all-or-nothing mentality, Danielle searched for an outlet. She tried alcohol for the first time at age fifteen and liked the way it made her feel. She was more carefree and less preoccupied with food—at least until the buzz wore off. She started drinking more in college and was soon doing it every day. She would sometimes attempt to curb her alcohol consumption by drinking just a few days a week or on alternate days. But that never lasted long. Danielle's bulimia facilitated her alcoholism, and at times she would drink before throwing up to help blunt the pain of purging. She carried on like this for years, juggling alcoholism and bulimia with a fear that she would never break free from either one. When she moved in with her partner, she could no longer binge and purge every night. Her behaviors lessened, but she still felt trapped. Hoping to find a reliable escape hatch, Danielle turned to books for guidance.

By that point, in 2019, she had been an alcoholic for five years and bulimic for nineteen. Yet she had never talked to anyone with similar struggles. In reading the 1988 book *Women's Secret Disorder: A New Understanding of Bulimia*, Danielle began to realize that her behaviors were common among people with the disorder. She also learned more about the devastating toll that bulimia can have on the body. Reading about these side effects didn't scare Danielle into stopping the behaviors, but one book did lead her to stop drinking: Ann Dowsett Johnston's *Drink: The Intimate Relationship Between Women and Alcohol.* In describing the risky rise of alcoholism among girls and women, Johnston details what alcoholism does to the brain. The book talks about how alcohol activates the reward system and increases dopamine levels, which are associated with pleasure. The more people use a substance, the more their brain adapts, becoming less sensitive to dopamine. They end up experiencing a reward deficiency and overcompensate by consuming more of the drug to recapture the pleasure they derive from it. When Danielle read about this in greater detail, she was distraught thinking about what alcohol had done to her brain. "It just clicked entirely for me, and I thought, *Why didn't I know this?*" Danielle said. She quit cold turkey and is now six years into sobriety.

As a recovering alcoholic, Danielle wishes she could abstain from food like she does with alcohol. Of course, this is not an option for anyone who wants to live. I know from my own experiences that the idea of abstaining from food can seem less overwhelming than the act of choosing what and when and how much to eat. When making these choices, we all navigate the gray area between all or nothing. But inhabiting this area is especially exhausting for people with eating disorders, who have difficulty trusting the sensations their brains get from their bodies: hunger and fullness, but also pain, temperature, and sensations that accompany emotions.

Researchers have found that people with eating disorders have altered brain connectivity and functioning in the part of the brain that's integral to interoception, a lesser-known sense that helps us feel what's going on inside our bodies—a fullness of the bladder, a racing heartbeat, a pang of hunger. These alterations may help explain the feeling of confusion or uncertainty that people like Danielle experience when faced with food-related questions.

Danielle's mind is like a racetrack on which these questions constantly run. *Should I eat this? Should I not eat this? Have I eaten enough? Have I not eaten enough?* She wishes she could make them stop, or at least slow them down, with answers. Sometimes the thoughts are so overwhelming that she purges in search of relief, only to end up feeling worse than before.

For years, Danielle has used journals to track the rare days she doesn't purge. Last year, there were only seven entries. She still has never talked with a therapist or sought inpatient or outpatient care—which is the case for many people with eating disorders. She did, however, recently receive a prescription for antidepressant medication, hoping it might help lessen her bulimic behaviors. In the months since, Danielle has refrained from binging and purging seven to eight days a month—a significant improvement from the previous year. She bought a new journal to track the days. "Meaningful change begins with small daily efforts," she wrote at the top of one of her entries, in handwriting that's much bigger than it used to be.

Danielle has also started weightlifting to gain strength and feel safer in her body. She said she hasn't felt safe since the childhood abuse, and she still worries she'll be abused again. But she's beginning to question whether invisibility is the best protector. "I've been thinking about how, if I'm small and weak, people could hurt me anyway. But if I'm not as small and not as weak, perhaps they won't hurt me and there will be more chance that I could get away," Danielle said, her voice cracking with emotion. "With weightlifting, I am actively getting bigger. I didn't take up any space before, and now I want to." Danielle admits that she doesn't know if she'll ever recover from bulimia, but she hopes these recent changes are signs of progress. She sees her recovery as a spiral staircase, where she is bound to take some steps downward but tries to ultimately move upward. "Maybe I won't ever get to the top," she says, "but I'm so much higher than when I was stuck."

At the end of our interview, Danielle said this was the first time she had ever spoken so openly about her eating disorder. Our conversation made me think about how important it is to not only talk freely about illness, but to expand our collective lexicon around sickness and recovery. Looking back on my college years, it's clear that I didn't know how to explain what I was experiencing: the perfectionism surrounding my writing and recovery, the obsessive thoughts about food and weight, that first binge my freshman year. Maybe if I'd had the language to describe these as slips, I could have sought help and prevented them from turning into a lapse and then a relapse. When we learn to identify possible triggers, when we talk openly about how symptoms can shift, when we have the words to describe recovery's imperfections, we can better navigate around the obstacles we'll encounter. Language that reflects lived experience can change our view of recovery—from a perfectionistic ideal to a realistic possibility.

Chapter Nine

The Middle Place

When I moved to St. Petersburg, Florida, for a fellowship opportunity after college, my father bought me a handheld GPS navigation system. It was 2007 (before smartphones had become popular), and many people at the time relied on these handheld devices for directions. "I don't want you to get lost driving around all these new roads," he said, worried I wouldn't be able to find my way in a new place that was far from home. Growing up, I had watched him hover over Rand McNally road maps on our kitchen table, tracing his fingers along the roads we would travel on trips through New England. These maps, marked by hundreds of little lines that zigzagged and crisscrossed, easily overwhelmed me. I was in awe of how easily my father followed them and how many different routes he could extract. It's a running joke in our family that my father takes a while to get wherever he's going—not because he's lost but because he opts for the most scenic routes, preferring back roads to main thoroughfares.

For a long time while I was sick, I had strayed from the family map and followed my disorder's directions instead. I lost my way, navigating uncharted territory that my father couldn't imagine, let alone access on a map. When I returned home from treatment and got my driver's license, Dad wanted to help me find my way—literally. Whenever I told him where I was going, he would unfurl one of his maps and show me which roads to take.

"Dad, nobody uses maps anymore!" I'd tease, annoyed but also appreciative. "I printed out directions and know how to get there."

"Oh, let me just show you!" he'd insist.

"I'm good, Dad . . ."

I wanted to arrive at places on my own, without my father telling me how to get there. But that changed when I moved to St. Petersburg, thirteen hundred miles from home. I longed for his guidance. In his absence, the handheld GPS became a cicerone of sorts, channeling me along unfamiliar roads and toward new destinations. I liked the pleasant voice of the digital woman: "Turn right at the top of the hill, drive straight ahead, veer to the left at the next intersection." When I made a wrong turn, which usually led to multiple wrong turns, the ever-patient voice redirected me every time. "Recalculating. Recalculating. Recalculating." It sounded like the opposite of my eating-disorder voice. And it reminded me of the grace I wished I could give myself whenever I made poor choices and needed to get back on track.

Even after I settled into St. Petersburg and learned my way around, I called on the GPS. At a time in my life when I felt lost, I liked being told where to go. I had moved to St. Pete for a year-long fellowship at The Poynter Institute, a nonprofit that offers training and resources for journalists around the world. I worked for the institute's website, writing and editing news stories about the media industry. It was 2007, a time when newspapers were in financial turmoil and laying off staff at unprecedented rates. I covered these stories with a heavy heart, as I interviewed journalists who had been let go from work they had done for decades. But I was also encouraged by the ways in which journalists were trying to adapt to the changes by experimenting with new forms of storytelling and new ways of engaging audiences. I gravitated toward telling the stories behind the stories—how a smalltown newspaper editor became a Pulitzer Prize finalist for his dogged reporting on civil rights cold cases, or how a reporter uncovered decades of abuse at a Florida reform school, sparking remedial action. As I reported on the industry and began writing a mix of breaking news and feature stories, my fellowship turned into a job. I got assigned bigger stories and interviewed some of the industry's most venerable journalists: Bob Woodward, Katie Couric, Tom Brokaw, Dan Rather, Bob Schieffer, Ted Koppel, and more. I liked seeing my byline multiple times a week and knowing my work was reaching a wide audience.

But my own story was one of chaos that hid behind every word in my articles. It was part of their making and yet completely invisible to every reader but me. Each assignment sparked unbearable anxiety that ended with a frenzied trip to the grocery store. I would report during the workday, from the office, then make a pit stop at the neighborhood Publix grocery store on my way home. I would load up on binge foods—ice cream, chocolate chip granola bars, Swedish fish, trail mix—and fidget at the checkout line, praying I wouldn't run into anyone I knew. I tried going to a different cashier's line each time, fearing I would blow my cover if I went to any one of them too often. I'd rush back into my car and drive home, feeling guilty whenever I inevitably passed people who lived rough on St. Pete's streets. There they were, begging for something to eat, and here I was, with a passenger seat full of binge food. I knew that half the food would wind up in the trash (where I would pour soap on it to render it inedible) or in the toilet (which became a literal dumping ground for food I wanted to flush away). The waste compounded my shame.

Alone in my apartment, I would sit at my kitchen table and write my stories with a half-gallon of Breyers Cookies and Cream ice cream beside me. I'd slide the spoon along the smooth surface of the ice cream, telling myself I would just skim the top layer and then put the container back in the freezer. But the longer I stared at the blank laptop screen, the bigger the bites got and the faster I ate them. When the remaining ice cream in the tub melted, I would scout for cookie chunks and dig them out with my spoon until I had eaten every last one. My gray tabby cat, Clara, kept watch, her head tilted to the side as though both curious and concerned. She was the lone witness to my binges, the only one I could trust to keep my secret.

When hunger came knocking the day after a late-night binge, as it always did, I would try to avoid food by drinking a few cans of Coke Zero and chewing gum until my jaw hurt. I'd feel bloated and unsatisfied; my stomach growled, sometimes in the middle of meetings. Other days, I resorted to the kind of food picking I had first done in college, with the cranberry-walnut bread. I would hunt through bags of trail mix, discarding the nuts but eating the chocolate pieces and dried fruit. For a time, I bought Fiber One granola bars almost every day. I'd pluck out the chocolate chips and discard the granola, paranoid that someone would catch me in the act. I longed to be able to eat whole foods—not the unprocessed sort but the complete kind. I wished I could just be "normal" and eat one whole handful of trail mix or one whole granola bar. But food picking had become an obsession, one that briefly calmed me but always left me feeling disgusted. I often wondered what the janitors thought when they emptied my trash can at night and saw the chewed-up gum, the half-eaten trail mix, the mounds of granola—proof that something was not right. Every night I vowed to do better the following day. But each day was a broken promise. To renege was to constantly wrestle with a question that had no easy answer: *What if I never get over my eating disorder?* This was my deepest dread.

A year or two after I started at The Poynter Institute, I told some colleagues and friends about my experiences with anorexia. But I always framed it as a past problem that I had since overcome. I spun a false narrative, weaving threads that became tangled in lies. It seemed easier to pretend I was the heroine of a coveted recovery narrative ("I was sick, then I got better") than to describe this strange place I found myself in—somewhere between acute sickness and full recovery. So, I told a recovery story that shaped people's perceptions of me, leading them to believe I was a "healthy eater" who took good care of her body and was fueled by willpower.

I became a vegetarian, finding it was a way for me to restrict food under the guise of a healthy diet. "I wish I had your discipline!" friends would say when I ordered a salad for lunch, not knowing I had inhaled thousands of calories the night before. During a work retreat one year, a colleague asked if I wanted some candy. He handed me a bowl of Hershey's Kisses, but before I could answer or grab one, another colleague interjected. "Oh, Mallary would never eat those!" she said, as though surprised anyone even offered. I wanted the candy, but my eating disorder dismantled my desire, reminding me I had a reputation to uphold. "Oh, no thanks," I said politely, pushing the bowl away. At Publix that evening, I bought a bag of Hershey's Kisses. Alone in my apartment, I inhaled every single one.

I had gotten so good at carving out a fake identity—outwardly free from my eating disorder but inwardly trapped by it—and I couldn't help but feel like a fraud. It seemed as though I was no longer battling my disorder but, rather, my recovery from it. I began to wonder if other people were hiding their hurts beneath the shield of their stories. As a journalist, I turned to media for answers. I was well aware of ways that "the media"—books, newspapers, magazines, television, and social media—perpetuate an ideal of thinness, portraying the body as a problem to be fixed. The media have lauded fad diets and fit bodies for decades, and every era has had its phases and crazes. I grew up in the 1990s, when the "heroin chic" aesthetic was in vogue. Models like Kate Moss popularized the look: emaciated bodies, pale skin, and wreaths of exhaustion circling the eyes.

The early 2000s saw the rise of "thinspiration" content online. Pro-ana (pro-anorexia) and Pro-mia (pro-bulimia) groups on forums, Tumblr, and YouTube glamorized these illnesses, with members who shared tips and encouraged one another's eating-disorder thoughts and behaviors. I was aware of these toxic groups at the time and saw occasional news coverage about them. I sometimes googled them myself, usually after bouts of binging that left me feeling ashamed and alone. *Maybe if I just take a quick look*, I would think, *these sites could inspire me to stop binging*. I peeked but never posted. Still today, pro-ana and pro-mia content persists on social media, despite a growing awareness of how harmful it is.

In truth, I was desperate to find stories about other people who were grappling with the ups and downs of recovery. I consumed news from a wide range of sources and knew where to turn for quality journalism. But I couldn't find in-depth stories about recovery from eating disorders. News and feature stories were few and far between, and the ones I found did not match my lived experience. They described people who had struggled with eating disorders and were now fully recovered. The stories had beginnings and ends, but they were missing middles—the setbacks and small victories that lie between the origins of a disorder and one's recovery from it. Recovery was often confined to one or two sentences marked by triumphant words: *overcame, achieved, conquered.* I saw my false narrative reflected in these stories, the one where I pretended to be "all better." But I didn't see my *actual* narrative, and that lack of a mirrored image left me feeling deeply misunderstood. I began to think that eating-disorder recovery was an untold—or at best half-told—story. As a journalist and lifelong writer, I found myself wanting to change that.

I stayed at The Poynter Institute for six years, all the while juggling two full-time jobs: my eating disorder and my role as managing editor of Poynter's website. Ready for a professional change, I called some of my mentors for advice. One of them urged me to apply for an executive director role at a small media nonprofit called Images and Voices of Hope (ivoh). The nonprofit's motto was "media as agents of world benefit." I was intrigued by the organization's mission, which aligned with my long-held belief that journalism is a public service that can spark meaningful awareness and change. I was hired, joining ivoh when it had begun to explore resilience as a theme in storytelling. The exploration was prompted by a *New Yorker* article about *The Newtown Bee*, a small newspaper that had gained national attention for its coverage of the 2012 Sandy Hook Elementary School shooting in Newtown, Connecticut. Twenty students and six adults were killed by a lone gunman, making it the deadliest school shooting in the United States at the time.

In the *New Yorker* article, journalist Rachel Aviv profiled *The Newtown Bee* editor Curtiss Clark, who wanted his newspaper to help the community heal. Instead of fixating on the gunman or the fatalities, the *Bee* spotlighted acts of benevolence as Newtown residents supported each other in the tragedy's aftermath. The paper, Aviv wrote, was "crafting a redemptive narrative." This notion of a "redemptive narrative" stuck with ivoh's founder, who thought it held promise not just for the *Bee* but also for the media industry at large. We enlisted other journalists to help shape language describing an emerging story genre: the restorative narrative. A primary part of my job was to define the genre, identify its key tenets, and make the case for its value. At a time when public trust in the media was in a free fall and traditional business models were failing, it seemed like an opportune time to propose a new way of telling stories that mattered and offered hope.

Along with reporting that held powerful people and institutions accountable, news organizations tended to prioritize stories of violence, trauma, and tragedy (and still do). In TV news, it became both motto and mentality: "If it bleeds, it leads." But a growing body of research was beginning to confirm what many had long suspected: that repeated exposure to trauma coverage can trigger stress, fear, and anxiety in those consuming the stories and in those telling them. Perhaps restorative narratives had the potential to deepen media coverage and connect communities in ways that traditional "doom and gloom" stories couldn't.

I came to define restorative narratives as stories that show how people and communities find resilience in the aftermath, or the midst of, difficult experiences. They're not fluff pieces that romanticize resilience but, instead, deeply reported stories that explore pain, sorrow, grief—and human determination in the face of all that. Rather than sensationalizing what's broken, or suggesting that it's already been fixed, restorative narratives probe how people move forward amid the breakage. They reveal meaningful progressions—a fuller arc from heartbreak to hope, illness to wellness, suffering to survival.

As part of my work, I partnered with people like Kevin Becker, PsyD, a Massachusetts-based trauma psychologist. Trauma recovery, he told me, is a developmental process. In other words, we can't simply recover from a trauma and then expect its effects to disappear. The pain is bound to resurface—during anniversaries, big life events, or, more likely, when we least expect it. Part of recovery involves learning how to deal with this pain as it ebbs and flows, rather than avoiding it or wallowing in it.

I wove that knowledge into our approach to journalism. "Restorative narratives are mindful of the fact that recovery is a process that takes time. These narratives may not come to fruition until months or years after a tragedy or period of disruption," I wrote in an article describing the genre. "Restorative narratives don't pretend that a person is 'fully recovered' or 'all better.' They recognize that it takes a while to recover, grieve, rebuild, etc., and that there will be setbacks along the way."

Over time, it dawned on me that I was exploring restorative narratives not just for the journalism profession but also for myself. It had taken me some time to realize this, partly because I had wrapped myself in a "fully recovered" identity. But the more I understood restorative narratives, the more I realized my romantic-heroine storyline hurt me more than it protected me. I was gaining a hard-won appreciation for the parts of our lives that can't fit neatly into boxes. My story had long been jammed into one of those boxes, adorned with a beautiful bow. But the pretty packaging was a cover-up. Now, I felt I could give myself permission to untie the bow and reveal the package's contents. After all those years of hiding, I had a framework for defining my own recovery and the freedom to reveal its imperfections.

I wasn't ready to write a restorative narrative of my own, but I searched for books that could help me think about how I eventually might. Among my favorites was Arthur Frank's *The Wounded Storyteller*, which outlines three types of illness narratives: the restitution narrative, the chaos narrative, and the quest narrative. Though similar in name, restitution narratives are different from restorative narratives in that they tend to oversimplify the recovery process, just like all those superficial stories I had read about eating disorders. As Frank writes, the restitution narrative has a basic storyline: "Yesterday I was healthy, today I'm sick, but tomorrow I'll be healthy again." This is the preferred narrative of the medical establishment, and it aligns with the modernist expectation that there is a remedy for every form of suffering. It's the same narrative that my family clung to when my mother was sick, with its promise of a happy ending that contradicted reality. It's a narrative that led me astray as a child and that I now view with great skepticism.

In reading about restitution narratives, I thought about the connections between my mother's illness narrative and my own. Our diseases were different in myriad ways. Cancer metastasizes from one part of the body to another, while eating disorders morph from one set of behaviors to another. Cancer thrives on the growth of cells, while anorexia does so on the shrinkage of a body. But the *Merriam-Webster Dictionary* definition of cancer is strikingly similar to the way I think about anorexia: something "evil or malignant that spreads destructively." My mother and I had both harbored uncurable diseases, gotten treatment, enjoyed a precarious recovery, then fallen hard back into sickness. Both our diseases were relentless, secretive, and all-consuming. Though my mother's illness story ended before mine began, it has continued to live on within me, shaping the way I see the world.

I thought of my mother, too, when I read Frank's description of the chaos narrative. The chaos narrative, as you'd expect, is the opposite of the restitution narrative. "Its plot imagines life never getting better," Frank writes. "All of us on the outside of some chaos want assurances that if *we* fell in, we could get out. But the chaos narrative is beyond such bargaining: there is no way out." The narrator of these stories may have a terminal illness or may never be able to conceive of a world in which they are better. My parents had told a restitution narrative in hopes of protecting me, but it seemed that my mother's lived experience was more in line with the chaos narrative, particularly after her cancer metastasized. I again saw parallels between us—both of us living out the heroine stories we wanted people to believe instead of revealing the true ones they needed to hear.

My mother didn't live long enough to experience what Frank calls the quest narrative. It aligns with Joseph Campbell's classic work on "the hero's journey," in which someone goes on an adventure, overcomes a crisis, and returns transformed. Campbell's work piqued my interest, but Frank's framing resonated with me more and reminded me of restorative narratives. "Quest stories tell of searching for alternative ways of being ill," Frank writes. "As the ill person gradually realizes a sense of purpose, the idea that illness has been a journey emerges. The meaning of the journey emerges recursively: the journey is taken in order to find out what sort of journey one has been taking." I cringed at the clichéd notion of a journey but was intrigued by the idea of figuring out what sort of trek I had been taking. I had been on this trek without any idea of where I was headed, let alone what my current coordinates were.

If the quest is the story, the map is its underlying structure. "Stories are a way of redrawing maps and finding new destinations," Frank writes in *The Wounded Storyteller*. As my father's daughter, I committed this line to memory and pictured myself tracing my finger along the map of my own story, which seemed like a vast continent of different plotlines. The "fake Mallary" (or the "eating-disorder self") and the "real Mallary" (the "healthy self") had mapped out disparate routes, wrenching me between the narrative I wanted everyone to believe and the one I actually lived. To bridge that chasm, I was going to have to figure out how to tell a cohesive narrative—one that would allow for these two selves to travel together on the same road. "The issue for most ill people," Frank writes, "seems to be keeping multiple selves available to themselves." The late journalist Stewart Alsop alluded to this in his book *Stay of Execution*, which chronicles his experience with acute myeloblastic leukemia. The book, he said, "was written by different me's." He writes of five different selves, including a self who was sick, a euphoric self who felt better for a brief period, and a present-day self who was navigating the recrudescence of a terminal disease.

In reading Alsop's memoir, I wondered if this might have been what Walt Whitman meant when he famously wrote "I contain multitudes"—different selves that come in and out of focus at different times in our life. I penned a thought in my journal: "If we recognize that we contain these different multitudes, and if we accept that they can coexist alongside each other *and* contradict one another, then we can gain a deeper sense of our whole self—one that's defined not by how we think we ought to be perceived but by who we authentically are." I was no doubt inspired by Audre Lorde, another literary hero of mine at the time, who had once said: "If I didn't define myself for myself, I would be crunched into other people's fantasies for me and eaten alive." In reading Frank, Alsop, Whitman, and Lorde in my mid-twenties, I developed an expanded language for my own story. An idea began to crystallize: Maybe if I shared my story from the perspective of my whole self, I wouldn't have to choose a narrative of *either* sickness or recovery. Maybe I could tell a more honest narrative—one that allowed room for both. Rather than a story that had my healthy self talk over my eating-disorder self, I could let the two be in conversation with each other, as they were in my daily life.

This pivotal thought prompted questions I had never before considered: What if, instead of framing stories solely around the extremes of "sickness" and "full recovery," we could explore the space in between? What if this space could invite conversations about the imperfections of recovery and the slips that happen along the way? It occurred to me that I had been living in this space with shame because I didn't think I was supposed to inhabit it. But if the stigma were removed, then maybe this space could be defined not by guilt but by growth. It felt like I was onto something, and after not so many moons, I gave this expanse a name. I came to call it the middle place.

I now live in this middle place, where recovery is an everyday act that takes effort. Life in the middle place has widened my aperture on recovery, pushing me to see past the limited lens through which I used to view it. To live in this space is to explore the realms of sickness and wellness, and the porous boundary in between. "Everyone who is born holds dual citizenship, in the kingdom of the well and in the kingdom of the sick," writes Susan Sontag in her seminal work *Illness as Metaphor*. "Although we all prefer to use only the good passport, sooner or later each of us is obliged, at least for a spell, to identify ourselves as citizens of that other place." Though Sontag was writing about cancer, her work has relevance for those with eating disorders. So many of us in recovery know what it's like to move back and forth from the kingdom of the sick to the kingdom of the well. And at some point, no matter where we settle, we all end up having to cross that space in between. Many of us in recovery not only pass through this space but also end up living out our lives there.

Others remain sick. Anorexia was long considered an acute condition that began in adolescence and lasted a relatively short time. But in the mid-1980s, academic articles began to use different words to describe it, referring to the "protracted" and "long-term course" of the disorder. Years later, the term *severe and enduring anorexia* emerged to describe the 15 to 20 percent of people who have chronic cases and don't respond to treatment (if they even get treatment in the first place). The treatment community has yet to reach a consensus definition of severe and enduring anorexia, and it's not an actual diagnosis in the *DSM-5*. "How, precisely, should this stage of illness be defined? How ill is 'severe,' how long is 'enduring'?" Timothy Walsh, MD, wrote in the introduction to *Managing Severe and Enduring Anorexia Nervosa: A Clinician's Guide*.

One team of researchers said those with severe and enduring anorexia are a "challenging and neglected population," adding that "the limited understanding of and paucity of treatments for [severe and enduring anorexia] represent a crisis in our field." To treat this population is to acknowledge the reality that full recovery may not be possible for everyone with an eating disorder. And not everyone seeks recovery as the ideal; some believe their eating disorder serves a purpose and don't want to part with it. Remaining sick isn't so much a choice, but rather a constant state of being stuck.

It has become popular in the eating-disorder field to say that eating disorders are not lifestyle choices. I wholeheartedly believe this, and at the same time I wish there were more exploration of whether *recovery* is a choice. Choosing recovery, and making a commitment to it, helps. But it's not a guarantee that the eating disorder will go away.

In one of the more interesting studies I've come across, researchers took a longitudinal look at recovery from anorexia nervosa and bulimia nervosa over a twenty-two–year period. The study showed that of the 246 participants, roughly 63 percent recovered at the twenty-two–year mark, compared with 31.4 percent at the nine-year mark. The 2017 study, which was led by Massachusetts General Hospital's Dr. Kamryn Eddy, showed that recovery is possible even after long-term illness. Though not a treatment study, it argued in favor of active treatment rather than palliative care. The findings speak to a question that has driven much of my work in the middle place: Why do some people fully recover, while others struggle for a lifetime? It's a question that defies easy answers, but part of the answer may lie in the stories we tell ourselves and the ways these stories shape our sense of self.

From a very early age, I came to identify with my eating disorder. "I like knowing I have anorexia because it makes me special," I journaled when I was in the psychiatric ward. "But I don't like the *X* in *anorexia*—it scares me." I didn't elaborate, but I remember feeling daunted by what the *X* symbolized: the crossing out of something that can still be seen but is deemed incorrect or unnecessary. As anorexia took over, it tattooed that big black *X* on my being. I let it slowly take hold of me, to the point where I stopped saying "I have anorexia" and started saying "I am anorexic." It was no longer a nameless force outside me; it was an undeniable part of who I was, how I saw myself, and how I wanted others to see me.

I would later learn that neurobiological factors were likely at play. It turns out that adolescents' development of self and identity is closely linked to brain development. When adolescents begin to establish their adult identity, connections are formed in the brain. To make these connections, the brain relies on white matter, which is made up of myelin—an insulating layer that surrounds the nerve cells. The production of myelin partly relies on a person's dietary-fat consumption. Starvation, then, significantly alters the brain's white matter. For adolescents and teenagers with anorexia, white-matter alterations can result in a distorted sense of self and altered neurodevelopment. These underlying neurobiological factors—which scientists have only recently begun to understand—could help explain why I was so fixated on my anorexic title all those years ago. With every hospital admission, I felt even more worthy of it. In the narrative I crafted about myself, my anorexia was the main character and everyone else was pushed to the margins.

I thought about this when speaking with psychologist Erin Parks, PhD, who is co-founder and chief operating officer of the Equip eating-disorders treatment program. "I sometimes worry how our treatment industrial complex puts people into a patient role so much that it becomes maybe more of their identity than it had to," Dr. Parks told me. "For some people, the eating disorder is a blip on their radar. And for some people, it's a part of how they see the world forever." Park's comment reminded me of the book *Strangers to Ourselves* by Rachel Aviv (the *New Yorker* writer whose story inspired my work on restorative narratives). Aviv, who developed anorexia at age six but quickly recovered, writes: "Mental illnesses are often seen as chronic and intractable forces that take over our lives, but I wonder how much the stories we tell about them, especially in the beginning, can shape their course. People can feel freed by these stories, but they can also get stuck in them. . . . There are stories that save us, and stories that trap us, and in the midst of an illness it can be very hard to know which is which." She cites the work of social historian Joan Jacobs Brumberg, who says anorexia can be divided into two phases: "recruitment" to the disorder and the subsequent stage in which it becomes a "career."

I would argue for a third category: an undesirable "side job"—one that doesn't take up your entire day but still demands time and energy that could be better spent elsewhere. I followed the eating-disorder career path throughout my early adulthood. But since I began framing my recovery around the middle place, my disorder has been demoted to a side job. It still takes up space in my life, but my livelihood no longer depends on it. It's still part of my narrative, but it's not the whole story.

Narrative psychologists say the way we tell our life stories has a direct impact on how we see the world. Dan McAdams, PhD, a pioneer in the field of narrative psychology, has researched what he calls "contamination narratives" (in which people view their lives as moving from good to bad) and "redemption narratives" (in which people view their lives as moving from bad to good). He has found that people who "find redemptive meanings in suffering and adversity, and who construct life stories that feature themes of personal agency and exploration, tend to enjoy higher levels of mental health, well-being, and maturity." In other words, it's not solely our life situations that determine our well-being but also how we choose to tell stories about these situations and where we place the chapter breaks. Stories alone can't save us, but they can steer us in the right direction.

The narrative psychology research reminds me of new research about the restorative narrative genre and its effects on readers. One study found that restorative narratives elicit positive emotions and prompt readers to want to help those in need—namely, the people featured in these stories and others like them. The study said restorative narratives are especially helpful when reporting crises and ongoing social issues, and it ended with a quote from one of my earlier pieces about the genre: "We're not saying, 'Don't cover the trauma or tragedy,' . . . We're saying the story doesn't end there. In many ways, it's just beginning."

The restorative narrative provides a framework for thinking more realistically about life after treatment. It's easy to assume that when eating-disorder patients leave treatment, they are ready to live out the final chapter of their eating-disorder story: full recovery. But there is so much storytelling that needs to happen before—and if—they turn the page to that final chapter. It's this part of the story—the messy middle—that too often gets overlooked. And because it's left out of the way we talk about illness, we often can't find words to explain it. The language we use to describe sickness and illness tends to be black-and-white: "sick" or "fully recovered." "Curable" or "terminal." "Healthy" or "unhealthy." But there's a semantic expanse between these pairs of words—a widening of vocabulary that would help us make better sense of eating disorders and recovery from them. Hence the side job and the middle place.

In her iconic memoir *Wasted*, Marya Hornbacher refers to her experience with anorexia and bulimia as "a very wordless time" in which she struggled to describe "the inarticulate process" of being sick and working toward wellness. When I surveyed people for this book, I asked each respondent to share one word to describe either their eating disorder or their recovery. Labels for their eating disorders included "insidious," "debilitating," "demonic," "lifelong," "inescapable," "suffocating," "unremitting," "torturous," "relentless," "destructive," "all-consuming," "treatment-resistant," and "disturbingly comforting." They called their disorder "a thief," "a drill sergeant," "a toxic friend," and "my oldest friend." Annelise, a thirty-four-year-old respondent from Kentucky, said she used to refer to her anorexia as "Reptar"—the creepy Tyrannosaurus rex from the 1990s cartoon *Rugrats*. Naming her disorder and being able to picture it helped Annelise see it for what it was: a monster.

Other survey respondents shared words for recovery: "hard-won," "life-changing," "enduring," "freeing," "foundational," "messy," "incremental," "complicated," "fragile," "flimsy," "exhausting," "unacknowledged," and my favorite, "yummy!" Interestingly, no one listed "full." Given how many people with eating disorders feel uncomfortable with physical fullness and try avoiding it, using "full" to describe recovery doesn't seem all that fitting.

Taylor, a twenty-six-year-old from Charlotte, North Carolina, referred to the same word multiple times when describing her recovery: "fun." While in the throes of binge-eating disorder, Taylor developed food rules for herself, many rooted in restriction. Like me, she denied herself the foods she wanted during the day, only to binge on them (or some variation) late at night. In recovery, Taylor began to heed her desires instead of depriving them. "I needed to do that after feeling like I was just being controlled by food and my fear of food and my rules around it for so long," she told me. "The recovery process has been just so delightfully fun, because food is fun, and it's supposed to be fun."

Annelise and Taylor were among the many people who said the idea of the middle place resonates with them. About 85 percent of my survey respondents said they have found themselves in the middle place or are still there. Many said they've inhabited a middle place for years without ever knowing what to call it. In the presence of a place that seemed ineffable, they remained silent.

Fueled by my own desire to give words to this place, I reconnected with four women who were treated with me at Boston Children's Hospital and Germaine Lawrence (which has since been shuttered). They each nodded at the notion of the middle place and, like me, have lived there for the past twenty-five years. "At this point, the eating disorder is a chapter of my life but not the whole book," said Katie, one of the girls who was on the Bader 5 psychiatric ward with me. "It creeps in and is more prominent in times of extreme stress. The fear of losing control is always there. The eating disorder played such a significant role in my life and shaped me in so many ways both positive and negative. I feel like it will always be a part of who I am."

Haniyah, who was also on the ward with me, compared the middle place to a stock market graph: some days her recovery trends upward, some days downward. "For so long, I pictured recovery as a very final state of mind/being—one without counting calories, scales, obsessive thoughts, and complete acceptance of who I am and how I appear. But I've finally accepted that recovery is about taking one day at a time, accepting my flaws, but also understanding that I am deserving of recovery," said thirty-nine-year-old Haniyah, who developed anorexia at age twelve. "I don't really know what full recovery means, but if it means being completely devoid of all eating-disorder–related thoughts, behaviors, and triggers, then I don't know that it's possible. And while that may sound pessimistic or hopeless, I actually find it comforting because it means that where I am right now, and the progress that I make every day, is okay."

Though I've been moved by how many people say they like the idea of the middle place, I also realize it's not a safe space for everyone. Because the middle place is often overlooked, those who occupy it are at greater risk of getting overlooked, too. "That place was triggering," said survey respondent Brianna, who is recovered from anorexia. "I felt like I wasn't well enough to go without treatment, but the medical community thought I was well enough, so I often relapsed to get the care I needed."

It's a devastating reality for many people with eating disorders, who may not qualify for treatment or insurance coverage but still need high-level support.

For some, the middle place can become too safe, luring them to settle for stagnancy rather than striving for growth. It can be a limbo where people get by without getting better. Viewed in this light, some might be tempted to equate the middle place with "quasi-recovery" or "pseudo-recovery." I've had to confront related questions in my own life: Am I just staying in the middle place because I'm too afraid to let go of my eating disorder? Am I not trying hard enough? Is my affinity for the middle place preventing me from attaining full recovery? I still don't know if I will ever reach full recovery, but I continue to aim for forward momentum. From this ill-defined middle, I've come to accept that my recovery is a path of imperfection, laden with slips and setbacks. Along the way, I've figured out where to place those yellow "Caution: Don't fall!" signs so that my slips don't become uncontrollable slides. Even with the signs, though, I sometimes lose my footing. But whereas I once viewed that as a failure, I now see it as proof of progress.

If I had to pick a poem to describe the middle place, it would be "Risk," which is credited to Anaïs Nin. The poem makes me think about the perils of sickness and the possibilities of progress. The poem reads:

And then the day came
when the risk
to remain tight
in a bud
was more painful
than the risk
it took
to blossom.
Life is a process of becoming, a combination of states we have

> *to go through. Where people fail is that they wish to elect a*
> *state and remain in it. This is a kind of death.*
> *Living never wore one out so much as the effort not to live.*
> *Life is truly known only to those who suffer, lose, endure*
> *adversity, stumble from defeat to defeat.*
> *Perfection is static, and I am in full progress.*

Though the poem was not about eating disorders, it occurs to me that "full progress" could be a fitting alternative to "full recovery." Whether we think about recovery in terms of the middle place, or a book chapter, or a stock market graph, it's ultimately about trying to make progress, even without knowing if it will lead to full recovery. The geography of recovery usually doesn't allow for a linear progression. And for those of us in the middle place, the map may point us forward but not necessarily to a final destination.

I spoke about this with several clinicians to get their take, including Mark Warren, MD, the recently retired chief medical officer of Accanto Health. Dr. Warren, seventy, was diagnosed with anorexia nervosa as a teenager and spent many years in the middle place. "I would say that I am really recovered at this point, but it was a thirty-year process," he told me, noting that aging helped him gain more confidence in himself and his body. "When you have focused on something for most of your life, the idea that you would just stop focusing on it is kind of absurd, really. There's no on/off switch in the head." Warren likes to use the word "remission" to describe the recovery process. "Remission is when you're not having the behaviors, the body is physically okay, you could have a family, you could have a life, you could have friends," said Warren, who's based in Cleveland, Ohio. "I think about it like cancer; it's like, yeah, the cancer's in there and you're going to have to see the cancer doctor every six months for the rest of your life. And it could come back, so you don't want to say you're 'cured.' But you can be hopeful, and you can be optimistic, and you can still have a really great life."

Carolyn Costin, the therapist who introduced me to the "healthy self" versus the "eating-disorder self," believes everyone can reach full recovery. It's "limiting" to think you can't, she said. "If you believe that you're not going to be fully recovered, you stay in that liminal place. I don't want to say that's necessarily bad; maybe you have a good life and maybe you feel like it keeps you humble and honest, and it keeps you always looking out and always trying to grow," said Costin, who has been recovered from anorexia for over four decades. "But me saying I'm 're-covered' doesn't mean I don't try to continue to grow and get stronger and better in my beliefs, my behaviors, my actions, my balance." She acknowledges that recovery is a nonlinear process with slips and slides, but says they can ultimately be overcome. She has crafted her own definition of what it means to be recovered and says it's "when the person can accept his or her natural body size and shape and no longer has a self-destructive relationship with food or exercise. When you are recovered, food and weight take a proper perspective in your life, and what you weigh is not more important than who you are; in fact, actual numbers are of little or no importance. When recovered, you will not compromise your health or betray your soul to look a certain way, wear a certain size, or reach a certain number on the scale. When you are recovered, you do not use eating-disorder behaviors to deal with, distract from, or cope with other problems."

It's a more comprehensive definition than most, and it reflects Costin's belief that people can not only achieve recovery but also maintain it. She refers to herself as someone who is "recovered" instead of someone "in recovery." "I think what we say to ourselves means something, and I think it's limiting to say 'in recovery,'" Costin said. "Someone can say 'I'm recovering from anorexia,' and they could still be severely underweight and just out of a treatment center and recovering, or somebody could say they're 'in recovery' when they've been weight restored and not using behaviors for twenty years. So, to me, the words 'recovering' and 'recovery' are vague."

This makes sense, and a lot of people who are recovered from eating disorders probably agree. But I still prefer the language of "in recovery" to describe my own experiences. There has always been a language barrier between me and full recovery, a lack of understanding about how to interpret it and how to translate it into action. When I talk with people who consider themselves fully recovered, I sometimes feel a tinge of longing for something that seems inaccessible to me—a life where the eating-disorder self is dormant, and my healthy self is always awake and in total control. I adopted the words "I'm recovered" when I got out of residential treatment, but they failed me. While stuck in my binge-and-restrict cycle, I didn't want to say I was "in recovery." I thought I had outgrown that language, and I worried that others might judge my use of it. "You are supposed to be **R**ecovered with a capital R," I journaled. In the same way that my family used to question, "Why can't you just eat?!" I found myself adopting a similar line of questioning. *Why can't you just recover, Mallary?*

The phrase "in recovery" has become acceptable when speaking of alcoholism, drug addiction, or perfectionism. But if you say you're "recovering" from an eating disorder over a prolonged period, there can be an assumption that you're somehow not trying hard enough or you're undermining yourself. Many of us in the middle place are trying hard as we can, though, all the while knowing we remain at risk. We are, indeed, "in" recovery. Margo Maine, PhD, prefers this wording, too. As one of the most well-known psychologists in the field, she has written seven books on eating disorders, including *Pursuing Perfection*, which focuses on why some adult women struggle with perfectionism and eating disorders.

"I like the idea of recover-*ing*, and I like it to be more fluid than static," she told me in an interview. "I don't ever use the word 'cure' because it's a fixed state. Recovery is a long-term process, and we have to talk about it that way." When Dr. Maine was doing her dissertation on anorexia in the 1980s, she said there were three shortsighted criteria for recovery: weight restoration, return of menstruation, and (believe it or not) marriage. The field has no doubt come a long way since then, but there is still room for improvement, not only in terms of how recovery is defined but also how it's framed. "To pretend that patients are a fixed entity—'recovered'—when they leave treatment is just so wrong," Dr. Maine said. "I don't think we do a good job preparing people for next steps when they are out in the world and in a new life stage outside the hospital or residential. We need to be better about preparing people for real life. Recovery *is* life; it has bumps and bruises. Recovery is a middle place; I think that's a really, really good metaphor."

Maine's words reminded me of the famous Viktor Frankl book title, *Yes to Life: In Spite of Everything.* It seems like a fitting motto for my own eating-disorder story, which has been rooted in hope despite all its despair. It began as a chaos narrative when I was sick, then morphed into a restitution story when I thought I had reached full recovery. Then it slid into a chaos narrative disguised by a restitution story as I relapsed. To arrive at a storyline that felt more authentic, I had to rewrite my narrative and be open to revisions along the way. I had to change the language I used—with a shift from "recovered" to "in recovery"—to show that my recovery is not a fixed state but a space that I still move through. The act of switching storylines made me feel vulnerable, but it helped me see that while the setting and plot had changed, I was not just a protagonist but also a true heroine. I was no less strong, no less competent, just because I hadn't reached full recovery. As a heroine, I don't want to fix my gaze so intently on one part of my story that I can't see beyond it; I want to hold a mirror up to myself and reflect the whole, authentic, imperfect me.

Chapter Ten

Love, Sex, and Marriage in the Middle Place

When I lived alone after college, I would often look in my bedroom mirror and catch glimpses of my mother. I started to resemble her more and more: thin lips, round cheeks, and blue eyes that narrowed into crescent moons when I laughed. I also found myself missing her in ways I hadn't before. My heart longed for her advice—on how to date, how to handle rejection, how to find a guy who wanted to be in a relationship.

I was nearing my mid-twenties and had never been in a serious relationship. When I was sick as an adolescent, my eating disorder held me back from flings and flirtations, and I had no interest in guys. At a time when my body should have been developing into a woman's, I was determined to stay small. It wasn't until the end of my time at Germaine Lawrence, at nearly sixteen years old, that I got my period, started wearing bras, and developed occasional crushes. I took these crushes as a sign of recovery—proof I had space in my heart and mind for something other than anorexia. But even then, I had little interest in casual dating; I yearned to be in a relationship. I thought love would overpower my eating disorder. And I hoped a committed relationship would buffer me from the frequent letdowns and losses that tend to accompany casual dating. Since losing my mother, the pain of any loss throbbed like an open wound.

My mother didn't live long enough to watch me go on my first date or to the prom with my high school crush. But she did offer a bit of counsel when I was ten. "Don't have sex until you're married," she told me one evening. "Then you can share that moment with someone who truly loves you." Without going into detail, my mother told me she was sexually abused as a child, losing her virginity without her consent.

"Promise me you'll wait?" she asked. It was more than a question.

"I promise, Mom," I said, determined to keep my word. "I promise . . ."

It was the only time she mentioned the abuse to me, and the only time she spoke to me about sex. I was so rattled by the revelation that I held on to every word for years to come. I vowed to honor my mother's wishes without really understanding their implications. For a long time, I wondered why she would share such traumatic news with me when I was so young. But I've come to believe she must have sensed death's imminence and wanted to protect her little girl as best she could before time ran out.

Post-college, when I started dating, I kept my promise top of mind. I would go out with someone for a few weeks—usually someone my friends had connected me with or who I knew through my journalism circles. There was the newspaper designer who oscillated between liking me for a few days and weeks of apparent disinterest. There was the light-fixture salesman; instead of coming to the door to pick me up, he would beep the horn of his old Camaro and blast Flo Rida hip-hop music loud enough to shake the car. There was the recently divorced writer who was fourteen years my senior and seemingly scouting for a rebound. There was the avid runner who acted enamored in his text messages but aloof in person. And there was the dapper Midwesterner who took me by surprise when he opened his car trunk on our first date to show me a set of bones. (Turns out he was a medical sales representative, and the bones, to my relief, were not real.)

It seemed impossible to find a guy who was not only interested in committing to a relationship but also willing to wait until marriage to have sex. I might as well have been wearing a shirt emblazoned with the word *RUN!* And most guys did. After a few dates, my text messages were met with blank spaces, my phone calls with silence.

"Guys like the chase," Gramz told me on more than one occasion, trying to teach me that this was normal.

"But Gramz, I don't want to keep running!" I once said in exasperation. "I want to find somebody who will run toward me—somebody who likes me and who *shows* me they like me."

"There's a lid for every pot, Mallary," she reassured me. "You'll find yours soon enough."

I wanted to believe her, but I was tired of hoping I had finally found my lid only to discover it didn't fit. I never revealed my eating disorder to the men I dated. With every rejection, I blamed not just myself but also my body. If I were thinner, then maybe guys would like me better. If I were prettier, they would stay. Rejections led to self-critiques of my appearance and day-long restrictions of food. During these vulnerable stretches, my eating disorder manipulated me into thinking it cared. It whispered that, unlike all those guys who had fled, it had stayed. Anorexia was, for better or worse, always with me.

My heart had never been broken, but after years of fizzled-out flings, it felt cracked. I talked about those cracks with my dear friend Kristyn, who was my roommate in college. Although we now lived in different parts of the country, we kept in touch via late-night instant-message chats. We'd jump online a few nights a week and indulge in woes about our empty love lives. Kristyn was good at weaving levity into heavy conversations, and she buoyed me with funny stories about her own unsuccessful attempts at dating. We were both single young women—virgins who had grown up Catholic in small Massachusetts suburbs. And we shared a fondness for *Sex and the City*. We lived vicariously through Carrie Bradshaw, the show's beloved lead character who worked as a love columnist. We liked her one-liners and made-up phrases, including *zsa zsa zsu*—"that butterflies-in-your-stomach thing that happens when you not only love the person, but you've got to have them." Kristyn and I used to joke that, at the rate we were going, we could one day co-author a love column of our own: *Abstinence in the Suburbs*. Funny as the title was, I cringed at the thought.

It seemed that if I wanted to change course, I needed to start looking for love in different places. In April 2010, a month before my twenty-fifth birthday, I joined the dating site Match.com. I was hesitant, fearing that others would see it as a sign of desperation. So, at first I just lurked, scanning only some of the messages that flooded my Match.com inbox each day. I suspected that most women on the site got inundated with messages, and that success in this cyber world involved determining which messages to respond to and which to ignore. I was easily turned off by most of them, which were variations of "Hey gurl" or "Hi beautiful, u want to chat?"

But there were a few that stood out, including one from a guy I had "winked" at—Match.com speak for expressing interest in someone by clicking a winking, smiley-faced emoji. Unlike most messages I received, this one was well written, with complete sentences free of typos and grammatical errors. Besides meeting this literary benchmark, the note seemed sincere, with questions about where I grew up and what kind of work I did as a journalist. His profile pictures were noticeably silly, making me think he must know how to have fun and laugh. There were photos of him careening down a Slip 'N Slide, dancing goofily at a party, and posing with funny faces and aviator sunglasses. We messaged back and forth for a week or so, tiptoeing forward through the written word before the spoken one. Then we decided to meet for dinner at Moon Under Water, a British pub overlooking the Tampa Bay. When I first saw Troy, my eyes were drawn to his smile. Warm and welcoming, it disarmed me. We hugged a bit awkwardly and exchanged hellos, then followed the hostess to our table.

"What's good here?" Troy asked, looking at the menu.

"I'm a vegetarian, so I like the Indian curry with tofu and veggies," I told him.

"A vegetarian, huh? I've never had tofu before, but I think I'm going to order some."

It felt validating, and I liked that he was open to trying new foods. We ate and talked for well over two hours, sharing stories about our upbringing, our work, our aspirations. He grew up in Arlington, Texas, went to Florida State University, and now was pursuing a master's degree in anesthesia. I noted how our narratives crossed and diverged, and I was moved when he told me that he, too, had lost a parent at a young age. When Troy was fourteen, his father was killed in a motorcycle accident. He never got to say goodbye. We talked about how the death of a parent is tragic no matter how they died, or whether or not you had time to prepare.

I barely knew Troy but felt comfortable with him. I studied his face: tan and undeniably handsome, with a dimpled chin and smoky-blue eyes. His voice was confident when he asked me the kind of questions that showed he had listened to what I said and wanted to learn more. I was relaxed enough with him to eat most of my meal. Troy ate most of his, too, declaring that he liked the tofu. By dinner's end, I made a private declaration to myself: I liked him.

One date turned into two, then three, then too many to keep track. Troy planned most of our early dates, which were equal parts adventurous and chivalrous. He took me parasailing, and together we soared above a clear-watered beach. He booked a Cessna plane ride that took us on an aerial tour of Tampa Bay. We admired the view and kissed amid the setting sun—my own *zsa zsa zsu* kind of moment. He booked us surprise reservations at some of St. Pete's best restaurants, and together we expanded our palates. We experimented with new foods: Japanese, Thai, Mediterranean. The first time he came to my apartment, I opened the door to see his hands behind his back. Then he presented me with an origami rose that he had folded from red construction paper. "That rose took me so long to make!" he said, laughing. I placed it on my dresser that night, delighted that he always seemed to remember the little details I shared with him, including my love for origami.

A month into our relationship, we began referring to each other as girlfriend and boyfriend. He was the first boyfriend I ever had, the first man I had met who didn't seem afraid of commitment. And he was the first one to be openly affectionate with me. He squeezed in kisses whenever he could, in private and in public. He massaged my shoulders when I seemed tense. And when we walked side by side, he always slipped his hand into mine. At first, my reaction was childlike befuddlement. *How long am I supposed to hold his hand? What if my hand gets sweaty? How will I know when it's time to let go?*

Growing up, I had never felt especially comfortable being touched. My parents were not the touchy-feely sort. When I was in treatment, I had to follow strict "no physical contact" rules and couldn't so much as tap someone on the shoulder. The rules were in place out of respect to the boundaries of patients, many of whom had a history of sexual trauma. When I dated guys prior to meeting Troy, physical contact was limited to kissing; anything more felt performative.

But with Troy, being touched felt natural, comforting, and sensual all at once. I saw his public displays of affection as signs he genuinely liked me and wasn't afraid to show it. One night, when I told him I didn't like how my legs looked, he responded by kissing them all over. "I love your legs," he said, and I knew he meant it. For years I couldn't look at my body without disrespecting it. Now here was this man who adored it. Troy respected my wishes not to have sex, and though there was no doubt he wanted to, he never pressured me. He told me several times a day that I looked beautiful, especially when my hair was in a messy bun and my face was bare of makeup.

Troy could sense my disdain for my body, but he didn't know the roots of it. I was still afraid that telling him about my history with an eating disorder would make him look at me differently. I worried he would no longer see me as his beautiful girlfriend but, rather, as a burden. As a defense mechanism, I made a list of what I didn't like about Troy, thinking it might soften the blow if he broke up with me. We weren't living together at that point, but I had been to his place enough times to see parts that perturbed me:

— He doesn't make his bed.
— He owns hardly any books.
— He leaves his clothes strewn across the room instead of putting them in the laundry basket.
— He doesn't like my cat and isn't a cat person in general.
— He says *whatnot* a lot.

The list came up comically short, and I was reminded that there was so much I loved about him and so little I didn't like. Seeking solace elsewhere, I turned to books. Among them was Elizabeth Gilbert's classic memoir *Eat, Pray, Love*, which had just been published. One passage in particular resonated with me: "To lose balance sometimes for love is part of living a balanced life." I jotted the quote in my journal and wrote my own response: "If you're too afraid of losing your balance, you'll never fall for anyone. The question I keep asking myself, though, is: What if you let go of that fear and no one's there to catch your fall?"

A few days later, I decided to tell Troy about my eating disorder. Over dinner one night, I outlined my past experiences and explained that the disorder was still part of my present. I didn't go into detail about the extent of my binging and restricting, but I told him that recovery remained a work in progress. With characteristic calm and curiosity, he asked questions about the disorder's origins, what the hospitalizations were like, and if I had any residual physical effects. He listened to what I had to say and reassured me that he would be there to support me along the way. My inner strength, he said, was one of the many qualities he admired. Troy caught my fall, making me realize that I could trust him—to be there for me, to stay.

If anything, telling Troy about my ongoing recovery drew him closer to me. Moving forward, truth became our love's super glue, binding us together as we navigated life's sticky situations. I began opening up to him more, letting him know about the nights I binged and the days I restricted. At times, it felt like I was juggling two relationships—a healthy one with a man I loved and a toxic one with a disorder I loathed. Being in a relationship hadn't magically erased my eating disorder in the ways I once hoped. But the more I talked with Troy about my struggles, the fewer slips I had and the more of myself I could bring to our relationship. I found truth in the adage shared in many twelve-step communities: "You're only as sick as your secrets." And I sought comfort in the wisdom of author bell hooks, who wrote that "commitment to truth telling lays the groundwork for the openness and honesty that is the heartbeat of love."

My relationship with Troy coincided with my work on the middle place, giving me a greater appreciation for how love can help us navigate the messiness of recovery. With Troy by my side, I felt a newfound desire to make progress in the middle place—not just for myself but also for us as a couple. I still wasn't set on "full recovery," but I found myself wanting to aim for "more recovery." I liked the idea that "more" could be open to interpretation—10 percent one day, 1 percent the other, but progress nonetheless.

Together, Troy and I came to learn that there's beauty not just in the acceptance of hard truths but also in the revelation of them. As the psychologist John Welwood once wrote: "When we reveal ourselves to our partner and find that this brings healing rather than harm, we make an important discovery—that intimate relationship can provide a sanctuary from the world of facades, a sacred space where we can be ourselves, as we are. This kind of unmasking—speaking our truth, sharing our inner struggles, and revealing our raw edges—is sacred activity, which allows two souls to meet and touch more deeply." For me, that sense of touch—in both the literal and figurative senses of the word—became a big part of what made me feel comfortable with Troy. The writer Diane Ackerman once said that "love is the great intangible," but for me, it didn't feel intangible at all. For the first time in my life, it felt like I could grasp love. It was around me and within me, both physically and emotionally. The days of wanting to remain in a child's body started to feel more distant and less relevant to the woman I had become.

Three months into my relationship with Troy, I decided to break my promise to my mother. I had toyed with the idea for weeks, feeling torn between fulfilling my own wishes and upholding my mother's. But I was weary of letting my past dictate my present, and I didn't think my mother would have wanted that, either. The first time Troy and I had sex, he was gentle and sweet. I, alas, was nervous and stiff. I didn't know what to do or how I was supposed to feel, and I worried my body would let me down. But Troy guided me in ways that felt comfortable and respectful. He made me, above all else, feel loved.

Afterward, we lingered in bed for over an hour. It was morning, and the autumn sunlight cast golden hues on our faces. Before meeting Troy, I had never been able to lie in bed and relax on weekends. I was too anxious to stay still, too self-critical to think of it as anything but being lazy. With Troy, though, I could sleep in and then go out for a leisurely late-morning brunch. I could watch two back-to-back movies in one sitting. I could let my body (and sometimes even my mind) take a respite. I came to love our carefree idleness, our languid evenings of having nowhere to be but by each other's side. Young and in love, we savored what the Italians call *dolce far niente*—the sweetness of doing nothing. It was during these times that we had some of our best conversations.

"I dated so many guys who didn't want to be in a relationship," I told Troy in bed on that first day we made love.

"I used to be that guy who didn't want to be in a relationship, partly because I knew I would be moving around so much during my clinical rotations in grad school," he said matter-of-factly.

"What changed?" I asked.

"You."

We kissed, sealing a moment that would become one of my favorite memories. When I opened my journal later that evening to capture the day's events, I paused after writing the date: October 10, 2010. It was, of all days, my parents' wedding anniversary. They married twenty-eight years earlier and stayed together until my mother's dying day. I looked at the clock and saw that it was 7:23 p.m. I stared at the clock until it struck 7:24—a symbolic time that has always made me think of my mother, who was born on July 24. It knew it was all pure happenstance. But I welcomed it as a sign that maybe my mother hadn't meant for me to take her advice so literally, that maybe she was really trying to say: "Wait for the one you love." By that measure, I had kept my promise.

Of all the love stories in the world, the one about me and Troy was my favorite. It was a story that I liked sharing with others, especially my father. The first time he and Troy met, about six months into our relationship, they stayed up until 3 a.m. talking about guitars and cars. My father gave me his stamp of approval the next morning, telling me I had found "a keeper." My stepmother, Gina, whom I have grown closer to throughout the years, agreed. Falling in love with Troy also helped me understand something I couldn't before: why my father had wanted to be in a committed relationship with Gina after losing the first love of his life. I came to see their relationship differently, from a place of acceptance.

A year and a half after Troy met my family, he told my father he wanted to ask for my hand in marriage. Dad approved, knowing I was entering a new phase in life, not as his little girl but as his grown daughter. He was reminded that parenting is a lifelong exercise in figuring out when to hold on to your children and how to let go. He shared these sentiments the way he usually does—in a letter he wrote me around Christmas of 2012, a few weeks after Troy and I got engaged. It was the first Christmas I would be spending with Troy's family instead of my own. "Every time I 'let go,' I think of it as 'let grow,'" Dad wrote. "It makes it easier for me." He went on to list some of the earlier times when he had to let go of me: when he released his hand from the handlebars the day I learned to ride my bike without training wheels; all the times he had to leave me in the hospital and at Germaine Lawrence; that late August evening when he kissed me goodbye on my first day of college. "Now, you are entering the next stage of your life," the letter concluded. "You have a wonderful man who loves you. You belong with him, so that you two can start a new chapter in your lives."

On my wedding day, my father and I both wept as we met in the church vestibule. I felt immense gratitude for the many years he took care of me, refusing to give up hope that I would one day get better. As we prepared to walk down the aisle together, I wrapped my arm around his and held tight on to my wedding bouquet. It was draped with lace from my mother's wedding veil, a reminder of my mom's lasting love—and the long arc of loss. I had learned that to commit to love, you must assume the risk of loss. True love is an acceptance of an inevitable reality: that your beloved will one day leave this world and so will you. I had no doubt that for as long as we were alive, Troy and I would remain together.

At the altar, Troy and I took the traditional vows: to be there for each other in sickness and in health, until death do us part. We both knew it was a promise that carries added weight when you marry someone who has endured an eating disorder for more than half her life, but it was a weight we pledged to share. "I have watched with pride as you have become a stronger and more confident woman," Troy said, reading his handwritten vows. "With you by my side, the future is a brighter place. As we marry, I contemplate our future together, as a family. I imagine the life we will lead, raising kids with compassion, ambition, and a combination of our values. All the things I imagine about our future, I imagine with us standing together, hand in hand. With this, I vow to love you forever."

My vows echoed his: "As your wife, I will listen to you, comfort you, and support you," I told Troy. "I will love you unconditionally and embrace your imperfections. I will always love you for the amazing man that you are."

Love—that great mixer of metaphors—had helped me see Troy not only as my husband but also as the sun in my sky, the home for my heart, the lid for my storied pot.

Troy and I have been married for eleven years, and our vows remain integral to our love story. As I think about how that story has evolved, I wish I could say that my eating disorder was confined to the earlier chapters. But the truth is, it remains a plotline, lurking in the margins on some days and finding its way into sentences and whole paragraphs on other days. I've come to realize this may always be the case while living in the middle place.

The eating disorder emerges during stressful periods at work, when I make everything and everyone but myself a priority, and when I neglect to get the sleep and nourishment I need. It raises its head at social gatherings where there are no vegetarian offerings and thus easy excuses for me not to eat. Or, when we're at a restaurant that lists calories on its menu, and I fixate on what my eating-disorder self thinks I should eat rather than what my healthy self wants. Troy sees all of this and intervenes—reminding me I need to take better care of myself, encouraging me to eat something at home after the social gathering, and reading menu items out loud so I can listen to the entrée descriptions rather than reading the numbers beside them. Sometimes, my disorder leads to arguments—never screaming matches, but tense discussions about how we should approach my struggles with food. We've learned to navigate the arguments with a shared understanding that we're in this together. Together, we try to defy the disorder so we're not diminished by it. Together, we try to be bigger than it.

Whereas anorexia and I used to be inseparable, we're now in more of a long-distance relationship. I've been able to distance myself from it with Troy's help, but my disorder still calls and visits more often than I'd like. I'm not sure if I'll ever figure out how to let all the calls go to voicemail, to let all the doorbell rings go unanswered. In her book *Life Without Ed*, Jenni Schaefer writes: "I have never been married, but I am happily divorced." She's referring to the separation from her eating disorder, which she calls "Ed" throughout the book. By personifying her disorder, she portrays it as an abusive spouse she needed to divorce in order to fully recover. When I first read *Life Without Ed*, before meeting Troy, I came away believing I would need to break up with my disorder before I could enter a loving relationship. Had I held myself to that belief, I don't know if I ever would have fallen in love. For me, it was ultimately more important to learn how to be with both, in hopes that my healthy relationship would grow strong enough to outshine the unhealthy one.

The same was true for one of my survey respondents, Sara, who developed anorexia nervosa at age fourteen. She went to residential treatment multiple times and found each stay left her more mired in her eating-disorder self. "The longer I had the eating disorder, the more I developed an illness identity," said Sara, who's now in her late thirties. "In treatment, there weren't many patients who were very recovery oriented. And once you've been in residential multiple times, as I was, you get some street cred from other patients for being super sick." Shortly after graduating college, she ended up in residential treatment again and realized she didn't want to be sick her entire adult life. She made a plan: Once she was discharged, she would go to graduate school, engage in activities outside of anorexia, and meet new people who didn't know her as "the girl with an eating disorder."

Sara followed through on her plan and went to graduate school to become a social worker. She made friends who didn't have eating disorders and had professors who saw her for her intelligence. She wasn't all better, but she was working toward a better life. "Embracing that middle ground and some degree of illness *while* I was living my life was beautiful," she said. "Instead of telling myself, *Don't go to grad school, you have to get better first*, choosing to live my life even with this illness is what allowed me to get past my disorder."

Ultimately, she fell in love with a woman whom she would eventually marry. "When I met my wife, I made a promise to myself I wouldn't lie to her about anything I was doing with my food," Sara said. "I just committed to being honest with her." That helped Sara move further away from her eating disorder; she gained the weight she needed to, and she stopped purging after meals. Her wife has been able to help her eat and exercise intuitively, becoming not just a cheerleader but also a teammate in Sara's recovery.

Rose, the mother of four mentioned earlier in the book, also considers her spouse to be a team player. She used to hide her behaviors from her husband and would downplay their severity. She thought that doing so might diminish the disorder's presence in their relationship. But she came to realize that the cover-ups weren't helping her recovery or her marriage. "My husband's never going to capitulate and pretend the eating disorder isn't there or pretend it's not that bad," said Rose, who has learned to be more honest with her husband about the days she struggles. "In the past, it really felt like me and the eating disorder were against him. And now it's more like the two of us are against the eating disorder. We are on the same team now, and I think that makes a big difference."

Having a partner's support can go a long way—so much so that new treatments have been developed to foster better communications between people with eating disorders and their partners. About a decade ago, experts specializing in cognitive behavioral therapy and eating disorders teamed up to create UNITE—a suite of couple-based interventions that engage partners in the recovery process. With a therapist's support, couples learn how to reduce secrecy and avoidance by communicating constructively about eating-disorder behaviors, body-image concerns, and issues concerning physical intimacy and affection. This treatment model is considered effective, and it dovetails with research showing that loving relationships can improve recovery outcomes.

In one study, researchers interviewed people with eating disorders—including anorexia, bulimia, binge-eating disorder, and OSFED—about the factors that were helpful in their recovery. Participants laid out seven key elements of recovery: (1) not allowing food to dominate life or resolve problems; (2) finding a life purpose; (3) identifying emotions and having the courage to express them; (4) experiencing less anxiety and depression; (5) fulfilling one's own potential instead of conforming to others' expectations; (6) having healthy social interactions; and (7) accepting oneself and one's body. The study found that "accepting oneself included feeling comfortable with other people in general and being able to function sexually and emotionally in a relationship with a stable partner. This feeling was closely linked to body acceptance."

The connections between sexuality and eating disorders date back to the late nineteenth century, when psychoanalysts noted that anorexia seemed to develop during adolescence, a time when young people typically begin to grow into their sexuality. Those with anorexia do the opposite; through starvation they slow their body growth and sexual development, as I did. The onset of menstruation is often delayed, keeping adolescent girls in a childlike state. The father of psychoanalysis, Sigmund Freud, is credited with being the first person to consider: "What does a lack of appetite *mean*?" He believed all appetites were expressions of the sex drive and posited that people with anorexia (those who seemingly had no appetite) were revolted by food *and* sex—the result of what he called "nutritional neurosis." In 1895, Freud wrote: "The famous anorexia nervosa of young girls seems to me (on careful observation) to be a melancholia where sexuality is underdeveloped."

One of Freud's contemporaries, psychoanalyst Pierre Janet, was similarly intrigued by anorexia, which he called "a deep psychological disturbance" that was "difficult to interpret." Like Freud, he believed that a lack of appetite was the result of underlying emotional difficulties. But he disagreed that people with anorexia were disgusted by food; he believed they had an appetite for it but were fixated on trying to control it. Among the women he studied was Nadia, a young middle-class woman struggling with anorexia in the late 1880s. Janet said that when Nadia began developing breasts, she was mortified by her changing body and tried to hide it by cropping her hair, wearing baggy clothing, and restricting her food intake. Nadia refused to eat in front of anyone, was repulsed by the sound of her own chewing, and feared sexual maturity. In a paper, Janet quoted Nadia as saying: "I didn't want to gain weight or grow or look like a woman because I would have liked always to stay a little girl."

Decades later, the pioneering eating-disorder psychoanalyst Dr. Hilde Bruch carried out the views of Freud and Janet, declaring that adolescents with anorexia have "seriously disturbed" attitudes toward sex and adulthood. "Under the fragile façade of normality, their whole development has been so distorted that it would be inconceivable if they functioned normally in this area," she wrote in her seminal 1973 book, *Eating Disorders: Obesity, Anorexia Nervosa, and the Person Within*. "Characteristically they are confused about their bodily sensations and feel unable to control their bodily functions. To them the changes of pubescence, the increase in size, shape and weight, menstruation with its bleeding, and new and disturbing sexual impulses, all represent a dangerous challenge for which they are unprepared, threatening what little control they had. The frantic preoccupation with weight is an attempt to counteract this fear of losing control."

These psychoanalysts' theories focused almost exclusively on women, as most eating-disorder research historically has. That's been changing in recent years, with greater acknowledgment that men and transgender people also struggle with eating disorders and sexuality. One man I interviewed—sixty-three-year-old Ken—said his eating disorder developed after he started experiencing stronger than usual desires for food and sex during his teenage years. As an Italian American who loved pizza, he would eat a slice or two and find himself wanting more. But that desire was accompanied by a growing sense of guilt. Once he started having sex, he felt similarly—wanting more of it but feeling ashamed and afraid of the desire. "I started cutting down on both things," said Ken, a longtime music journalist who lives in California. "I just had this great fear that if I kept eating the pizza I'd get fat. And I worried about what would happen to me, or who I would turn into, if I kept wanting sex." Ken said that while he was sick, his libido was so low he had no interest in romantic relationships. Starvation had stripped him of life's pleasures, and he felt devoid of desire.

Ken continued restricting his food intake for decades, until he had a debilitating stroke at the age of forty-five. "I couldn't do anything; I was like a baby," recalls Ken, who lost feeling and strength on the left side of his body for several months. "You lose your coordination temporarily, too. Every time I stood up, I felt like falling over." He was suddenly a writer who couldn't hold a pen, a middle-aged man who needed help bathing himself and tying his shoelaces. Ken said his primary care physician had warned him many times that his organs were giving out, but he had considered himself invincible. "The stroke punctured the delusion of invincibility and made me realize that I would die if I didn't change," Ken told me. "Everything I believed had been shattered. Suddenly, I felt mortal and stripped of my coat of armor. It was terrifying."

After two months in the hospital and another two and a half months of rehabilitation, Ken regained feeling and strength as his balance returned. He didn't immediately stop his eating-disorder behaviors once he got home, but the stroke laid the foundation for his recovery. He began dating again and met a woman (a gourmet chef, no less) who would eventually become his wife. Being in a committed relationship helped Ken resurface his desires for sex and food without feeling ashamed of them. He now considers himself fully recovered and is vocal about issues he didn't feel comfortable discussing when he was sick. Chief among them is sexuality—a topic he wishes the eating-disorder field and the media talked about more. "The most overlooked story angle," he said, "is the intimate connection between food and sex in eating disorders."

While sexuality was a focal point for psychoanalysts' early work on eating disorders, it has been under-researched and underdiscussed in recent decades. "This is such an important area for growth in our field," said Dr. Beth McGilley, the Kansas-based psychologist mentioned earlier. "A lot of therapists are uncomfortable talking about it, so we don't bring it up as an area of concern for a lot of our patients." Dr. McGilley started practicing in the early 1980s, when the eating-disorder field was in its infancy. At the time, she told me, the clinical focus was on helping patients manage their symptoms. This frame expanded to address the various factors that contribute to eating disorders, including family systems, culture, and trauma. And psychologists began to address sexuality in the treatment of people who had both sexual trauma and eating disorders. But Dr. McGilley says it was—and still is—largely left out of eating-disorder treatment as a whole.

Some clinicians are trying to change that, including Ashley Moser, a clinical education specialist for the Renfrew Center, a national eating-disorder treatment center. "Sex can be an uncomfortable, taboo topic, but I think we just all have to get over our discomfort and lean into it," Moser told me. "It helps our clients decrease shame when they can talk about it with us." As I know from my own experiences, and as Moser has seen in her patients, some people with anorexia have trouble expressing their sexual desires and equate pleasure with overindulgence. "The restriction of enjoyment and of wants and needs goes so much more beyond just food; it shows up in sexual relationships, too," Moser said. "Patients will sometimes say, 'I don't know how to ask for sex when I want it.' Or, 'I don't know how to ask for the food that I want, and I have to wait until someone tells me it's okay before I can choose it for myself.'" She helps patients to identify their needs, wants, and desires (or lack thereof) concerning both food and sex. "I work with a lot of cisgendered female patients who feel a sense of obligation not just to be thin but to be highly sexual in order to be lovable and to maintain that lovability in their relationships," she said. "But eating disorders often decrease sex drive, so trying to force physical intimacy when there isn't that biological or physiological desire and connection can feel like a real betrayal of self, and the sex can feel performative."

One study of women with anorexia, bulimia, and OSFED found that sexual dysfunction is common across eating disorders but "is rarely discussed as an important component of treatment except in the context of sexual abuse and trauma history." Of the women surveyed, 67 percent reported a decreased sexual desire, 59 percent reported increased sexual anxiety, and 45 percent reported either absence or avoidance of sexual relationships. The study noted that people with anorexia tend to have a later onset of sexual activity compared to people without eating disorders and even those with bulimia. It cited several likely reasons, including malnutrition—which can lead to lower production of estrogen in women and testosterone in men, often resulting in a reduced sex drive. Distorted body image and body dissatisfaction can also lead to sexual anxiety and avoidance of sexual relationships.

My own body distortion and dissatisfaction have mostly stemmed from my inner critic, and not from others' comments. But I know that people in larger bodies face pressures I have not had to face—ones that make them feel as though they need to take up less space in the world in order to be loved. "The way that you are treated in medical situations, in professional situations, in social situations, in romantic relationships, is really, really unpleasant when you are larger—or at least it has been for me," said survey respondent Stacey, who experienced a painful breakup because of her weight. Stacey, who's in her thirties, has lived in a larger body her entire life and is in recovery from atypical anorexia. She began restricting her food intake at age eleven—sending her down a slippery slope that led to anorexia by the time she was twelve. She lost weight but was never considered underweight. Her naturally big body disguised her disorder, making it easier for family members and medical providers to overlook her need for care. When she was fifteen, she was eating so little that she fainted. But her pediatrician declared he could find nothing wrong with her. Stacey, who grew up in the United States and now lives in Europe, has dreaded going to the doctor's office ever since. On more occasions than she can count, primary care physicians have offered her Weight Watchers vouchers, not knowing about her history with anorexia. She, like so many people who don't "look the part" of someone with an eating disorder, has never had an official diagnosis.

Stacey fell into a binge-and-restrict cycle during her undergraduate years at a university in England, and then again while earning her master's and doctoral degrees. Once she had the pressures of school behind her, she began to make progress in her recovery. She met a man who seemed to accept her body, and she moved with him when he received a job assignment in a new city. As their relationship progressed, though, Stacey questioned her partner's support. He began telling her she needed to lose weight but didn't want her to engage in restrictive or disordered eating, which he knew she had done in the past. "There was this expectation of effortlessly becoming thinner," Stacey said. "We live in a society where there is this demand to lose weight, and yet there is this expectation that you do it invisibly and without complaint, and that you hide it and magically undergo a transformation." The experience led Stacey to reengage in eating-disorder behaviors to the point where she lost a significant amount of weight and relapsed. The relationship fell apart.

Stacey sought therapy and stopped dating for a couple of years to protect herself from getting hurt again. It helped that her choice coincided with the pandemic, making it easier to stay home and have time to herself. As the pandemic restrictions lifted, she began dating again and now has a new partner. Yet she remains wary. "My current boyfriend is great, but then again, I am significantly smaller than I was before," said Stacey, whose weight has fluctuated a lot throughout her sickness and recovery. "I don't know what it would be like if I were in a larger body than I am now, and I don't really want to find out." Though she considers herself to be in recovery, she still engages in behaviors she believes will prevent her from gaining weight—namely, the "the daily labor" of counting calories, exercising, and weighing herself. "It seems impossible to be in a body in this society without some degree of ongoing efforts at weight manipulation, and I have resigned myself to walking a fine line of tolerable restriction without letting it overwhelm my life," Stacey said. "At the end of the day, I still live in a larger body than the structures of society deem to be acceptable, normal, and worthy."

Another woman I spoke to, named Ella, also grew up in a larger body. Ella developed anorexia nervosa at age eighteen and spent her college years in and out of inpatient treatment. She began restricting, hoping it would help her lose weight and feel better about herself. But no matter how much weight she lost, and no matter how many times she was hospitalized, she still never felt thin enough. It was ultimately a romantic relationship—not her disorder—that helped her feel more comfortable in her own body. There's that old axiom, "If you do not love yourself, you will be unable to love anyone else." But for Ella, the reverse turned out to be true. She started dating her now husband right after her last hospitalization, when she was at one of her lowest points. "So many people told me, 'You probably shouldn't be super-invested in a relationship; you should work on yourself first,'" said Ella, who is now an eating-disorder psychologist. "And it's funny, because as a psychologist, I want to say that's what you should do. But my lived experience tells me that it's not one-size-fits-all. I had to meet someone who loved me in order to learn how to love myself."

When her disordered thoughts creep in, Ella shares them with her husband. He listens but doesn't lecture—an approach that Ella appreciates. She continues to go to therapy for additional support. "I don't want my husband to have to play that sole role of being the only person who's helping me to stay in recovery," she said. Early on in her recovery, Ella would turn to her husband when she had urges to restrict or count calories. Whenever her in-laws engaged in diet talk at family gatherings, he held her hand and squeezed it to let her know that he acknowledged it was hard for her. Then he would redirect the conversation. Now, six years into her recovery, Ella doesn't have as many urges and can speak up if she's uncomfortable with the way people are talking about food and bodies. When she's struggling with body image, she confides in her husband, who usually responds by saying, "I'm sorry you're struggling with that; I'm here for you and love you."

"He's learned (and I've helped him) that it doesn't help to respond with 'You're so beautiful, though!' because that still centers on my appearance," Ella said. "I've come to the realization that body image really has nothing to do with what I actually look like, or with what other people think I look like; it's more about my feelings of being inadequate. By decentering my appearance and instead centering on empathy and how he feels about me as a person, it helps me refocus on things that matter more to me than my body."

Ella found that talking with her husband about recovery helped her develop more words to describe it. But she finds that her descriptions change with her audience. "If I were talking to an eating-disorder researcher, I'd have to say I'm fully recovered because it seems there's no middle for them. I feel like it's very black-and-white; you're either recovered or you're not, you're either well or sick," Ella said. "I totally understand the need to protect patients and make sure you're conducting yourself ethically, but I don't think you have to be fully recovered to do any kind of work."

Outside of professional circles, Ella likes to say she's "in committed recovery"—a recognition that she's dedicated to continuously trying to get better. "I think of myself as being in a long-term relationship with recovery, but we're not married," said Ella, who lives in New England. "We've lived together for a really long time, and we're super-comfortable with each other. But I'm still afraid of commitment. I know the eating disorder is something I'm going to have to work on for a very long time—maybe the rest of my life, maybe not."

As we spoke, Ella was cradling a big part of her future—her two-month-old daughter, who cooed in the background while feeding. I listened intently, thinking about how fitting it all seemed—to hear Ella share her recovery story and to see the continuation of it as she nourished her newborn baby girl.

Chapter Eleven

Pregnancy in the Middle Place

When I was at my sickest, Gramz warned me that anorexia could upend my future. "If you keep this up, you're never going to be able to have kids," she told me when I was thirteen, shortly after my first stay at Bader 5. Wide-rimmed glasses swallowed her face, which was worn not just by age but also by a worry about what had become of me. She worried, in particular, that the damage I was doing to my body would leave me infertile or unable to carry a baby to term. It was a fear she shared many times when I was sick, hoping it might scare me into recovery. At the time, I knew I didn't want to be sick for the rest of my life and that I wanted children someday. But I was so consumed by anorexia that it was hard for me to imagine a future without it, let alone a future with children.

Gramz lived to see Troy and me marry. But she died at age ninety-two—one month before I found out I was pregnant. I was devastated by her death and coped with it in the best way I knew how: by writing her eulogy. I reflected on the ways she helped raise me after my mother passed away, referring to her as "a reservoir of advice and a strong-willed woman who proved that when we lose someone we love, when we think that feeling of emptiness will never go away, someone else often steps in or enters our life to fill the void and ease the pain." Now, it seemed the same truism was unfolding: My grandmother had left this world, and my unborn child was entering it.

Troy and I had been trying to conceive only for a few months and were elated it happened so quickly. Within hours of finding out, I downloaded pregnancy apps on my phone so I could track the milestones. All the apps compared the fetus's size to fruits and vegetables; for once, I had a fun and playful way to think about the size and shape of food. When our baby was no bigger than a blueberry, Troy and I watched it wiggle around in the sonogram image and heard the loud lub-dub of its heartbeat.

During that first prenatal appointment, I told my obstetrician about my history with an eating disorder. She noted it in my charts and then moved on. I was hoping she would ask questions about it or offer to be a resource if I had trouble with nutrition or weight gain during pregnancy. But she didn't—not at that appointment or any that followed. I stuck with her, knowing I would be hard-pressed to find an obstetrician who knew much about treating eating disorders.

By my second appointment, I began to literally face the numbers on the scale. It was a new position for me, one I hadn't assumed in more than a decade. For years, I dreaded looking at those numbers. I feared that if they were too high, I would slip into restriction, then slide my way into a relapse. But when I was pregnant, I wanted to see my weight; I knew if I didn't eat enough or gain enough, I could lose my baby. Now, food haunted me in a new way; I imagined scenarios in which I would binge and drown my baby in food, or restrict and shrink my baby into an irreversible invisibility. I read literature about how pregnant women should avoid soft cheeses, shellfish, high-mercury fish, raw meat, raw eggs, raw sprouts, unpasteurized juice, caffeine, alcohol. I told myself I could not go near these foods and drinks, and I was predictably rigid about this rule, vowing not to consume even a nibble or a sip. I took all sorts of mental notes about warnings I read in pregnancy books and blogs: "You're not actually supposed to eat for two; it's more like eating for one and a half—or one and a quarter. . . . The more weight you gain now, the more you'll have to lose later. . . . 'Breast is best'—for your baby, for postpartum weight loss, and for reducing your risk of breast cancer." I learned I could burn hundreds of calories a day by breastfeeding/pumping and potentially reduce my risk of breast cancer by 4.3 percent for every year of breastfeeding.

When the fetus was the size of a banana (or a Belgium endive, depending on your produce preferences), we learned we were having a girl. I received the news with an outward thrill and an inner shudder. I knew that of the thirty million people who suffer from an eating disorder in the United States, two-thirds are women. Determined to not have my daughter become part of that statistic, I told myself I needed to model good behaviors that she could learn from, even while in the womb. For starters, I found an eating-disorder dietitian who helped plan meals designed to keep me from regressing. With her help, I tried not only to be honest about my cravings but also to honor them. Instead of sneaking in bites of ice cream when no one was looking, as I would have done pre-pregnancy, I took whole bites in the middle of the kitchen with Troy by my side. Instead of peeling off a quarter-slice of cheese and putting the rest back in the container, I ate the whole slice. Instead of saying I couldn't have an afternoon snack because I had eaten a hearty lunch, I ate the snack. Newly equipped with knowledge of what I craved, Troy indulged me with mocha-almond-fudge ice cream from Publix. We would curl up on the couch, our bodies pressed together, our lips occasionally meeting, and eat straight from the carton. Some nights, the ice cream came with a familiar side of guilt. But I kept scooping out spoonfuls for myself and our unborn baby. In between bites, Troy would run his hands along my belly, feeling for a connection as he had done every night since we saw those double pink lines on the pregnancy test. I trusted that no matter how big my body got, he would always love me.

I outgrew my usual wardrobe and embraced the comfort of maternity clothes; I liked the way they respected the curves of my body and accommodated its changes. Sometimes I wore body-hugging dresses that accentuated my growing belly and widening hips. When I studied the mirror, I barely recognized myself. *Who was this young woman who felt comfortable showing off her belly, who was unashamed of overlapping thighs?* I was fully aware of the fragile state of the middle place, where favorable reflections are fleeting. But now I thought of my belly as a globe—a world of bodily beauty my baby called home. I wanted to make it as comfortable for her as I could and hoped that even after I gave birth, I would have the strength to admire my changing body. I remembered my mother, standing in front of the mirror with her own changing body, and I still longed to tell her she was beautiful.

The one time I tried to run while pregnant, I imagined my baby bouncing around inside of me. *That's uncomfortable*, I told myself, speaking for both of us. I walked the rest of the way, happy for an excuse to slow down. I swapped my running shoes for a yoga mat, completely at ease in lopsided tree poses and my not so graceful dancer poses. For the first time I could remember, I didn't push myself past the edge. I lapsed in child's pose when my body wanted to rest. I accepted the lavender-scented eye patches and burgundy blankets the yoga instructor offered during *shavasana*—the restorative pose at the end of each session. I listened to the steady beat of the instructor's meditation drum, a far better sound than the noise in my head. The more I deepened my yoga practice, the more these split seconds of stillness multiplied into whole minutes. Lying on my yoga mat like a still snow angel, I thought about my daughter and my mother.

So much had changed since those years when I tried to stay small in the aftermath of my mother's death. Now, I no longer wanted to lose weight to feel closer to my mother; I wanted to gain it to feel closer to my daughter. But the fear of loss still lurked. I dreaded I would die when my daughter was a newborn, or that she would die in my womb. I found myself studying the birthmarks on my body, looking for discolorations and irregularities. I had never paid much attention to my moles before, but suddenly they seemed like breeding grounds for cancer. (A visit to the dermatologist confirmed they were not.) I examined my breasts in the shower and in the mirror, fearful I would find a lump. (I never did.) I pressed my fingers into my belly, which felt as hard and as heavy as a pumpkin, hoping my baby would kick. (She often would.) Every time I went to my prenatal checkups, I expected the worst—but always left with the obstetrician's reassurance that nothing was wrong. Still, I fretted: *Is my baby okay in there?* I wanted constant proof that the little being within me was alive.

I wondered if my mother had experienced similar worries, if she ever lay awake at night scouting for signs of life. *What were each of her trimesters like? How did she feel when she learned she was having a daughter? What worried her most about bringing a baby into this world?* I yearned for any wisdom she could have passed on. During my third trimester, I flipped through the baby book she had kept for me, searching for clues that could give me insights into her pregnancy and maybe my own. On those pages, yellowed by thirty years, I learned that my mother craved fried clams, french fries, and (like me) coffee ice cream. Her handwritten lists revealed that I received many colorful baby gifts: a thin white blanket, a pink-and-white heart dress, a blue sailor suit, a yellow bunny outfit. Paragraphs described when and where I was born, the doctor who delivered me, and the TV character I was named after: Mallory Keaton, from the 1980s hit TV show *Family Ties.* The irony wasn't lost on me that Justine Bateman, the actress who played Mallory, had suffered in silence from anorexia.

On difficult days during my pregnancy, I tried to name my struggles out loud. Whenever I was tempted to serve myself less food at mealtimes, or skip my morning and afternoon snacks, I would turn to Troy. While on a work trip halfway into my pregnancy, I told him about the knots I was in so that we could untangle them together. "I ordered room service last night and ate an entire small pizza," I confided one morning. "I was so hungry, but then just felt gross and guilty." I thought I needed to "make up for it" by not eating breakfast, as though on a quest for the perfect equilibrium of calories in and calories out. "You have a baby inside of you!" Troy said, reminding me my food choices were no longer about me alone. "Our daughter needs food. You need food. I know it's hard, but you can't let one meal throw you off course." Heeding Troy's advice, I went down to the hotel lobby and bought a yogurt parfait. The volume rose on my eating-disorder thoughts: *Why would you eat after all that pizza you had last night? You're not even that hungry. You should have just waited until lunch. Now you'll have to skip your next meal.* These were scolds I hushed, not wanting my unborn baby to hear. Before getting pregnant, disordered thoughts like this may have resulted in a full day of restriction, an uncontrollable binge or, more likely, both. But now my swelling belly had a way of convincing me to listen to, then lower, anorexia's din.

By the forty-week mark I had gained the weight I needed to, and my baby was about the size of a plump watermelon. I was eager to be done with pregnancy and hold our baby in my arms, to feel her soft skin against mine. At forty weeks and two days, I started to feel contractions—piercing pains that seemed to mimic the chaos I used to feel in my stomach when I binged. "I think I'm in labor," I told Troy as he was about to leave for a long shift at work.

"Are you sure?"

"*YES!*"

We drove to the hospital, where the nurse looked at me and said: "Wow, girl, you're tiny! You're all belly!" I felt a perverse surge of pride—a sign of anorexia's imprints and a reminder that comments about pregnant women's bodies are better left unsaid. The nurse told me to walk the hallways until my contractions were closer together and I was more dilated. Troy had one hand on my forearm and another on my back as I minced down the hall. I was in so much pain I couldn't engage in conversation, but I loved knowing he was by my side, guiding me and ready to catch my fall. As we shuffled forward, I tried to focus on the shiny white tile floor, the beeping of monitors in nearby rooms, and the smooth wood of the handrail. In that hospital hallway, the past seemed to collide with the present, and I found myself thinking about my mother's hospital days and my own. It had been seventeen years since I was last hospitalized, while in the trenches of anorexia as a motherless daughter.

As an expectant mother, I viewed my past not with shame but with an acceptance of how it had molded me. "The past," Virginia Woolf wrote, "only comes back when the present runs so smoothly that it is like the sliding surface of a deep river. Then one sees through the surface to the depths. . . . But to feel the present sliding over the depths of the past, peace is necessary." This is true, too, of recovery. Progression through the middle place requires a revisitation of the past—to understand and be at peace with how our experiences shaped who we once were and who we came to be. This prepares us for the reality that we may always carry hardships, grief, baggage. But over time, we can disperse their weight in ways that no longer drag us down.

In the labor and delivery room, I lay in a fetal position and studied family photos that Troy propped up alongside my hospital bed pillow. A few weeks earlier, I had gone through shoeboxes of photos and selected ones that captured memories of the mother and grandmothers who came before me. The contractions intensified and the time between them condensed, urging my body toward a new future. I stared at the photographs, overcome with an immeasurable sense of loss, love, and gratitude. I felt not a sense of closure (can there ever such a thing?) but, rather, of continuation and closeness. I recalled Gramz's admonishment: "If you keep this up, you're never going to be able to have children." I imagined my grandmother and mother with me in the maternity ward; if they were there looking at me, I know their eyes would have reflected pride.

The hours of labor continued, and I found myself wanting to abandon my birth plan. I had promised myself I would give birth naturally and push through the pain as I had done all my life. But after eleven hours of labor, I wanted to pull away from the pain. I requested an epidural, which no longer seemed like surrender but, instead, a show of strength in my ability to ask for what I wanted and for what my body needed. As an anesthetist, Troy had prepared me intellectually for some of what to expect, but we couldn't predict the range of realities. Less than an hour from arriving, the baby's heart rate began to drop, slightly at first and then precipitously. Nurses scurried into the room in choreographed chaos. They shifted my body from one side to the other, trying to find a position that might increase the baby's heart rate. But it plummeted, and I panicked.

The obstetrician calmly took my hand, her eyes meeting mine: "We need to get your baby out now. I'm going to need you to push as hard as you can. You can do this. You've got this!" It was like being cheered through the final mile of a marathon. My legs were numb from the epidural, but I could feel the pressure of my push. I kept pushing, breathing, pushing, breathing, pushing, panting. I was driven by both the desire to see my daughter and an unshakable fear I would lose her. Loss had a way of following me, and it might find me again. I heard "Now!" then saw my obstetrician pulling out a pair of forceps. In a painful blur that lasted seconds but felt like hours, I gave birth to my baby girl.

The doctor lifted her into the air and placed her on my chest. And there we met, skin to skin, heart to heart. Troy wrapped his arms around us in an embrace that felt impossibly perfect, wholly loving. We gazed at Madelyn Joelle, in awe of her unexpected red hair and resounding wail. She was here. She was healthy. She was, undeniably, alive.

As Madelyn grasped my index finger, she stuck out her tongue and started moving it around her lips. She looked as though she was trying to tell us something. But what? The nurse came over and interpreted for us.

"She's hungry!"

Of course; she had labored with me for thirteen hours and needed to be nourished. I fumbled, unsure of how to begin, as the nurse helped position my baby's body against mine. With Madelyn's head next to my heart and her lips beside my breast, I fed my daughter.

As the days passed, I became increasingly enamored by Madelyn, with her button nose, her adorable coos, and her tiny fingers grasped tightly onto mine. *I'm a mother!* I thought, still in disbelief. *And she's my daughter!* My love for Madelyn was vast, like an ocean that stretches far beyond the horizon. But it was harder for me to fall in love with motherhood; learning how to mother my child was difficult in ways I hadn't expected. The challenges started with breastfeeding, which felt like a damning descent into the unknown. On our first night home from the hospital, I tried feeding Madelyn by mimicking the cradle pose the lactation consultant had shown me. After a few seconds, she latched on. But just as quickly, she pulled away and started crying. We tried again and again, repeating one unsuccessful attempt after another. As I fumbled in the darkness, my pre-baby life dimmed like a distant star. Motherhood brought a constellation of doubts.

Troy woke and saw me clumsily cradling our baby.

"She won't latch!" I said with anxiety and annoyance. "I can't do this!"

"Why don't you try the football hold?" he suggested, referring to one of the nursing positions the lactation consultant had shown us. In my sleep-deprived stupor, I snapped.

"The football hold?! That is such a guy thing to say. I HATE the football hold; it doesn't work!"

"Okay, I get it!" he said, sounding perturbed. "It was just a suggestion!" Like all new parents, we were both unsure of ourselves and unaware of how best to help our baby. Troy offered to hold Madelyn, who eventually fell asleep in his arms. He placed her in the bassinette and then crept back into bed and cuddled up next to me. He slid his hand into mine and squeezed it three times, just as he had done every night for years. Like always, I returned the three squeezes—one for each word. I. Love. You.

We had begun mastering the art of staying quiet while Madelyn was asleep, but she was awake again in minutes. Her cries were contagious;

whenever she began wailing, I did, too. My difficulty breastfeeding made me feel like a failure. And her difficulty latching made me wonder if it was an early sign she would grow up to have difficulty eating. I couldn't help but project my past onto her future, couldn't help but worry I had passed on my disorder to my newborn daughter. These fears, irrational though they may seem, made me want to get it right.

Within a few days I figured out how to position Madelyn properly, and she learned how to latch. We slowly fell into a familiar rhythm of feeding, an easier togetherness. Breastfeeding became my superpower; it calmed Madelyn down when nothing else could. Sometimes Madelyn would look up at me as she fed and then stop midway to give me a smile. I beamed back. I watched with admiration as she pulled away from my breast after she'd had enough to eat, her cheeks glistening with milk. She would bury her milk-drunk face in my chest and fall asleep. I'd stay awake and rock her, thinking maybe I could learn something from Madelyn's own superpower: eating when she was hungry and stopping when she'd had enough.

At Madelyn's six-week follow-up appointment, the pediatrician said she was at a healthy weight and told me to keep up the good work breastfeeding. At my own six-week follow-up appointment, my obstetrician said my body was healing well from the birth and noted I was already back to my pre-pregnancy weight. I had peeked at the numbers on the scale and liked knowing I had lost so much weight so quickly. I was on a losing streak—but felt like I was winning.

Disordered thoughts followed me out of the appointment. I couldn't stop thinking about the numbers on the scale. I toyed with a twisted desire to lose more. *Just a few pounds*, I told myself. *It's time to get your stomach back to where it was.* My doughy belly was stretched out from the pregnancy. Instead of praising my changing body, as I had done during pregnancy, I now scolded the extra folds. I wanted to reinhabit my former figure, to replace the folds with flatness. But I knew that if I started restricting my food intake, it could send me spiraling and affect my milk supply. So, I crafted another plan: If I breastfed more, I could keep my supply up and bring my weight down. I reasoned that more breastfeeding would also have another important effect: reducing my already higher than average chances of getting breast cancer, which had taken my mother's life at forty and my maternal aunt's at fifty.

It was evident to me that my milk was Madelyn's sole source of food, the thing that kept her alive. When she began sleeping through the night, I should have used it as an opportunity to get sleep and let my milk supply adjust accordingly. But I worried the supply would quickly dwindle, leaving Madelyn without enough. I didn't want her lack of food to be my fault, and I mistakenly thought that using formula would mean I was a less than perfect mom. So, while she and Troy slept, I woke up twice a night to pump. During the day, I breastfed Madelyn as much as she would let me and pumped in between. Bottles began to fill our refrigerator shelves—signs of reassurance that Madelyn had ample food. The supply multiplied until I needed to start freezing the milk. Soon it became too much to store. Pumping had become a quiet compulsion, disguised by my desire to provide for my daughter. It seemed that the obsessive-compulsive disorder I had struggled with as a child had been hibernating and was suddenly wide awake. Now, instead of jumping, I was pumping.

Excessive pumping led to restrictive eating, mimicking a pattern I had observed most of my adult life: When one disordered behavior begins and sticks, others almost always follow. I wasn't severely restricting, but I wasn't eating enough to account for all I was expending. I downplayed the seriousness of it all. I didn't even tell Troy, who was so distracted by early fatherhood that he didn't notice. Although I had gotten better about struggling aloud during pregnancy, the novelty of my disordered pumping behavior scared me back into silence. I thought that as a mother, I should have known better, should have *been* better. I carried on like this for several months, until my daughter's body sent me a warning sign. At her nine-month doctor's appointment, the pediatrician said

Madelyn had fallen below her growth curve. She was born right around the fiftieth percentile for weight, then fell into the twenty-fifth percentile at four months, the tenth percentile at six months, and below the third percentile at nine months. Despite these dips, the pediatrician hadn't expressed any concerns, so neither did I. This dip, though, was far too low.

"What are you feeding her?" the pediatrician asked.

"She's getting breastmilk several times a day and one pouch of pureed food per day," I said, thinking she'd be proud that I was still breastfeeding.

"Ah okay. . . . That explains it."

My heart sank the way it always does when I realize I've done something wrong.

"You're not feeding her enough. We need to increase her solids intake. She should be getting closer to six pouches per day."

"Closer to six? Oh, my god," I said, in disbelief of my own ignorance. "I'm so sorry. I had no idea. I thought she was getting enough calories from my breastmilk. . . ."

The outpatient lactation consultant had told me that Madelyn mostly needed breastmilk until she turned one, at which point she could begin eating more solids. I didn't pry for details, partly because her counsel validated my belief that I was doing right by my daughter. But anorexia's long shadow had clouded my judgment, discouraging me from asking better questions and seeking input from multiple sources. I hadn't known any better, and neither had Troy—a sobering reminder that parenthood doesn't come with all the answers. As we were learning, there are inherent challenges to feeding children—ones that can be especially hard to navigate when you have a history of being unable to properly feed yourself.

As Madelyn began to breastfeed less and eat more solid foods, she gained weight, and I stopped losing it. I quit pumping at night and still produced enough milk during the waking hours to pump twice a day at work. By the time she was eleven months old, Madelyn was nursing just once in the morning and once before bedtime, and I no longer had to pump. She gobbled up the solid foods she most liked—Cheerios, bread, applesauce, puffs—and threw the ones she didn't. The wall by her highchair was splattered with so many spoonfuls of yogurt, avocado, and banana slices that it looked like a culinary Jackson Pollock painting. I admired Madelyn's playful attitude toward food and her ability to communicate which foods she did and didn't like.

Then, just before Madelyn turned one, Troy and I found out that we were about to have another opportunity to put into practice what Madelyn had been teaching us: Baby number two was on its way.

Pre-kids, I naively hoped that motherhood would one day make me all better. I thought my life would come full circle: I developed an eating disorder after my mother died, and I would recover after becoming a mother. If this narrative proved to be true, I reasoned, then losing a mother and becoming one would be the beautiful bookends for my cyclical story. But postpartum, it became clear that the narrative I had envisioned turned out to be too neat, the ending too premature.

Pregnancy with my son, Tucker, mirrored the one with Madelyn, marking a nine-month stretch when I gave my body the nourishment it needed and respected its changing shape. Labor was far easier with Tucker. And when he arrived, I knew to start feeding him right away. We bonded quickly, and he fit perfectly in my arms and heart. But as Troy and I juggled life as two working parents with two children under age two, I felt increasingly overwhelmed. "When you have kids, your life is no longer your own," I remember Gramz telling me after I got married. The sentiment had always struck me as overly dramatic. Now I knew exactly what she meant. I was living for my children, who seemed to control my life's—and my body's—schedule. As I nursed Tucker at home and pumped milk for him back at work, I began fixating on my body again. At times in life when I'm faced with an unfamiliar situation, the eating disorder is quick to offer a familiar solution.

Family and friends applauded my dedication to breastfeeding and told me I was lucky to have such a strong milk supply. But I knew it was less about luck and more about a compulsion hidden in the jagged edges of my recovery. By the time Tucker was done breastfeeding, I had so much leftover milk that I donated 1,255 fluid ounces—nearly ten gallons—to a local milk bank. I wrote an article about this for *The Dallas Morning News*, espousing the benefits of breastfeeding without exposing the hard truths beneath. The article could have been an opportunity to talk about the challenges of breastfeeding as a mother in the middle place, and about the reality that "breast isn't always best" for those with eating disorders (or women in general, for that matter). But I was too afraid to admit what I had done, too ashamed to publicly acknowledge what I knew to be true: My efforts to lose weight have always diminished my opportunity for growth.

I did eventually tell Troy about my pumping problem, but I otherwise kept this secret. At the time, I had never heard of anyone else who pumped as a form of purging, and I still don't hear many people talk about it today. I've attended sessions at eating-disorder conferences on perinatal complications, and excessive pumping has never come up. Research on the topic is almost nonexistent, though in recent years a couple of related studies have emerged. A 2023 study led by psychologist Katie Thompson, PhD, found a direct association between obsessive-compulsive symptoms and perceived pressures to breastfeed. It concluded that healthcare providers should screen perinatal patients for obsessive-compulsive and eating-disorder symptoms whenever discussing breastfeeding. I nodded my head in agreement when reading this and thought about how I was never asked about these symptoms while pregnant, even though I told my OB/GYN and primary care physician that I had a history of both OCD and anorexia.

"OCD is very common postpartum. It's a hallmark feature of postpartum depression, and there are many women who experience OCD symptoms postpartum who don't have them at any other time in their lives," said Leah Susser, MD, a reproductive psychiatrist and an assistant professor of clinical psychiatry at Weill Cornell Medicine in New York. "The kind of symptoms that women can get postpartum can feel very distressing if they haven't been warned about them. But learning about the possible symptoms before they happen makes them feel much less embarrassing and much less scary."

In 2023, Dr. Susser and colleague Suzanne Straebler, PhD, wrote an article stating that maladaptive breastfeeding and pumping often go undetected in eating-disorder patients. The dearth of attention stems, in part, from reluctance to challenge the popular message that "breast is best." "For many women, breastfeeding is wonderful, and the positive effects can outweigh the difficulties. But that's not always the case," Dr. Susser told me. "It's often taboo to say that publicly, though. We were even nervous when we were writing the paper about what backlash there might be to any suggestion that breastfeeding may not always be the best thing to do depending on the circumstances, such as if it is negatively impacting that woman's mental health." Dr. Susser and Dr. Straebler said they didn't receive any negative feedback, but they are also not aware of any researchers who have examined the issue further yet.

Dr. Straebler, clinical director of the Center for Eating Disorders at NewYork-Presbyterian Hospital, told me there's a need for more discussion and research about how eating-disorder behaviors are influenced by societal norms and trends. In recent years, she has noticed an increase in maladaptive breastfeeding/pumping among her patients, as well as increased use of laxatives. Some patients view them as a cheaper alternative to GLP-1 drugs like Ozempic and Mounjaro, even though the drugs work very differently. "In the eating-disorder field, we've become a little bit pigeonholed about what kind of weight-control methods and compensatory methods are known and talked about it," said Dr. Straebler, a psychiatric nurse practitioner. "I think we need to step back a little bit and think: What has changed in the last twenty or thirty years? What other behaviors might we be seeing, or no longer seeing? And what behaviors could have benefits, like breastfeeding and exercise, but when used to excess can be really harmful?"

In another recent paper, Dr. Straebler and Dr. Susser analyzed ways eating disorders can affect reproductive health. Indeed, fertility issues are prevalent among women who are actively restricting. Specifically, malnourishment can suppress the hypothalamic-pituitary-ovarian axis, the system that controls female reproduction. It also can depress levels of the hormone GnRH, which is critical to a healthy reproductive system and sexual development. Suppressed GnRH can cause anovulation—the medical term for an inability to ovulate. People who have binge-eating disorder and are in larger bodies can also develop hormonal imbalances that cause anovulation.

Women are the focal point of most research on eating disorders and fertility issues, but men are of course affected, too. "When a male's body is undernourished, it causes changes to testosterone, and it causes changes to a male's ability to create and produce sperm," said Dr. Straebler, who has seen many male eating-disorder patients with fertility problems.

Evidence suggests that recovery can ameliorate these issues. Two large population-based studies showed no differences in rates of pregnancy, infertility treatment, or reported infertility for women who had recovered from anorexia nervosa compared with the general population. "If you have a prior eating disorder, you should be able to regain fertility if you would have been able to otherwise," Dr. Susser said. "That's very hopeful, especially for people entering treatment."

Such messages often get lost, though, in conversations between eating-disorder patients and fertility specialists, the latter who lack eating-disorder training and report feeling ill-equipped to detect these disorders. "Fertility is an area where it would be really helpful to have health professionals with more eating-disorder training," said Diana Lemly, MD, medical director of the Eating Disorders Collaborative Care

Clinic at Massachusetts General Hospital. Dr. Lemly told me she has treated patients who underwent IVF without ever being screened for an eating disorder. This can be problematic for people with all eating disorders, including those who have binge-eating disorder and are in larger bodies. These patients may be told they need to lose weight to receive fertility treatment, without any consideration of their disorder and the related weight stigma they face. Dr. Lemly has also had patients with anorexia who lost their period in their early forties and were misdiagnosed with perimenopause. Up until recently, there were no rapid screening tools for obstetricians to identify patients with eating disorders. One such tool was developed in 2022, signaling a step in the right direction. But it can take years for such tools to be implemented in clinical practice, even on a small scale.

Studies suggest that most OB/GYNs report having had little to no residency training in diagnosing and treating eating disorders. To complicate matters, women don't tend to disclose their disorders. "A lot of times, doctors don't know what do with that information, and patients know this, so they avoid the conversation. There's already an extremely high amount of medical avoidance, even prior to pregnancy," Angela Kaloudis, a New York–based mental health counselor who treats eating-disorder patients and specializes in perinatal issues, told me. "And if someone in a larger body becomes pregnant, the first message they hear from the doctor might be, 'You have to lose weight.' So, disclosing their eating disorder doesn't feel safe."

That avoidance can lead to serious complications for both pregnant women and their babies. Women with a history of any eating disorder are at greater risk of developing depressive and anxiety symptoms during and after pregnancy, and those with a history of bulimia nervosa and binge-eating disorder are especially prone to developing postpartum depression. Women with anorexia are at higher risk of losing their babies, carrying babies who are small for their gestational age, having a pre-term delivery, and delivering babies with low birth weights, decreased Apgar scores, and microcephaly—a condition in which a baby's head is abnormally small.

Health psychologist Alice Domar, PhD, told me she has witnessed other, lesser-known risks that are rarely discussed, including women with eating disorders who decide not to follow through with a pregnancy. "This breaks my heart, but I've had patients who did IVF, got pregnant, and then between twelve and sixteen weeks terminated the pregnancies because they couldn't handle showing; they just couldn't handle the weight gain," said Dr. Domar, who is chief compassion officer at Inception Fertility and an associate professor of obstetrics, gynecology, and reproductive biology, part-time, at Harvard Medical School. She said her field has long focused on obesity and its detrimental effects on fertility. There's far less discussion, however, about the dangers of being underweight. "Eating disorders are so common, and we need to know how to better support patients with them," Dr. Domar said. "We shouldn't just be taking a woman with an eating disorder and, without any discussion, putting her on drugs to get her pregnant; she may not be physically or psychologically ready for that."

Dr. Domar's stories struck a painful chord. I found myself once again grateful that pregnancy helped me progress in recovery rather than prompting a slide. Some studies have found that pregnancy triggers relapse among women with a history of an eating disorder, with one reporting a relapse rate as high as 33 percent. Not surprisingly, pregnancy also appears to be a period of vulnerability for the onset and continuation of binge-eating disorder. Other studies have found that pregnancy can lead to a decrease in concerns about weight, partly due to "a maternal sense of responsibility for recovery." But these findings come with an important caveat: Women who say pregnancy helped lessen their eating-disorder behaviors tend to report a worsening of behaviors postpartum. The range of research findings reflects the myriad stories I've heard from mothers in the middle place. Like me, these women were healthy enough to have children but dealt with vulnerabilities that demanded vigilance.

Such was the case for Marielle, a thirty-something woman from the Midwest, who had acute anorexia as a teenager and has been in the middle place her entire adult life. Though she has made strides in her recovery, she still sometimes restricts and slips back into other disordered behaviors. "This feels awful to admit, but I'm not sure I have ever actually wanted to be fully recovered," Marielle told me. "But when I was pregnant, I felt very solidly recovered. I told myself, 'I'm going to be very well nourished and super healthy.' I was not worried about gaining weight, and the numbers on the scale didn't mean the same thing to me." Once Marielle began breastfeeding, the disordered thoughts started creeping back in. "There was a certain thrill knowing that I was basically just expressing calories from my body. I was making a lot more than my kids were drinking, and at one point I thought, *Oh, I can just pump like crazy and donate lots of milk and lose weight faster.*" She said she ultimately didn't have the time it would take to excessively pump, nor did she want to make time for it.

But other women I spoke with said eating-disorder thoughts intensified during pregnancy. Weight gain was especially difficult for forty-year-old Renee, who is in recovery from bulimia. She faced weight stigma throughout childhood and developed bulimia after years of disparaging messages about her body; her aunts and grandparents all chastised her for being the family's lone "chubby kid." "Both my parents came from super-traditional Chinese families, where the boys got to eat as much as they wanted but the girls did not. I was taught that you need to be skinny in order to be pretty, and you need to be pretty in order to get married," said Renee, who lives on the West Coast. "One thing my grandparents would always say to me is, 'Your sister's going to get married first because she's the pretty, skinny one.' It all tied together into how I measured my self-worth."

Obsession with weight has trailed Renee ever since, and it chased her during pregnancy. As she gained weight, she had to consciously work to counteract her disordered thoughts by prioritizing her values. Renee told me: "The weight gain was anxiety provoking, and I had to remind myself all the time, *I am choosing motherhood. This is what I want to do, and if I give in to this voice that's telling me not to eat, then I'm not going to be able to accomplish my goal and bring this baby to term. I really want to grow my family. And that's more important than feeling good about not eating a cookie, right?*" As a new mother in the middle place, Renee said recovery is about "consciously deciding to ignore the eating-disorder voice—because I don't think that voice is ever going to go away."

It's no secret that many women deal with depression, anxiety, and weight-related concerns during and after pregnancy, regardless of whether they've ever had an eating disorder. In a society steeped in fatphobia and diet culture, women face immense pressure to "bounce back" to their pre-pregnancy weight in record time. Almost two-thirds of pregnant and postpartum women report experiencing weight stigma, which has been linked to depression and increased stress levels. And an estimated 40 percent of women are concerned about their weight during pregnancy.

But for women who are in recovery from eating disorders or actively struggling, that concern often leads to debilitating ruminations, which can trigger restriction, binge eating, purging, and other behaviors. It's like listening to a radio being switched from one station to the next, except your eating disorder is choosing the stations and setting the volume. Reclaiming control of the volume—and retaining it—is a job so many of us take on while in recovery from an eating disorder.

Meaghan, a thirty-five-year-old from New York, knows this job well. When we spoke, she had just given birth to her second child and was noticeably exhausted—not just because she had a newborn but also because her eating-disorder thoughts were literally keeping her up at night. "I should be sleeping when the baby's asleep, but instead I'm lying in bed anxiety-spiraling about losing my pregnancy weight," said Meaghan, who is in recovery from anorexia and bulimia. "I constantly fantasize about restricting nonstop. I wonder what it's going to take to feel good about my body again, even though intellectually I know that even at my lowest weight, I never felt good about my body." Meaghan told me she was working hard to keep old behaviors at bay, determined to stay healthy enough to breastfeed her daughter. But she admitted that being pregnant, and then breastfeeding, made her feel she had lost control of her body, which became a home for her fetus, then her baby's primary food source. It no longer felt like her own.

Some therapists I've talked with say they work with women to grieve the loss of their pre-pregnancy body and life. I feel that. There have been moments when I've longed for my pre-kid life, for a time when I had fewer responsibilities, fewer demands of my time, fewer mouths to feed. But alongside that loss there is also an expansion—of my life as a mother and as a woman who now works toward recovery not just for herself but also for her family. I thought of this during a recent call with Haniyah, one of the girls who was on Bader 5 with me all those years ago. We talked about how we are both in the middle place, and how motherhood challenges us to keep getting better. At the end of our Zoom interview, we asked our kids to join us. So much of our conversation had been about our shared past, and now we wanted to bear witness to our hard-won present. I called the kids into my office and told them I was talking with someone special whom I had known for a very long time. As I saw the two images on my computer screen—of Haniyah and her eleven-year-old son Jacob, and of me with my seven-year-old Madelyn and six-year-old Tucker—I thought about how much space we all took up in that frame. In that moment, from within the middle place, there was no room left for anorexia.

Chapter Twelve

Motherhood in the Middle Place

When the kids and I were drawing together one Sunday afternoon, I let them have a Ziploc bag filled with colorful Sharpies. Permanent markers are typically off-limits in our house because Troy and I know we'll find marks everywhere but on the paper they were meant for. But sometimes I relent. Our kitchen table is a landscape of sticky fingerprints and crumb-covered placemats, paint stains and glitter glue streaks, origami creations and crumpled paper. It's an imperfect place where meals are enjoyed, where little hands make big art, where stories are told. It's just as I hope my children will remember it: free from restriction and filled with abundance.

"Mom, I wish I had a Sharpie eraser," Tucker said, while drawing Godzilla, his latest monster of interest.

"That would be so nice, Sweet Pea," I responded. "I wish I had one, too."

There are moments when I've wished I could erase the painful parts of my past. If my life were a sketchbook, with big moments illustrated on each page, what would happen if I erased my mother's death? Would the illustrations of my eating disorder then disappear? If one never existed, would the other have ever emerged? I realize I will never know the answers to these questions. But still, I sometimes search. I wrestle with the contradiction of wanting life's hardships to be removable while accepting their Sharpie-like permanence.

This is, of course, the predicament we face in the middle place: wanting to get rid of our disorder but accepting the obstinate reality it may never fully go away. Some people have asked if writing this book has caused me to slip. Others have asked if it has helped me move forward. The answer is yes and yes—and yet, I'm still very much in the middle place. The longer I navigate this place, the bigger the space becomes and the less temporary my inhabitance seems. I am not sandwiched between the extremes of acute sickness and full recovery; I roam between them at my own pace and on my own terms.

I've come to believe we're all and always navigating some sort of middle, even if we don't describe it as such. I was reminded of this recently when talking with my ninety-seven-year-old maternal grandmother. She had moved into a nursing home after having lived in the same house for roughly seventy-five years, and she was adjusting to her new day-to-day life. "This middle you find yourself in is fascinating. I think that's a good place to be—neither the best nor the worst," she told me. "Right now, I'm trying to find the middle because this has been such a big change for me. We all have a thing we're trying to beat, and we can't always do it. But if we work at it, then we can get to the middle, and that seems like a comforting place to be."

It *is* comforting, knowing I don't have to be perfect in this place and there is always potential for progress. The real Mallary can acknowledge the child I was and the woman I've become, and recognize how much my disorder has shrunk as I've expanded my life beyond it. I can eat meals with my family; go on dinner date nights with Troy; exercise without obsession; stand in front of the classroom confidently as a journalism professor; and move through my days without anorexia consuming my mental space or enervating my body. At the nadir of my illness, my gaze was so laser-focused on my disorder that it was all I saw, all I ever thought about, all I ever wrote about. The sun now casts light on parts of my life once so hidden I thought I'd never see them again. But shadows remain, reminding me I still have work to do.

As far as I know, I don't have any residual physical side effects from when I was acutely sick. But in the middle place, I still take small bites of food, just as I did as a sick child. Whenever the taste of food lingers in my mouth—from a garlicky pasta dish or a salad with raw onions—I find myself feeling full and uncomfortable for hours after the fact, regardless of how much or how little I ate. When sitting down, I tend to twist my body into a tight pretzel, sometimes to the point of soreness, because I've never learned how to take up space. During stressful stretches, I tend to lose my appetite and overly fret about my weight. It takes concerted effort to nourish myself during these times—and to realize my beliefs about my body's needs almost always skew toward restriction. When I think I've had "too much" to eat or "just the right amount," I typically have not had enough. When I do eat to the point of fullness, I feel an instant urge to exercise the calories away. I have to remind myself that compensatory behaviors like this are easy to fall into but immensely difficult to climb out of. I confide in Troy, with hopes that one slip won't turn into a slide. And I work through the slips with my therapist, whom I started seeing for additional support while writing this book. In conversations with her, I've become aware of how restriction seeps into other aspects of my life: my tendency to be financially frugal when I don't need to be; the way I hang the "privacy please" sign on my hotel room door when traveling because I don't think I need the "luxury" of housekeeping; the way I squeeze the smallest bit of hand lotion or shaving cream onto my body, afraid to indulge in excess.

During an interview, I described some of my ongoing struggles to my former Boston Children's Hospital doctor. She responded that she was so proud of how much better I am now than when she treated me as a teenager. I told her that I'm in the middle place and not fully recovered, to which she replied, "Make sure you're not holding yourself to a standard that most average women wouldn't achieve. I mean, how many women in America of your age would be thinking about their weight and calories? I'd venture to say quite a few." It was the first time I had spoken to Dr. Forman in twenty years, and I remembered why I liked her so much. Her words stayed with me, reminding me how hard it is to recover in this society.

In my related research, I came across something called *normative discontent*—the notion that most women experience some level of discontent with their weight, making that discontent more the norm than the exception. The term first emerged in 1984, with more recent research showing that this discontent is pervasive among men, too. At an eating-disorders conference, I spoke with the woman who coined the term: psychologist and longtime eating-disorder researcher Ruth Striegel Weissman.

"Women's physical appearance cuts all the way down to our identity and what it means to be a woman. It gets rewarded in terms of social success, career success, academic success," Weissman told me. "Of course, the pressure on women to be beautiful goes way, way back. But the difference that emerged culturally around the mid-twentieth century was sort of a democratization in a bad way of attaining the ideal. Women in America began to feel like everybody could obtain it, and that made it even more toxic." The problem, she said, has only gotten worse in a commercialized society with a $76 billion diet industry: "There are all these industries that profit from the discontent. In other businesses, if the product doesn't work, we blame the product. But in the beauty business, if you don't become beautiful, we blame you. It's not the cream or the diet or the exercise equipment; it's you. We internalize this so readily rather than pushing back."

As a mother in recovery, I'm perhaps more aware than most that both my son and my daughter are growing up in a society of normative discontent, fueled by messages about what they should and shouldn't eat and how their bodies should and shouldn't look. And I know they have a higher risk of developing anorexia because of me. Research shows that females who have a relative with anorexia are eleven times more likely to develop the disorder themselves compared to individuals without a family history. *Eleven times more likely.* This statistic looms like a distant tornado that threatens to move closer as my children get older. My fear of it has undoubtedly shaped the mother I've become, making me hyper-vigilant about the messages I share with my children and the home environment Troy and I foster for them. We cannot control the genes we have passed on to our children; they exist deep within us in that Sharpie-like way. So, I focus my efforts on shaping what surrounds them.

Since becoming a mother, I've often thought back to that Bader 5 staffer named Glen, who introduced me to the axiom "Fake it till you make it." Though I wish it weren't so, I sometimes have to fake it when teaching my children lessons I have trouble honoring myself. When I talk with them about food and bodies, words flow out of me with hope and hypocrisy. "All bodies are worthy of respect, no matter how big or small, no matter how short or tall," I tell Madelyn and Tucker, optimistic they'll genuinely believe this—and well aware I believe it to be true for everyone but myself. Even though my mind is unkind to my body, I keep critical thoughts to myself. I know my children are always listening and watching, even when I think they're not, and I don't want them growing up with a mother who insinuates that her body is a problem in need of fixing. When taking photos with the kids, I never demand a redo if my hair is askew or the camera angle is less than flattering. Instead, I look at the photos and pay more attention to the view of my kids than of myself; with my gaze fixed on them, I am happiest.

When Madelyn and Tucker are brushing their teeth and looking at themselves in the mirror, I often stand behind them and tell them how strong, kind, and smart they are. Occasionally, I'll poke gentle fun at my son's wild cowlick or at my daughter's annoyance at having to brush her teeth "every . . . single . . . morning." But I make it a point not to overly focus on their appearances. I want my kids to see themselves as more than "pretty" or "handsome"—to know their worth is not dependent on how they look but on who they are. I tell them this, realizing that society will try to convince them otherwise.

With maddening ubiquity, diet culture permeates television shows, social media, advertisements, and much to my dismay, school assignments. When I was picking up the kids from summer school a couple years ago, Madelyn handed me two paper plates. On one plate were pictures of an apple, salad, almonds, grilled chicken, and chicken nuggets. On the other plate were pictures of an ice cream sundae, nachos, cake, a hamburger, and a baked potato. I immediately knew what Madelyn's assignment had been, but I asked her to describe it anyway. "We had to put healthy foods on one plate and unhealthy foods on the other one," she told me. Her teacher, who was standing beside us, looked at the pictures and told Madelyn that the chicken nuggets probably should have gone on the unhealthy plate and not the healthy one. I saw the look of confusion on my daughter's face and was taken back to my seventh-grade health class, where I learned to categorize foods as "good" and "bad." It was a hits-close-to-home reminder that the same lessons are being taught in schools thirty years later.

Struck by this, I wrote about the experience in a piece for *The Washington Post*. I described what happened in my daughter's class and explained how such lessons can contribute to eating disorders in kids. I included interviews and research showing that weight-focused public health interventions for children "rarely result in health improvement or sustainable weight loss and are instead associated with disordered eating and greater weight gain." My article spurred more comments than I had ever before received on a single piece, with hundreds of readers thanking me and hundreds more lambasting me for having the audacity to criticize "healthy eating" when adolescent obesity rates have quadrupled since 1990. I understand these readers' frustration, but I doubt they have endured a debilitating eating disorder or cared for someone with one. I've interviewed dozens of mothers who have lived experience with an eating disorder, and nearly all of them expressed how hard they're working to lay an anti-diet foundation for their children—one that ascribes to the belief that food is not "good" or "bad," "healthy" or "unhealthy." As I tell my own kids, food is fuel, and it's what their bodies need.

Through my words, and sometimes through my actions, I'm trying to teach Madelyn and Tucker that "all foods fit"; a carrot is not inherently better than carrot cake, nor is a cherry pie inherently worse than a bowl of cherries. This is eating-disorder recovery speak, but for me it's also eating-disorder prevention speak. I don't buy low-fat, fat-free, or sugar-free foods like I once did. With the exception of Wheat Thins (which I've liked and eaten for as long as I can remember), I don't buy "thin" or "skinny" foods. I roll my eyes when I walk down the aisles of the grocery store and see foods like Skinny Pop popcorn, Skinny Cow ice cream, Oreo Thins, and the horribly redundant ThinSlim bread.

I want my children to grow up knowing they are deserving of the real thing, without needing some slimmed-down version. I want them to grow up to eat intuitively, rather than ascribing to diets that will undoubtedly fail them. From my days of binge eating, I know that when you deprive yourself of what you want, you always end up desiring it more. There were so many times when I would want to eat an "unhealthy" food but told myself I couldn't. Instead of eating a full chocolate cookie, for instance, I would opt for a small bowl of fruit as a "healthy" alternative. Still unsatisfied, I would eat a cookie-flavored protein bar while thinking about the actual cookie the whole time. I would finally reach for the cookie itself and vow to take only one small bite. But one bite would become two, then three, then four. One whole cookie would turn into many more. *I already ate one cookie*, I'd think. *I might as well eat them all.* Once I was full past the point of discomfort, I'd look at the empty box of cookies in disgust. Intuitive eating is about just eating the cookie to begin with. It's about honoring your hunger and letting it guide your choices about what and when to eat.

This, of course, is easier said than done. Many of us learn in childhood that we shouldn't eat the cookie or even that it's wrong to want it in the first place. When parenting, we can impose these same beliefs on our children, lamenting that all they want is "junk food," without understanding the biological reasons why. "So much of the work and the growth and the development that's happening in a child is in their brain, which requires a lot of carbohydrates," says Sumner Brooks, an Oregon-based dietitian and author of the book *How to Raise an Intuitive Eater: Raising the Next Generation with Food and Body Confidence*. "So, there are reasons why young children prefer quickly digestible carbohydrates and sugars and very little protein; it's biologically necessary. Very early on, we begin the self-fulfilling prophecy of 'See, all they want is the carbs; that's all they want.' And if we can step back and look at the science and look at development and growth, it's very true—that is what they want, and it's because it's what they need." When we deprive kids of foods deemed "unhealthy," we imply that they can't be trusted to listen to their bodies. "If kids are getting a little bit less than what they need because they're told they can't have the extra bread or the cookies or whatever it may be, they're going to be more likely to sneak food, to hide food, or to eat more of the restricted foods when their parents aren't around," Brooks told me. "This happens so early on when there's over-control and rigidity around food."

Sometimes my rigidity swings in the opposite direction, and I go to extremes trying to prevent my kids' exposure to harmful messaging. I realized this one day when, unknown to me, Tucker checked out a library book titled *The Berenstain Bears and Too Much Junk Food*. The book was published in 1985, the year I was born; I loved the Berenstain Bears as a kid, so it's quite possible I had once read it. Tucker hadn't yet learned to read, so Madelyn sat next to him on the living room couch and started reading the book to him. I walked into the room as she was narrating a part about Mama Bear, who had noticed that her baby cubs were eating "too much junk food." She observed that "they were chubbier from the side, they were chubbier from the front, and from the back" and promptly decided they must stop consuming so much junk.

"But Mama!" the cubs say. "We're growing bears, and we need those snacks!"

"You're growing all right," Mama Bear responds. "The trouble is you're growing from side to side as much as you are up and down! Sometimes cubs get into bad habits, and you've gotten into the habit of eating altogether too many sweets and goodies."

My own Mama Bear came out as I ran toward Madelyn and snatched the book from her hands.

"Mom! What are you doing?!" she snapped.

"I don't want you reading that book!" I said.

"But why?!"

"Because it has bad messages."

Madelyn and Tucker started fussing, and I walked away, hiding the book on the top shelf of my closet. Later that night in bed, I realized I could have handled the situation better. I apologized the next morning, explaining that I took away the book because the story upset me. I reminded them that food isn't junk; it's fuel that helps them grow. I so fiercely want to protect Madelyn and Tucker, and yet I'm well aware that the older they get, the harder it will be. I find comfort in knowing that Troy and I are doing what we can to shield them from harmful messaging, but I realize our armor isn't ironclad. We're trying to help them develop their own armor, with the shared understanding that you can't be at peace with your body if you're always at war with food.

Instead of framing food as junk, I try to make it fun. Every couple of weeks, the kids and I bake banana bread together. We make "puffy pancake," referring to an ingredient-stained recipe from one of my mother's old cookbooks, and we stand in front of the windowed oven door to watch it rise. We make "taco muffins" by stuffing tortillas into the oversized cups of muffin tins, baking them to a crisp, and then filling them with Tex-Mex foods. I eat these foods with them, beside them, and for them. From my perch in the middle place, I tend to portion out less food for myself than for everyone else—a problem I'm addressing but haven't yet resolved. I am, and always will be, a work in progress. Motherhood has made me all the more aware of this; it has been both a magnifier of flaws and a marker of progress, especially during mealtimes.

My kids are at the stage when they'll eat only a small rotation of foods for dinner: Annie's mac and cheese, corndogs, hotdogs, buttery pasta, hamburgers. Anything else tends to elicit a thumbs-down or (if I'm lucky), a sideways thumb.

"Do you like it?" I'll ask, ever hopeful they'll enjoy the meal I spent an hour making after a long day at work.

"Ew, no. It's gross!" they'll say when served a vegetable-heavy dish, their thumbs turned down and their noses up.

Other nights, I might get a begrudging "It's okaaaayyy," with a sideways thumb to indicate that at least it's better than other meals I've made.

I used to question myself when figuring out what to feed them, and I'd expend an ungodly amount of mental energy figuring out what to pack in their Bentgo lunch boxes. I would often settle on a peanut butter and jelly sandwich, a bagel with cream cheese, or chicken nuggets, coupled with a rotation of nutritious sides: mixed nuts, avocado, fruit salad, raisins, carrots, cheese sticks, granola bars. In the small, circular section of the boxes, I would put a tiny treat: one Hershey's Kiss, two or three gummy bears, three or four M&Ms. But day after day, they would come home with lunch boxes half full. Madelyn left the granola bars and cheese sticks. Tucker ignored the mixed nuts and avocado. The carrots, in both lunch boxes, were never touched.

When Madelyn was old enough have a school lunch account, I added an extra $25 so she could buy ice cream on Fridays with her friends. But after a couple of weeks, I got an email saying the account was low. I scanned the transactions online and saw that Madelyn had been buying a bag of Doritos or a package of Oreos almost every day, plus ice cream sandwiches on Fridays.

When I asked her about it, she looked ashamed. "I'm sorry, Mommy," she said. "It's just that . . . I like these foods. And I get hungry at lunch."

"I know, sweetie," I said. "And that's okay to like those foods."

I realized that, as much as I had been trying to embody the idea that "all foods fit," I was imposing limits on my children. Madelyn, to her credit, found a way to counteract those restrictions. In the days that followed, I decided it was better to pack foods my kids would *actually* eat rather than ones I hoped they would eat. I started buying Oreos, and I began filling the circular compartment with as much candy as it would hold. *No one should have to eat just two gummy bears*, I whispered to myself. *That's true for you, too.* Soon, my children started coming home with more satisfied tummies and mostly empty lunch boxes.

But they are still almost always hungry right before dinner.

"Mommy, can I have a snack?" they'll ask a half hour before we sit down to eat.

"Mommy, can I have a granola bar?"

"How about a bag of popcorn?"

"What about a bowl of cereal?"

"A little pack of gummy bears?"

"Mommy? . . . Mommy, which one can I have?"

These questions, day after day, were so hard for me to hear that my first instinct was to scream back "NO!" I wanted to respond in a way that satiated their hunger and saved their appetite, but their questions spurred my own, clouding my judgment with uncertainty.

What if they eat too much and get full right before dinner? I'd think to myself. *What's "too much," anyway? Maybe I could give them half a bowl of cereal, but will that seem restrictive? An individual pack of gummy bears wouldn't fill them up, but should they really have candy right before dinner?*

On some evenings, I would say yes to one food but not to the other. On others, I would say no altogether, giving mixed messages that confused Madelyn and Tucker. And there were evenings when I just deferred to Troy. "Ask your father," I'd say, walking out of the kitchen and away from the situation. Troy would usually say no to the snack requests, knowing that it's hard enough as is getting the kids to eat dinner. After many months of this back-and-forth, I came up with a compromise that has more or less worked. Now, when the kids are hungry right before dinner, I tell them they have two options: fruit or cheese. They can choose whatever kind of fruit or cheese they want. If they don't choose either, they can wait until we sit down to eat as a family.

I was proud of myself for finding this middle ground, rather than being stuck between the extremes of yes and no. I thought of how crucial middle spaces have been in both my parenting and my recovery, and how good children are at listening to their hunger cues. I've heard kids tell their parents that they're hungry, only to have the parents quip, "No you're not! You just ate!" It's an understandable response, especially in moments of chaos or distress. But it's one I try to avoid. At this point in life, my kids are the best judges of whether they're hungry or full. As someone who is far from my own best judge, I have a lot to learn from them.

"Can I be full?" the kids will often ask at the kitchen table, when their tummies are satisfied before their plates are empty.

"Yes," Troy and I tell them. "You can be full."

I have not yet told my children about my history with anorexia. They think my book is about my mother, and I'm okay letting them believe that for now. But the day will come when I have to tell them about my eating disorder and how it all began. For many years I oversimplified my disorder's origin story, blaming it on my mother's death. We tend to shorten our storylines over time, narrowing them to the most obvious truths. But in the process, we render them only half-true. In recent years, as I've paid greater attention to the many plot points that contributed to my eating disorder, I've realized there was a confluence of factors at play: my mother's death, my desire to stay small, my suppressed grief, the health class, the consumption of eating-disorder stories in teen magazines, possible genetic components. Eating disorders always stem from a complex set of factors, but for many years scholars and clinicians blamed them on a sole culprit: mothers.

Mother-blaming abounds in the early literature about anorexia, schizophrenic, autism, and other mental health disorders, hearkening back to Sigmund Freud, who expounded on the long-term effects of early parent-child interactions. Post–World War II scholars pathologized the mother-daughter relationship, characterizing mothers of girls with anorexia as overbearing, rigid, and overcontrolling women who were "enmeshed" in their daughter's lives. As one scholar put it in 1949, anorexia was the result of "an insoluble conflict with the patient's mother," which served as "a dynamic force precipitating as well as perpetuating the child's illness." Mother-blaming continued well into the late twentieth century, with several eating-disorder experts and news stories attributing the development of anorexia to parents and overarching family dynamics. Psychotherapist Salvador Minuchin, MD, a pioneer of family therapy, coined the term *anorexigenic* in the 1970s to describe families who contributed to a child's anorexia. A 1974 *New York Times* article titled "Children Who Starve Themselves" declared: "Few in the psychiatric community doubt that anorexia nervosa is anything other than a family-caused disorder." It went on to say that children with anorexia were born to mothers who didn't feed them correctly as babies, and that these children could only get better if they were separated from the mother and hospitalized. "If the child is ever to return to the family in anything like health, the mother, at least, will probably need psychiatric treatment," the article read.

Around the same time, in the early 1970s, eating-disorder psychiatrist Dr. Hilde Bruch described the mothers of girls with anorexia as "frustrated" career women who gave up their professions for motherhood and became overly conscientious in their maternal roles. Feminist author and counselor Kim Chernin, PhD, who wrote several books about eating disorders in the 1980s, continued this narrative by describing "the hidden drama between mother and daughter that ultimately gives rise to eating problems." She posited that daughters of women who couldn't pursue careers were afraid of surpassing their mothers and developed anorexia as a way of holding themselves back. "The mother of the modern day is a woman who knows that the world of larger possibilities stands open before her but has not yet been able to make the choice to enter it," Dr. Chernin wrote in *The Hungry Self*, published in 1985. "Mothers and daughters of the modern era face one another, therefore, as beings in a struggle for a self—the older woman having already failed in this quest as the younger starts out on it. This is the psychological background of the epidemic of eating disorders among women today."

This line of thinking lingered when I was in treatment. During that first Boston Children's hospitalization in 1998, doctors gave my father several handouts about anorexia, including one from a Harvard University mental health newsletter that read: "According to some psychodynamics theories, a young woman has come to this desperate pass because her parents have never responded adequately to her initiatives or recognized her individuality." As a parent, I would not have known what to make of that.

In recent years, there has been a shift away from parent-blaming with the emergence of family-based treatment models that view parents as allies instead of scapegoats. With a rise in research, discussions around the etiology of eating disorders have moved away from theory and toward scientific testing. Genetic research in particular has lifted the burden of blame, showing that parents alone do not have the power to categorically cause eating disorders. This finding is reversing decades of inappropriate pathologizing, but it has also had an unintended consequence: a reluctance to explore questions about the environmental risks parents pose when they're actively struggling with an eating disorder. When I broached this topic during interviews with clinicians and people with lived experience, their sentiments didn't always align. Sometimes in the same day I would interview clinicians who said parents are never to blame, only to then have conversations with survey respondents who told me they got sick after growing up with parents who suffered from eating disorders, or who chastised them for their body size and eating behaviors. How does one acknowledge this parenting reality without laying blame? And how can we better help families by treating the parents and identifying the prevention measures that can lessen the chances their children will develop eating disorders? If we avoid tough questions like these, we do a disservice not only to parents but also to children who may be at a higher genetic *and* environmental risk of developing an eating disorder.

Psychologist Shiri Sadeh-Sharvit, PhD, told me the field is long overdue for prevention programs geared to older children and teenagers of parents with eating disorders. Dr. Sadeh-Sharvit helped develop an evidence-based program for high-risk families with children under age five. Her work is inspired by family-based treatment for eating disorders, as well as prevention models that have been successful for children with genetic risks for anxiety and depression. She is working on a similar program for high-risk families with adolescent children, but she says it's been hard to gain traction. "The main challenge is that families are unsure they want to address this topic when their kids are adolescents, especially if their kids are experiencing problems. And researchers and clinicians do not want to touch it" due to fear of parent-blaming, said Dr. Sadeh-Sharvit, an associate professor at Palo Alto University and coauthor of the book *Parents with Eating Disorders: An Intervention Guide.* "These high-risk families need the support. Just sweeping everything under the carpet and saying that the problem doesn't exist won't help anyone."

Dr. Sadeh-Sharvit's work offers hope for other mothers like me, and for children who have to bear witness to their parents' struggles. Makenna was one of these children. She spent her adolescence watching her mother cycle in and out of treatment for anorexia nervosa. As a child, Makenna was close to her mom, but anorexia wedged its way between them. When Makenna was in the seventh grade, her mother became so ill that she was hospitalized and put into a medically induced coma. She was restabilized and eventually returned home. But the following year, while visiting family in Florida, she was admitted to the hospital again. She sent handwritten letters to Makenna, who was a thousand miles away at their home in Texas. Makenna couldn't bring herself to open the letters, let alone talk with her mother. "I was so angry; I couldn't believe she had gone back to the hospital. And at the time, there was still so much about eating disorders that I didn't understand," said Makenna, who ultimately did open the letters, which were filled with words of love and longing. "I only went and saw her in the hospital once or twice, and then never again. I just really did not like seeing her like that."

Having this kind of up-close exposure could trigger some children to develop eating disorders of their own. But for Makenna, it was motivation to *not* develop one. As young as age twelve, she found ways to protect herself against anorexia. Every time she ate a meal, she would start off with her least favorite food and then work her way up to her favorite food. This way, she could ensure she ate everything on her plate. "I felt like my extended family, especially my aunt and grandma, were all really worried about me getting an eating disorder," said Makenna, who lives in Austin, Texas. "I kind of developed that as a mechanism to prevent myself from going down that path."

Her mother, Kimber, told me how hard it was to have anorexia while parenting a young child. So often, she felt ashamed and misunderstood. Family and friends couldn't comprehend why she wouldn't eat, and they chastised her for getting hospitalized and leaving her daughter behind. "There were times I'd wish I had cancer because people at least understand cancer," Kimber said. I winced when she said this, but I knew exactly what she meant. Kimber eventually went into residential treatment, which helped her ferret out the eating disorder's underlying causes. "I can honestly admit that I initially went to residential treatment just to save my relationship with my daughter," said Kimber, who lives in Dallas. "It had nothing to do with getting better. But I thought, *If I don't do something, she's never going to speak to me again.*"

Kimber and Makenna went through therapy together and spent years rebuilding their relationship. They have regained closeness and share the belief that their relationship is stronger than anorexia. Kimber says she's better than she was years ago, but she still contends with the disorder and with kidney failure—a fallout of earlier laxative abuse. "I'm always going to have anorexia," she acknowledged. "I feel lucky to be alive, and I have a good life now; eighty-five percent of the time, I control the disorder and it doesn't control me. But at almost fifty-two, I think I've lived almost my entire life in survival mode, and I am tired." Makenna supports her mom through recovery, often assuming a maternal role herself. At age twenty-three, she has not developed an eating disorder and says she doesn't worry about getting one, despite the environmental and genetic risks.

Research shows that the heritability of anorexia and bulimia is 50 to 60 percent, while that of binge-eating disorder is around 40 percent. A large twin study has shown that ARFID (avoidant/restrictive food intake disorder) is also highly heritable, at 79 percent. Genes clearly influence the risk for developing eating disorders, but they don't act alone. I spoke about this with the University of North Carolina's Dr. Cynthia Bulik, who began conducting studies on the heritability of eating disorders in the 1980s. Known for groundbreaking research on genetics, Dr. Bulik pointed to four key elements that determine a person's risk for developing an eating disorder: (1) genetic protective factors, (2) genetic risk factors, (3) environmental protective factors, and (4) environmental risk factors. The protective parts piqued my interest and have since expanded my understanding of what scientists mean when they refer to the difference between nature and nurture. It turns out that risk is not a matter of nature *versus* nurture; it's a mix of nature *and* nurture.

"There are protective environmental factors that allowed you to be here today—that got you to the point where you're not a statistic of someone who didn't survive anorexia. This is therapy. This is family. This is friends," Dr. Bulik said, making me think about how lucky I've been to have support. "And then there are the protective genetic factors. We know a lot less about these, but they could be genes that turn off or quiet or buffer the genetic risk factor." The four factors are like the four suits in a deck of cards: spades and clubs (for risk and protective genetic factors) and diamonds and hearts (for risk and protective environmental factors). We are each dealt a hand, one we carry throughout our lives. We don't have any say over how many spades or clubs we hold, but our number of diamonds and hearts may change over time, depending on how we grow up, how we care for ourselves, and how we respond to the events that shape our lives. In other words, eating disorders are the result of what happens not just within us but also around us. "You can never understand someone's risk for an eating disorder just based on their genes," Dr. Bulik said.

This is such an important message to convey to people with eating disorders and their relatives, who may believe they are "genetically doomed" because of their family history. I've interviewed many people who fear they will pass their "bad genes" on to their children, and some who have decided not to have children at all because of related fears. One woman I spoke to, named Carmen, developed anorexia nervosa as a twelve-year-old and has a strong family history of the disorder; her mother, maternal aunt, and two cousins on her mother's side have all had it. "I have no intention of having my own kids," said Carmen, who is in her thirties and lives in the Pacific Northwest. Carmen works at a youth eating-disorder treatment program and has watched intergenerational trauma unfold as mothers with a history of an eating disorder put their children in treatment for the same disorder. "Parents come into my clinic all the time and get hit with the reality of the genetic piece. I see how difficult it is for them to have to watch their kids struggle with something they struggled with themselves," Carmen said. "It has made me think a lot about the fact that really the last thing I would ever want is to have a kid and have them develop an eating disorder. I know there's a chance this wouldn't happen, but there's also a big chance that it would. I'm not willing to roll the dice on it."

Others are more willing to see how the dice fall. Isabella, a thirty-something woman from New England, said she and her husband plan to have children, even though they're both in eating-disorder recovery and have a family history of other illnesses. On the day I spoke with Isabella, she was at her childhood home caring for her father, who was undergoing treatment for breast cancer. When the question of genetics and eating disorders came up, she noted that she wasn't aware of the risk. "I remember my husband asking, 'Is there a genetic component? And I said, 'Honestly, I don't know.' I didn't learn about that in medical school," said Isabella, who is studying to be a doctor. When I told her what I'd been learning about genetics, she responded: "I tell my husband that breast cancer will very clearly be a risk factor for me and for our children, and I don't necessarily see the eating disorder as being different. We have to be aware of the risk for both," Isabella said. "For me, it's not that I don't want to have children. It's just a question of . . . How are we going to make sure our lingering eating-disorder behaviors don't inadvertently perpetuate behaviors in our children?"

Genetic research has no doubt helped us better understand the complex interplay of genes and environment, but it is far more advanced for other disorders and diseases, such as breast cancer, cystic fibrosis, and Down syndrome. For many years, people have been able to undergo genetic testing for these disorders to better understand their risk. In my mid-thirties I had genetic testing for breast cancer. While I do not carry the BRCA gene mutation, my lifetime risk of developing breast cancer is more than two times greater than the average woman's.

The genetic test results provided a reality check: I need to get more frequent screening than women who have no family history. I consulted a breast specialist and followed her recommendation to get both a mammogram and an MRI every year. As I take those precautions, I can't help but wonder: *What if we knew as much about the genetic risk for eating disorders as we do for other disorders and could implement processes for early screening, intervention, and detection? How many more lives would be spared from the devastating toll of living with an eating disorder—or dying from one?*

Cancer research is so sophisticated that doctors can now make specialized treatment recommendations (e.g., different types of chemotherapy) based on the person's genetic profile. Dr. Bulik, the UNC genetics researcher, wants the eating-disorder field to advance in similar ways. She has spent the past several years conducting large-scale genome-wide association studies, which help scientists identify genes associated with a particular disease, including genetic variations that contribute to a person's risk of developing the disease. Genetic research on eating disorders is complicated, Dr. Bulik said, because there are hundreds, if not thousands, of genes that influence a person's risk in this area. (To put this into perspective, we each have roughly 30,000 genes.)

"Anybody who ever says 'I have the eating-disorder gene' doesn't understand genetics," she told me with a laugh. Scientists like Dr. Bulik use genome-wide association studies to calculate a person's polygenic risk score, which is a measure of one's disease risk due to genes. These scores look at thousands of variants across a person's genome. This makes them less accurate than tests for the BRCA variant, which is "monogenic," meaning it's a variant in a single gene that affects a person's disease risk. The complexity of polygenic risk scores makes them vulnerable to misinterpretation, which is one reason why they're not yet used in clinical settings.

A high polygenic risk score, for instance, doesn't mean someone will develop an eating disorder, nor does a low score guarantee a person will be spared. "You might actually have a fairly low polygenic risk score for anorexia, but you still got the illness because of the trauma of losing your mom," Dr. Bulik said, referring to my own eating disorder. "Someone else who never develops anorexia nervosa might have a high polygenic risk score, but their environment has never been such that it triggered dieting or negative energy balance," she added. "They go through their whole life with a fairly high polygenic risk score but never develop the illness."

In 2019, Dr. Bulik published findings from the Anorexia Nervosa Genetics Initiative (ANGI), a global genome-wide association study that was the first of its kind. ANGI compared the genomes in DNA samples from 16,992 people with anorexia and 55,525 people without anorexia. Put simply, a genome is all the DNA located in one cell in your body; almost every cell contains a complete copy of your genome.

ANGI was groundbreaking in that it identified eight loci (regions on the genome) that influence the risk for anorexia nervosa. In earlier, smaller studies, only one region was identified. The large sample size of ANGI suggests that increasing sample sizes in future research will lead to the detection of even more genes associated with the risk for anorexia. Additionally, ANGI revealed that the genetic factors associated with anorexia also influence physical activity and overlap with depression, anxiety, schizophrenia, and OCD. Reading these results brought me back to my obsessive jumping days and helped me make better sense of why I have always been highly active. ANGI also found the genetic basis of anorexia overlaps with metabolic traits. Specifically, some of the same genetic factors associated with increased risk for anorexia are associated with decreased risk of type 2 diabetes and obesity. According to Dr. Bulik, anorexia should be reframed as a "metabo-psychiatric disorder."

"I used to say, 'Anorexia is a psychiatric illness and obesity is a metabolic illness; we've got to talk about two different things.' But I changed my tune when I saw these results," she told me. "We've never been able to answer the question of why people who develop anorexia *can* develop anorexia. Everybody isn't able to lose weight, keep it off, and keep losing; their bodies pull them back up again. But for people who are genetically predisposed to anorexia, their bodies let them lose weight and then they free-fall and keep losing. And even after we renourish them, their bodies pull them right back down there again. And that's the piece that I think these metabolic correlations are picking up." This suggests that people who leave treatment programs before they reach their ideal body weight could be at greater risk of relapse metabolically. Getting back up to an ideal body weight—and maintaining this weight over a sustained period of time—may be essential to giving a person's metabolism and brain the opportunity to recalibrate without the downward metabolic pull.

Dr. Bulik and colleagues just completed a new study that further reveals the metabolic aspects of anorexia. The study examined stool samples of hospitalized individuals with anorexia and those of healthy controls. The samples were put into a device called a bomb calorimeter, which calculates how many calories are excreted in one's stool. "We actually found that in the beginning of treatment, patients with anorexia were excreting more calories than controls. And they did once they were partially renourished too, which means their guts can't adequately absorb the food that we're feeding them," Dr. Bulik said. "We're saying food is medicine, right? Well, they're pooping their medicine right out."

This isn't to say that people with anorexia can't absorb any food, or that they'll never gain weight. But it suggests they may need to eat more than previously thought as their stomach regains the ability to absorb food. Their metabolism, in other words, may be working against them in ways we're just now beginning to understand. Dr. Bulik and other clinicians I interviewed said they've always been taught that if patients with eating disorders don't gain weight in an inpatient setting, it's because they're hiding food or secretly purging. Patients sometimes *do* engage in such behaviors, but those who don't and are wrongfully accused can come to mistrust clinicians. "Throughout my entire career, it's always been a 'blame the patient' kind of situation," said Dr. Bulik, whose new study could help inform refeeding and treatment approaches. "We suck at treating anorexia, especially in adults. If we can identify the metabolic mechanisms of the disorder and figure out ways to target them, it might make recovery a lot less painful, a lot more tolerable. It might even work."

Dr. Bulik is now leading the largest ever genome-wide association study for the range of eating disorders, which could help crack the genetic code of these disorders. Called the Eating Disorders Genetics Initiative (EDGI), the study will soon deliver findings about the genes associated with anorexia nervosa, bulimia nervosa, binge-eating disorder, and ARFID. Dr. Bulik hopes the study will lead to actionable findings that can be used in clinical settings, including new pharmacological developments and customized treatment models based on a person's genetic predisposition (similar to what's being done for breast cancer patients).

Dr. Bulik and her team of researchers made a concerted effort to gather a diverse sample size for EDGI, saying a lack of diversity in genetic research can have long-term repercussions, including health disparities. "If a medication was developed on the basis of a genome-wide association study that only had people of European ancestry, then all of a sudden we save all the white girls who have anorexia. But there is no guarantee that the same genetic profile of people of European ancestry is going to pop up in people of African ancestry or people of Asian ancestry," Dr. Bulik said. "If, however, we get large enough samples from other racial and ethnic groups and other genders (because most of what we have right now is women), we can make sure that whatever we do moving forward in terms of treatment development will actually target everyone who has the illness." She envisions that one day, genetic research could offer clues about who is predisposed to having chronic cases—a reality that could pave the way for customized treatment models aimed at preventing people from living their whole adult life with an eating disorder, or worse, losing their life to one.

If our understanding of eating disorders was a black-and-white sketch when I was sick, it's now a detailed painting with new brushstrokes being added each day. It's an ever-evolving, unfinished work of art. As I look ahead, I'm optimistic that scientific research will lead future generations to receive better care than I could as a child. One day, perhaps in the not too distant future, we will know more about the biological and genetic factors that keep people stuck in their eating disorders and then develop interventions for helping them get unstuck. One day, maybe the middle place will be far less populous.

I say all this with my family, and my next stage of life, in mind. When this book is published, Madelyn and Tucker will be seven and nine—about the same age I was when my mother received her cancer diagnosis. And I will be forty—the age my mother was when she died. As I begin a decade of life my mother never got to experience, I am struck by the sinking reality that I cannot control whether I contract the disease that killed her. But at this point, I do have a fair amount of control over the disorder that nearly claimed my life and over the way I frame my recovery from it. It's through this framing that I will one day share my eating-disorder story with Madelyn and Tucker.

I don't think we can ever fully shield our children from our thoughts, behaviors, or slips. But we can shape how they see our response; we can regain our footing when we slip, we can celebrate progress, and we can be honest about where we find ourselves. To live in, and to name, the middle place is an act of bravery. This is especially true in a society that pushes for full recovery from eating disorders and prefers illness narratives with protagonists who are triumphant.

I am not a soldier fighting a losing battle, nor am I a survivor who defeated a disorder. And I am no longer a girl who believes she needs to be sick to be special. I am a woman who works hard to keep moving forward in the middle place. I sometimes look back at the long distance I've traveled and wonder how it's possible I still have so far to go. On days like this I remind myself that even though I haven't reached full recovery, I am in full progress. And for me, for many of us, that's a good place to be.

Epilogue

While writing the final chapter of this book, I had a scare. A lump formed underneath the left-hand side of my collarbone, causing pain that radiated down my neck and arm. That same week, my routine mammogram came back with indeterminate results due to a possible asymmetry in my left breast. When I read that asymmetries can be associated with breast cancer, my fears surfaced, then pulled me down under.

"I'm afraid I have cancer," I told Troy through tears that fell faster and harder than they had in all my years as a mother. "I mean, what else could it be?" I pictured my diagnosis: Breast cancer that had spread to the lymph nodes near my collarbone. I had long known that breast cancer sometimes spreads to lymph nodes in the neck, armpit, and chest. My mother used to run her fingers along these spots, ever fearful that her cancer would make its way through her body like a flame that sparks, then suddenly spreads.

"We're going to take you to the doctor tomorrow. We'll figure out what's going on," Troy said, pulling me close. "But I'm staying optimistic, Babe." I had trouble sharing his outlook. I wondered if I would be drafting the final chapter of my book while entering the final stage of my life. It was macabre of me to conjure up such a connection, but the writer in me couldn't help but search for symbolism. I hoped that what I imagined wouldn't turn out to be true, but all I could think about was the possibility that I would die young of cancer and leave my family all too soon, just as my mother had. The timing didn't help; it was April, almost exactly thirty years to the date when my mom was first diagnosed.

My breast specialist ordered a series of tests: two ultrasounds, one CT scan, and one contrast-enhanced mammogram. Uncertainty depleted me in the days that followed. Then the results came in: no cancer. The mammogram also showed that I did not have an asymmetry in my breast after all. And the CT scan revealed that the lump below my collarbone was benign. Rather, it was something the radiologist referred to as a "bony bridge" that was "most consistent with a congenital rib fusion anomaly." *A bony bridge?* The term seemed so off-putting. I thought back to my childhood, when I was sick with anorexia and wanted everything about my body to be bony. Now as an adult in recovery, I no longer want my body to be associated with the word. My doctors and I don't know exactly why the bony bridge had become noticeably palpable or why it started hurting. We suspect it may have been because I'd been traveling with a much-too-heavy workbag slung across my shoulder, causing it to get irritated and inflamed. Within a week of getting the results, the pain subsided and my mood lifted.

"Mommy, why have you seemed so sad?" Madelyn asked me in her characteristically perceptive way.

Tucker, sweet as could be, chimed in. "Are you okay, Mama?"

"I thought I might be sick, Sweeties, but I'm not," I replied gently. "Mommy's better now."

"I'm glad you're a little more better," Tucker said, repeating a phrase he uses whenever someone's been sick and is on the mend.

That evening, Madelyn started working on an art project she didn't want me to see. "It's a surprise!" she said from the kitchen table. "Don't look!"

Naturally curious, I glanced over at Madelyn a few minutes later to see what she was up to. I couldn't tell what she was drawing, but I could see she had a framed photo in front of her—one of me and my mom. In the photo, I'm a three-year-old with thick blonde bangs hanging just above my eyes, and gemstone clip-on earrings dangling from my ears. I'm sitting beside Mom, who has her arms wrapped tightly around me. It's one of my favorite photos, which I keep safe in a heart-shaped frame on my desk.

The following day, Madelyn declared her art project was done. She handed me a sheet of paper, which I quickly realized was a cover for this book. On the top of the page, she had written the book's title in black Magic Marker and its original subtitle in hot pink. Below it she had drawn the mother-daughter photo, adding a note to my mother's shirt that said: "Love my dater like myself." (By "dater," she meant "daughter.") In the right-hand margins, there was a syringe alongside a box of tissues with the word *love* on it. Adorning the left-hand margins were several blue, green, and purple Band-Aids.

"I absolutely adore this!" I told Madelyn, my words laced with love. "You put so much thought into this! Can you tell me about it?"

"Since your book is about your mommy, I drew a picture of you and her on it," she said.

"It's beautiful," I told her. "And what are the Band-Aids for?"

"For sickness *and* recovery," she replied, emphasizing the *and*.

I took a deep breath. Then I held the drawing close, embracing Madelyn's interpretation of her mother's ever-unfolding story.

Illustration courtesy of Madelyn Joelle Tarpley

Acknowledgments

There are so many people who helped me transform the story I lived into the story I wrote.

I owe huge gratitude to my agent, Melissa Danaczko, for being a steadfast champion of this book. You buoyed me and never gave up hope that *Slip* would one day be published. To my amazing editor, Emily Graff, for sharing invaluable feedback and asking smart questions that pushed me to dig deeper. You helped me make this book as good as it could be, all while honoring my vision for it. A huge thanks to the whole Simon Element team for expanding the audience for this book and putting it out into the world. I couldn't ask for a better support system.

To Leah Miller for believing in this book and taking a chance on it. And to Jacqui Banaszynski for helping me navigate this book's structure and strive for clarity. Your brilliance knows no bounds.

To Julie Tate, my fact-checker extraordinaire. You know where errors like to lurk, and you helped find them when I couldn't. Thank you for helping me check the veracity not just of facts but of memory.

Writing this book required a revisitation of the past—an exercise I undertook with vigor while pursuing a Master of Fine Arts at Goucher College. I'm indebted to the Goucher College faculty who challenged me to interrogate storylines that time and memory had oversimplified: Porscha Burke, Suzannah Lessard, Maggie Messitt, Michelle Orange, Leslie Rubinkowski, and early reader Meline Toumani, whose editorial advice has always prompted me to think deeper and write better.

To my other early readers who gave me peace of mind at a time when I felt vulnerable about putting such a personal book out into the world: Julie Moos, for being by my side during the circuitous path to publication; Tamara Bell, for your unwavering support and wealth of creative ideas; Stephen Buckley, for your kindness and thoughtful editorial advice; Kristyn Dusel, for being a dear friend and sounding board; Jenny Harris, for pushing me toward "more recovery"; Margo Maine, for understanding and appreciating the middle place; and Beth McGilley, for being the bridge to so many connections and for cheering me on every step of the way.

I have immense appreciation for the Alfred P. Sloan Foundation for providing me with grant funds to advance public understanding of the science behind eating disorders. The foundation's support enabled me to pursue the kind of rigorous science reporting that a book like this requires. Thank you, Carrie McAdams, for being my trusted science advisor and expanding my scope of understanding. And to Lauren Breithaupt and Laura Berner for sharing research-backed, science-based insights.

Thank you to the University of Texas Libraries for providing me with endless access to research, and especially to librarian Meryl Brodsky for your assistance. To my UT students, past and present: I have become a better writer while teaching you and learning from you. And to the man who hired me at UT when I was thirty weeks pregnant, Rosental Alves; you gave me the greenlight to pursue my MFA while working full-time, teaching part-time, and mothering two young children during a pandemic. It probably seemed crazy to most because it *was* crazy, but you knew what I was working toward and made sure I had the support to fulfill my goals.

To Roy Peter Clark, my fellow Providence College alum, for helping me pursue my passion for writing. You've taught me so much of what I know as a writer, and your mentorship helped me get where I am today.

To Sarosh Arif, for helping me think through how to fairly and accurately describe a diverse mix of individuals, cultures, and beliefs so that the book would be inclusive of, and relevant to, a wide range of readers.

As a first-time author, I'm indebted to my readers. Thank you, thank you, thank you for your support. To my readers who have lived experience with an eating disorder and who are in the middle place, I hope that *Slip* helps you feel less alone and reminds you that recovery is possible but never perfect. Don't let the slips stop you.

I'm grateful to everyone who agreed to share their stories and expertise with me as I wrote this book. This includes the hundreds of people from around the world who filled out my survey and agreed to be interviewed. To most of you, I was a stranger. But you confided in me as though I were a best friend. Even though you don't all appear in this book, you each helped make it better. I also owe huge thanks to the many clinicians and researchers who shared their wisdom with me. I appreciate all the work you're doing to advance the field and treat people with eating disorders. You give me hope.

I'm especially grateful to the clinicians who helped me when I was in treatment, including Dr. Sara Forman and Kerry Healy. And to the middle-school teachers who helped me in the aftermath of my mother's passing, including Sarah Currie, Kathleen Meade, and Anne Fallon.

I'm lucky to have many maternal figures in my life, including Barbara Howland, Mary Ellen Tenore, Gina Tenore, and Kathy Tarpley. I wouldn't be where I am today if it weren't for my father, who always believed I would get better. As a parent myself, I can't imagine having to endure what you went through when I was sick. My love for you runs deep.

To my mother, who sent my first handwritten book—titled "Mallary: The Girl Who Loves Ducks"—to a company that bound and printed it when I was eight years old. When you gifted me that book, I felt like a real-life author. I have chased that feeling ever since.

To my husband, Troy, my favorite person and my first reader. Thank you for believing in me, for watching the kids when I went on reporting trips, and for being the best sounding board a wife and writer could ask for. You helped me through the most difficult passages.

Lastly, to my children, Madelyn and Tucker. I'm sure you will one day read this book, and when you do, I hope the hard truths in it won't sting. Let them be a guiding light that illuminates your understanding of me and helps you through life's dark patches. When I was writing *Slip*, you sometimes asked me what the last words of my book would be. I didn't yet know, but now I do: I love you, always.

Endnotes

Author's Note

xii *Intrinsic motivation is an important part*: Josie Geller, Sarah Cockell, and Danae Drab, "Assessing Readiness to Change in the Eating Disorders: The Psychometric Properties of the Readiness and Motivation Interview," *Psychological Assessment* 13 (Summer 2001): 189–98.

xii *yield more positive outcomes*: Anita Federici and Allan S. Kaplan, "The Patient's Account of Relapse and Recovery in Anorexia Nervosa: A Qualitative Study," *European Eating Disorders Review* 16 (January 2008): 1–10.

Chapter One: The Trigger

10 *near the end of life*: Alessio Molfino, Carmen Gallicchio, Giovanni Imbimbo, Michele Melena, Silvia Antonini, and Antonietta Gigante,

et al., "Evaluation of Anorexia in Cancer and Its Association with Autonomic Nervous System Activity Assessed by Heart Rate Variability," *Nutrients* 15, no. 23 (2023): 1–11.

14 *parents avoid conversations about death*: Atle Dyregrov, *Grief in Children: A Handbook for Adults* (Jessica Kingsley, 2008), 21.

14 *complicated (or prolonged) grief*: Victoria H. Raveis, Daniel Karus, and Karolynn Siegel, *Children's Psychological Distress Following the Death of a Parent: Journal of Youth and Adolescence* (Springer, 1999), 165–80.

14 *the reality of death*: Katherine M. Shear, "Complicated Grief," *New England Journal of Medicine* 372, no. 2 (2015): 153–60.

14 *their closest surviving family member*: Hope Edelman, *Motherless Daughters: The Legacy of Loss* (Delta, 1995), 102.

16 *"We ought to give it a try"*: Barbara Ehrenreich, "How Positive Thinking Wrecked the Economy," blog, November 6, 2009, http://ehrenreich.blogs.com/barbaras_blog/2008/09/how-positive-thinking-wrecked-the-economy.html.

16 *a predominant pillar of cancer care*: May McCreaddie, Sheila Payne, and Katherine Froggatt, "Ensnared by Positivity: A Constructivist Perspective on 'Being Positive' in Cancer Care," *European Journal of Oncology Nursing: Official Journal of European Oncology Nursing Society* 14, no. 4 (2010): 283–90.

16 *"Positive thinking seems to be mandatory"*: Barbara Ehrenreich, *Bright-Sided: How Positive Thinking Is Undermining America* (Metropolitan Books, 2009), 26.

16 *led to changes in survival rates*: James Coyne, Thomas F. Pajak, Jonathan Harris, Andre Konski, Benjamin Movsas, Kian Ang, et al., "Emotional Well-Being Does Not Predict Survival in Head and Neck Cancer Patients : A Radiation Therapy Oncology Group Study," *Cancer* 110 (Winter 2007): 2568–75.

17 *"a storyline resistant to evidence"*: James C. Coyne, Howard Tennen, and Adelita V. Ranchor, "Positive Psychology in Cancer Care: A

Story Line Resistant to Evidence," *Annals of Behavioral Medicine* 39 (Winter 2010): 35–42.

17 *rituals that were commonplace at the time*: Hope Edelman, *The After-Grief: Finding Your Way Along the Long Arc of Loss* (Random House, 2020), 15–17.

17 *Kübler-Ross first articulated these stages*: Elisabeth Kübler-Ross, *On Death and Dying* (Macmillan, 1969).

17 *quickly overcome in a linear fashion*: Edelman, *The AfterGrief*, 18–24.

18 *ongoing bonds with deceased loved ones*: Dennis Klass and Edith Steffen, eds., *Continuing Bonds in Bereavement: New Directions for Research and Practice* (Routledge, 2018), xvii.

21 *suppressing them as a result*: William J. Worden and Phyllis R. Silverman, "Parental Death and the Adjustment of School-Age Children," *OMEGA—Journal of Death and Dying* 33 (Winter 1996): 91–102.

21 *can get "stuck" in childhood*: Edelman, *Motherless Daughters*, 46–47.

22 *alcohol and drug abuse*: Edelman, *Motherless Daughters*, 57–58.

Chapter Two: The Spiral

24 *obesity rates among children were rising*: Hedwig E. Lee, Dohoon Lee, Guang Guo, and Kathleen Harris, "US Trends in Body Mass in Adolescence and Young Adulthood, 1959–2002," *Journal of Adolescent Health* 49, no. 6 (2011): 601–608.

25 *The food pyramid and Nutrition Facts labels*: Sandy Skrovan, "The Origins and Evolution of Nutrition Facts Labeling," *Food Dive*, October 16, 2017, https://www.fooddive.com/news/the-origins-and-evolution-of-nutrition-facts-labeling/507016/.

25 *"healthy," "reduced fat," and "fat-free"*: National Library of Medicine, "History of Nutrition Labeling," in *Front-of-Package Nutrition Rating Systems and Symbols: Phase 1 Report*, ed. Ellen Wartella et al. (National Academies Press, 2010).

34 *much stronger than it is today*: S. Bryn Austin, "Accelerating Progress in Eating Disorders Prevention: A Call for Policy Translation Research and Training," *Eating Disorders* 24 (Winter 2016): 6–19.

34 *gender, race, or ethnicity*: Frank Q. Nuttall, "Body Mass Index: Obesity, BMI, and Health," *Nutrition Today* 50 (Spring/Summer 2015): 117–28.

34 *body compositions of women and minorities*: Carly Stern, "Why BMI Is a Flawed Health Standard, Especially for People of Color," *Washington Post*, May 5, 2021, https://www.washingtonpost.com/lifestyle/wellness/healthy-bmi-obesity-race-/2021/05/04/655390f0-ad0d-11eb-acd3-24b44a57093a_story.html.

34 *Today, 40 percent of children*: Kristine A. Madsen, Hannah R. Thompson, Jennifer Linchey, Lorrene D. Ritchie, Shalika Gupta, Dianne Neumark-Sztainer, et al., "Effect of School-Based Body Mass Index Reporting in California Public Schools: A Randomized Clinical Trial," *Journal of the American Medical Association, Pediatrics*, no. 75 (Spring 2021): 251–59; Hannah R. Thompson and Kristine A. Madsen, "The Report Card on BMI Report Cards," *Current Obesity Reports*, no. 6 (Summer 2017): 163–67.

34 *"BMI report cards"*: Virginia Sole-Smith, *Fat Talk: Parenting in the Age of Diet Culture* (Henry Holt, 2023), 188.

35 *a 2023 study at Harvard University*: Mary Kathryn Poole, Steven L. Gortmaker, Jessica L. Barrett, Stephanie M. McCulloch, Eric B. Rimm, Karen B. Emmons, et al., "The Societal Costs and Health Impacts on Obesity of BMI Report Cards in US Schools," *Obesity*, vol. 31 (August 2023): 2110–18.

35 *no evidence showing these screenings are effective*: "Body Mass Index (BMI) Measurement in Schools," Centers for Disease Control and Prevention, information sheet, August 9, 2022, cdc.gov/healthyschools/obesity/bmi/bmi_measurement_schools.htm.

35 *school-based obesity-prevention programs*: "School Obesity Programs

May Promote Worrisome Eating Behaviors and Physical Activity in Kids," *Science Daily*, June 4, 2014, www.sciencedaily.com/releases/2012/01/120124151207.htm.

35 *adolescents were especially vulnerable*: Jessica A. Lin, Grace Jhe, Richa Adhikari, Julia A. Vitagliano, Kelsey L. Rose, Melissa Freizinger, et al., "Triggers for Eating Disorder Onset in Youth with Anorexia Nervosa Across the Weight Spectrum," *Eating Disorders* 31 (Winter 2023): 553–72.

35 *The CDC endorses nutrition education*: "Healthy Eating Learning Opportunities and Nutrition Education," Centers for Disease Control and Prevention, information sheet, January 10, 2023, https://www.cdc.gov/healthyschools/nutrition/school_nutrition_education.htm.

35 *lessons about "healthy eating"*: "Overweight & Obesity Statistics," National Institute of Diabetes and Digestive and Kidney Diseases, information sheet, September 2021, https://www.niddk.nih.gov/health-information/health-statistics/overweight-obesity.

35 *Many are rooted in diet culture*: Mallary Tenore Tarpley, "Healthy Eating Curriculum May Contribute to Eating Disorders in Kids," *Washington Post*, August 21, 2023, https://www.washingtonpost.com/parenting/2023/08/21/curriculum-trigger-eating-disorder/.

35 *In 1998, my pediatrician didn't recognize*: Paul Rohde, Eric Stice, Heather Shaw, Jeff M. Gau, and Olivia C. Ohls, "Age Effects in Eating Disorder Baseline Risk Factors and Prevention Intervention Effects," *International Journal of Eating Disorders* 50 (Winter 2017): 1273–80.

36 *children as young as five or six*: See the National Eating Disorders Association Parent Toolkit, at www.nationaleatingdisorders.org/wp-content/uploads/2012/06/ParentToolkit-946.pdf; Rachel Aviv, *Strangers to Ourselves: Unsettled Minds and the Stories That Make Us* (Farrar, Straus and Giroux, 2022), 4.

36 *how to screen for or treat eating disorders*: Diana C. Lemly, Melissa Dreier, Shana Birnbaum, Kamryn T. Eddy, and Jennifer J. Thomas. "Caring for Adults with Eating Disorders in Primary Care," *Primary Care Companion for CNS Disorders* 24 (Winter 2022).

37 *have been on the rise*: Caroline Hopkins, "Eating Disorders Among Teens More Severe Than Ever," *NBC News*, April 29, 2023, https://www.nbcnews.com/health/health-news/eating-disorders-anorexia-bulimia-are-severe-ever-rcna80745.

37 *the increase was 93 percent*: "Trends Shaping the Health Economy: Behavioral Health," Trilliant Health, website report, March 2023, https://www.trillianthealth.com/hubfs/2023%20Trends%20Shaping%20the%20Health%20Economy%20Report.pdf.

37 *suicide being among the leading causes*: "Social and Economic Cost of Eating Disorders in the United States of America: Report for the Strategic Training Initiative for the Prevention of Eating Disorders and the Academy for Eating Disorders," Deloitte Access Economics, report, June 2020, https://cdn1.sph.harvard.edu/wp-content/uploads/sites/1267/2020/07/Social-Economic-Cost-of-Eating-Disorders-in-US.pdf: 23.

37 *But still, eating disorders get overlooked*: Ann F. Haynos, Amy H. Egbert, Ellen E. Fitzsimmons-Craft, Cheri A. Levinson, and Jessica L. Schleider, "Not Niche: Eating Disorders as an Example in the Dangers of Overspecialisation," *British Journal of Psychiatry* 224 (Spring 2024): 82–85.

38 *research dollars and illness severity do not align*: Stuart B. Murray, Eva Pila, Scott Griffiths, and Daniel Le Grange, "When Illness Severity and Research Dollars Do Not Align: Are We Overlooking Eating Disorders?" *World Psychiatry* 16 (Fall 2017): 321.

38 *around $55 million annually*: "Estimates of Funding for Various Research, Condition, and Disease Categories (RCDC)," National Institutes of Health, report, May 14, 2024, https://report.nih.gov/funding/categorical-spending#/.

38 *That was compared to $239 per person*: "Social and Economic Cost of Eating Disorders."

38 *Peer Reviewed Medical Research Program*: Eating Disorders Coalition, status report, 2022, https://www.eatingdisorderscoalition.org/inner_template/our_work/previous-policy-initiatives.html.

38 *during the Covid-19 pandemic*: "HHS Awards Nearly $1 Million to Address Eating Disorders in Adolescent Girls," Department of Health and Human Services, press release, September 20, 2022, https://www.hhs.gov/about/news/2022/09/20/hhs-awards-nearly-1-million-address-eating-disorders-adolescent-girls.html.

39 *Under Dr. Austin's leadership*: "Screening, Symptom Recognition, and Referral to Treatment for Eating Disorders in Pediatric Primary Care Settings," American Medical Association Ed Hub program, https://edhub.ama-assn.org/boston-childrens-hospital-edu/provider-referrer/13431?resultClick=1&bypassSolrId=Q_13431.

39 *Only about 30 percent of people*: Jaime A. Coffino, Tomoko Udo, and Carlos M. Grilo, "Rates of Help-Seeking in US Adults with Lifetime DSM-5 Eating Disorders: Prevalence Across Diagnoses and Differences by Sex and Ethnicity/Race," *Mayo Clinic Proceedings* 94 (Summer 2019): 1415–26.

39 *implement screening tools*: "New Tool Launches to Help Primary Care Clinicians Screen for Eating Disorders," UNC Health, press release, July 13, 2022, https://news.unchealthcare.org/2022/07/new-tool-launches-to-help-primary-care-clinicians-screen-for-eating-disorders/.

39 *genetic, environmental, and neurobiological factors*: Jennifer Gaudiani, *Sick Enough: A Guide to the Medical Complications of Eating Disorders* (Routledge, 2018), 9.

40 *People with ARFID limit their food intake*: Jennifer J. Thomas and Kamryn Eddy, *Cognitive-Behavioral Therapy for Avoidant/Restrictive Food Intake Disorder: Children, Adolescents, and Adults* (Cambridge University Press, 2019): 1–2.

41 *despite "significant weight loss"*: American Psychiatric Association, *Diagnostic and Statistical Manual of Mental Disorders, Fifth Edition, Text Revision* (American Psychiatric Association, 2022).

41 *6 percent of them were underweight*: Martine Flament, Katherine Henderson, Annick Buchholz, Nicole Obeid, Hien Nguyen, Meagan Birmingham, et al., "Weight Status and DSM-5 Diagnoses of Eating Disorders in Adolescents from the Community," *Journal of the American Academy of Child & Adolescent Psychiatry* 54 (Spring 2015): 403–11.

41 *instead of those who aren't*: Kate Siber, "You Don't Look Anorexic," *New York Times*, October 18, 2022, https://www.nytimes.com/2022/10/18/magazine/anorexia-obesity-eating-disorder.html.

41 *Up to 25 percent of people with anorexia*: James Hudson, Eva Hiripi, Harrison Pope, and Ronald Kessler, "The Prevalence and Correlates of Eating Disorders in the National Comorbidity Survey Replication," *Biological Psychiatry* 61 (February 2007): 348–58.

41 *The LGBTQ+ population is at increased risk*: Lacie L. Parker and Jennifer A Harriger, "Eating Disorders and Disordered Eating Behaviors in the LGBT Population: A Review of the Literature," *Journal of Eating Disorders* 8 (Fall 2020): 51.

42 *have a low BMI*: Timothy B. Walsh, Kelsey E. Hagan, and Carlin Lockwood, "A Systematic Review Comparing Atypical Anorexia Nervosa and Anorexia Nervosa," *International Journal of Eating Disorders* 56 (Spring 2023): 798–820.

43 *The wealthy-woman stereotype*: Samuel Fenwick, "On Atrophy of the Stomach and on the Nervous Affections of the Digestive Organs," *Glasgow Medical Journal* 16 (1881): 124–25.

43 *"selectively befalls the young, rich, and beautiful"*: Hilde Bruch, *Golden Cage: The Enigma of Anorexia Nervosa: A Guide to the Medical Complications of Eating Disorders* (Vintage, 1978), vii.

43 *"urgent need to prioritize accessible eating disorder treatment"*: Kathryn M. Huryk, Catherine R. Drury, and Katharine L. Loeb,

"Diseases of Affluence? A Systematic Review of the Literature on Socioeconomic Diversity in Eating Disorders," *Eating Behaviors* 43 (Winter 2021): 10, 1548.

43 (*sometimes referred to as "the SWAG stereotype"*): K. R. Sonneville and S. K. Lipson, "Disparities in Eating Disorder Diagnosis and Treatment According to Weight Status, Race/Ethnicity, Socioeconomic Background, and Sex Among College Students," *International Journal of Eating Disorders* 51 (Summer 2018): 518–26.

43 *Black, Indigenous, and People of Color (BIPOC)*: Anne E. Becker, Debra L. Franko, Alexandra Speck, and David B. Herzog, "Ethnicity and Differential Access to Care for Eating Disorder Symptoms," *International Journal of Eating Disorders* 33 (Spring 2003): 205–12.

43 *and transgender people*: Reggie Casanova-Perez, Calvin Apodaca, Emily Bascom, Deepthi Mohanraj, Cezanne Lane, Drishti Vidyarthi, et al., "Broken Down by Bias: Healthcare Biases Experienced by BIPOC and LGBTQ+ Patients," in *AMIA Annual Symposium Proceedings* (American Medical Informatics Association, 2021), 275–84.

43 *Black girls are 50 percent more likely*: Michelle S. Goeree, John C. Ham, Daniela Iorio, "Caught in the Bulimic Trap? Socioeconomic Status, State Dependence, Unobserved Heterogeneity," Working Paper Series from RePEc (Winter 2009).

44 *compared to their white peers*: Rachel C. Uri, Ya-Ke Wu, Jessica H. Baker, and Melissa A. Munn-Chernoff, "Eating Disorder Symptoms in Asian American College Students," *Eating Behaviors* 40 (Winter 2021): 101, 458.

44 *compared to cisgender students*: Elizabeth W. Diemer, Julia D. Grant, Melissa A. Munn-Chernoff, David Patterson, and Alexis E. Duncan, "Gender Identity, Sexual Orientation, and Eating-Related Pathology in a National Sample of College Students," *Journal of Adolescent Health* 57 (Summer 2015): 144–49.

44 *Biases in our healthcare system*: Rachel W. Goode, Adelia Wilfred Salomé, and Mae Lynn Reyes-Rodríguez, "From Disparities to Equity: Striving for More in Our Treatments for Feeding and Eating Disorders," *Trends in Molecular Medicine* 30 (Spring 2024): 308–10.

44 *were formed with white populations*: Cynthia Feltner, Christine Peat, Shivani Reddy, Sean Riley, Nancy Berkman, Jennifer Cook Middleton, et al., "Screening for Eating Disorders in Adolescents and Adults: Evidence Report and Systematic Review for the US Preventive Services Task Force," *Journal of the American Medical Association* 327 (Spring 2022): 1068–82.

44 *trauma, racism, and/or oppression*: Rachel W. Goode, Kashonna C. Webster, and Rebecca E. Gwira, "A Review of Binge-Eating Disorder in Black Women: Treatment Recommendations and Implications for Healthcare Providers," *Current Psychiatry Reports* 24 (Winter 2022): 757–66.

45 *complications due to anorexia a decade earlier*: "Karen Carpenter's Second Life," *New York Times*, October 6, 1996, https://www.nytimes.com/1996/10/06/magazine/karen-carpenter-s-second-life.html.

45 *cultural food preferences*: Priya Krishna, "Is American Dietetics a White-Bread World? These Dietitians Think So," *New York Times*, December 7, 2020, https://www.nytimes.com/2020/12/07/dining/dietitian-diversity.html.

46 *Full recovery and early detection*: Janet Treasure and Gerald Russell, "The Case for Early Intervention in Anorexia Nervosa: Theoretical Exploration of Maintaining Factors," *British Journal of Psychiatry* 199 (Summer 2011): 5–7.

Chapter Three: The Disorder

48 *chapped and bleeding*: Jennifer Gaudiani, *Sick Enough: A Guide to the Medical Complications of Eating Disorders* (Routledge, 2018), 60.

48 *whose bodies instinctively try to keep them warm*: Gaudiani, *Sick Enough*, 22.

48 *can lead to heart failure*: D. Friars, O. Walsh, and F. McNicholas, "Assessment and Management of Cardiovascular Complications in Eating Disorders," *Journal of Eating Disorders* 11 (January 2023): 13, https://doi: 10.1186/s40337-022-00724-5. PMID: 36717950; PMCID: PMC9886215.

49 *Here, it was a sign my body*: Renata Strumia, "Skin Signs in Anorexia Nervosa," *Dermato-Endocrinology* 1 (Fall 2009): 268–70.

52 *and rid myself of it*: Christina Scharmer, Sasha Gorrell, Katherine Schaumberg, and Drew Anderson, "Compulsive Exercise or Exercise Dependence? Clarifying Conceptualizations of Exercise in the Context of Eating Disorder Pathology," *Journal of Clinical Sport Psychology* 46 (Winter 2020): 101, 586.

55 *to maintain basic life functions*: Gaudiani, *Sick Enough*, 12–14.

55 *The physiologist Ancel Keys*: Leah M. Kalm and Richard D. Semba, "They Starved So That Others Be Better Fed: Remembering Ancel Keys and the Minnesota Experiment," *Journal of Nutrition* 135 (Summer 2005): 1347–52.

56 *forty to sixty packs a day*: Todd Tucker, *The Great Starvation Experiment: Ancel Keys and the Men Who Starved for Science* (University of Minnesota Press, 2017), 124–25.

56 *unable to feel satiated*: Elke D. Eckert, Irving I. Gottesmam, Susan E. Swigart, and Regina C. Casper, "A 57-year Follow-up Investigation and Review of the Minnesota Study on Human Starvation and Its Relevance to Eating Disorders," *Archives of Psychology* 2 (Spring 2018): 1–19.

56 "*Insurance companies, with their lack of*": Gaudiani, *Sick Enough*, 30.

57 *eating disorders during residency*: Connie Ma, Diana Gonzales-Pacheco, Jean Cerami, and Kathryn Coakley, "Emergency Medicine Physicians' Knowledge and Perceptions of Training, Education, and Resources in Eating Disorders," *Journal of Eating Disorders* 9 (Winter 2021): 4.

57 *accommodate large volumes of food*: C. Laird Birmingham and Janet Treasure, "Complications of Nutritional Therapy," in *Medical Management of Eating Disorders* (Cambridge University Press, 2019), 69–86.

57 *This causes bloating and upper stomach pain*: Mark Norris, Megan Harrison, Leanna Isserlin, Amy Robinson, Stephen Feder, and Margaret Sampson, "Gastrointestinal Complications Associated with Anorexia Nervosa: A Systematic Review," *International Journal of Eating Disorders* 49 (Spring 2016): 216–37.

57 *helps the stomach speed up its emptying time*: Gaudiani, *Sick Enough*, 26–27.

58 *And since my heart was likely smaller*: Katherine V. Sachs, Ben Harnke, Philip S. Mehler, and Mori J. Krantz, "Cardiovascular Complications of Anorexia Nervosa: A Systematic Review," *International Journal of Eating Disorders* 49 (Spring 2016): 238–48.

58 *As I began eating in the hospital*: Hisham Mehanna, Jamil Moledina, and Jane Travis, "Refeeding Syndrome: What It Is and How to Prevent and Treat It," *BMJ* 336 (Summer 2008): 1495–98.

58 *larger amounts of food in treatment*: Katherine Sachs, Debbie Anderson, Jennifer Sommer, Amy Winkelman, and Philip S. Mehler, "Avoiding Medical Complications During the Refeeding of Patients with Anorexia Nervosa," *Eating Disorders* 23 (Fall 2015): 411–21.

58 *In recent years, new research has suggested*: Graham Redgrave, Janelle W. Coughlin, Colleen C. Schreyer, Lindsay M. Martin, Anne K. Leonpacher, Margaret Seide, et al., "Refeeding and Weight Restoration Outcomes in Anorexia Nervosa: Challenging Current Guidelines," *International Journal of Eating Disorders* 48 (Winter 2015): 866–73.

58 *In some cases this "underfeeding syndrome"*: Debra K. Katzman, Andrea K. Garber, Michael Kohn, Neville H. Golden, "Refeeding Hypophosphatemia in Hospitalized Adolescents with Anorexia Nervosa," *Journal of Adolescent Health* 71 (Fall 2022): 517-522.

58 *(descriptors partially determined by BMI)*: Andrea K. Garber, Susan M. Sawyer, Neville H. Golden, Angela S. Guarda, Debra K. Katzman, Michael R. Kohn, et al., "A Systematic Review of Approaches to Refeeding in Patients with Anorexia Nervosa," *International Journal of Eating Disorders* 49 (Spring 2016): 293–310.

58 *one year after hospitalization*: Graham W. Redgrave, Colleen C. Schreyer, Janelle W. Coughlin, Laura K. Fischer, Allisyn Pletch, and Angela S. Guarda, "Discharge Body Mass Index, Not Illness Chronicity, Predicts 6-Month Weight Outcome in Patients Hospitalized with Anorexia Nervosa," *Frontiers in Psychiatry* 12 (Winter 2021): 641, 861; James Lock and Iris Litt, "What Predicts Maintenance of Weight for Adolescents Medically Hospitalized for Anorexia Nervosa?" *Eating Disorders* 11 (2003): 1–7.

58 *Most of the physical side effects*: Dara Friars, Orla Walsh, and Fiona McNicholas, "Assessment and Management of Cardiovascular Complications in Eating Disorders," *Journal of Eating Disorders* 11 (Winter 2023): 13.

58 *Among them is low bone density*: Madhusmita Misra and Anne Klibanski, "Evaluation and Treatment of Low Bone Density in Anorexia Nervosa," *Nutrition in Clinical Care* 5 (Winter 2002): 298–308.

59 *Maximal increases in bone-mass accrual*: Madhusmita Misra and Anne Klibanski, "Anorexia Nervosa and Osteoporosis," *Reviews in Endocrine & Metabolic Disorders* 7 (Summer 2006): 91–99.

59 *One study found that roughly 40 percent*: Steven Grinspoon, Elizabeth Thomas, Sarah Pitts, Erin Gross, Diane Mickley, Karen Miller, et al., "Prevalence and Predictive Factors for Regional Osteopenia in Women with Anorexia Nervosa," *Annals of Internal Medicine* 133 (Winter 2001): 790–94.

59 *meaning their bone density is low*: Madhusmita Misra and Anne Klibanski, "Anorexia Nervosa and Bone," *Journal of Endocrinology* 221 (Summer 2014): 163–76.

59 anosognosia, *a medical term to describe*: Walter Vandereycken, "Denial of Illness in Anorexia Nervosa—A Conceptual Review: Part 2 Different Forms and Meanings," *European Eating Disorders Review* 14 (Fall 2006): 352–68.

60 *Several areas of the brain*: Roberto Esposito, Filippo Cieri, Massimo Giannantonio, and Armando Tartaro, "The Role of Body Image and Self-perception in Anorexia Nervosa: The Neuroimaging Perspective," *Journal of Neuropsychology* 12 (Spring 2018): 41–52.

60 *People with anorexia also tend to*: Eva C. Gregertsen, William Mandy, and Lucy Serpell, "The Egosyntonic Nature of Anorexia: An Impediment to Recovery in Anorexia Nervosa Treatment," *Frontiers in Psychology* 8 (Winter 2017): 2273.

60 *Neurobiological research has shown*: Amy Harrison, Niamh O'Brien, Carolina Lopez, and Janet Treasure, "Sensitivity to Reward and Punishment in Eating Disorders," *Psychiatry Research* 177 (Spring 2010): 1–11.

61 *If reward is not very important to decision-making*: Walter H. Kaye, Christina E. Wierenga, Amanda Bischoff-Grethe, Laura A. Berner, Alice V. Ely, Ursula F. Bailer, et al., "Neural Insensitivity to the Effects of Hunger in Women Remitted from Anorexia Nervosa," *American Journal of Psychiatry* 177 (Summer 2020): 601–610.

61 *These issues can persist*: Ella Keegan, Kate Tchanturia, and Tracey D. Wade, "Central Coherence and Set-Shifting Between Nonunderweight Eating Disorders and Anorexia Nervosa: A Systematic Review and Meta-Analysis," *International Journal of Eating Disorders* 54 (Spring 2021): 229–43.

61 *the findings of a major 2022 study*: Esther Walton, Fabio Bernadoni, Victoria-Luise Batury, Klaas Bahnsen, Sara Lariviere, Giovanni Abbate-Data, et al., "Brain Structure in Acutely Underweight and Partially Weight-Restored Individuals with Anorexia Nervosa: A Coordinated Analysis by the ENIGMA Eating Disorders Working Group," *Biological Psychiatry* 92 (Winter 2022): 730–38.

61 *The brain is made up of gray matter*: Anthony A. Mercadante and Prasanna Tadi, *Neuroanatomy, Gray Matter* (StatPearls, 2023).

63 *a "psycho-biological conflict"*: Guido Frank, Marisa C. DeGuzman, and Megan E. Shott, "Motivation to Eat and Not to Eat—The Psycho-Biological Conflict in Anorexia Nervosa," *Physiology & Behavior* 206 (Summer 2019): 185–90.

64 *conducted brain imaging scans*: Guido Frank, Megan E. Shott, Joel Stoddard, Skylar Swindle, and Tamara Pryor, "Association of Brain Reward Response with Body Mass Index and Ventral Striatal-Hypothalamic Circuitry Among Young Women with Eating Disorders," *Journal of the American Medical Association, Psychiatry* 78 (Fall 2021): 1123–33.

64 *"I really believe that medication"*: Guido Frank, "Pharmacotherapeutic Strategies for the Treatment of Anorexia Nervosa—Too Much for One Drug?" *Expert Opinion on Pharmacotherapy* 21 (Summer 2020): 1045–58.

64 *He typically prescribes*: Guido Frank, "Aripiprazole, a Partial Dopamine Agonist to Improve Adolescent Anorexia Nervosa—A Case Series: Aripiprazole in Adolescent Anorexia Nervosa," *International Journal of Eating Disorders* 49 (Spring 2016): 529–33.

64 *Combinations of these drugs*: Lisa Adler, "Revisiting Dopamine Neurocircuitry for the Use of Aripiprazole and Olanzapine in the Treatment of Anorexia Nervosa," *Journal of the American Academy of Child and Adolescent Psychiatry* 62 (Fall 2023): S333.

65 *Still today, there is no FDA-approved drug*: Rachel Gutman-Wei, "We Have No Drugs to Treat the Deadliest Eating Disorder," *Atlantic*, September 7, 2023, https://www.theatlantic.com/health/archive/2023/09/anorexia-drug-resistance-eating-disorder/675246/.

65 *including psilocybin*: Stephanie Knatz Peck, Samantha Shao, Tessa Gruen, Kevin Yang, Alexandra Babakanian, Julie Trim, et al., "Psilocybin Therapy for Females with Anorexia Nervosa: A Phase 1,

Open-Label Feasibility Study," *Nature Medicine* 29 (Summer 2023): 1947–53.

65 *ketamine*: Anya Ragnhildstveit A., Matthew Slayton, Laura Kate Jackson, Madeline Brendle, Sachin Ahuja, Willis Holle, et al., "Ketamine as a Novel Psychopharmacotherapy for Eating Disorders: Evidence and Future Directions," *Brain Sciences* 12 (Spring 2022): 382.

65 *ayahuasca*: Adele Lafrance, Anja Loizaga-Velder, Jenna Fletcher, Marika Renelli, Natasha Files, and Kenneth Tupper, "Nourishing the Spirit: Exploratory Research on Ayahuasca Experiences Along the Continuum of Recovery from Eating Disorders," *Journal of Psychoactive Drugs* 49 (Fall 2017): 427–35.

65 *symptoms in people with anorexia*: Natalie Gukasyan, Colleen C. Schryer, Ronald R. Griffiths, and Angela S. Guarda, "Psychedelic-Assisted Therapy for People with Eating Disorders." *Current Psychiatry Reports* 24 (Winter 2022): 767–75.

65 *Though highly preliminary*: Stephanie Knatz Peck, Hannah Fisher, Jessie Kim, Samantha Shao, Julie Trim, and Walter H. Kaye, "Psychedelic treatment for anorexia nervosa: A first-hand view of how psilocybin treatment did and did not help," Psychedelics (Fall 2024): 1-4.

Chapter Four: The Treatment

69 *engaging in mealtime rituals*: Simona Calugi, Elisa Chignola, and Riccardo Dalle Grave, "A Longitudinal Study of Eating Rituals in Patients with Anorexia Nervosa," *Frontiers in Psychology* 10 (Winter 2019): 15.

70 *"My anorexia is so powerful"*: Lucy Serpell, Janet Treasure, John Teasdale, and Victoria Sullivan, "Anorexia Nervosa: Friend or Foe?" *International Journal of Eating Disorders* 25 (Spring 1999): 177–86.

71 *The Bader building*: "The CHB Walking Trail: A Walking Tour of

Children's Hospital Boston," Children's Hospital Boston, https://bcrp.childrenshospital.org/wp-content/uploads/2017/07/History Walking-Tour.pdf.

71 *We'd stare at one another's bodies*: Reout Arbel, Yael Latzer, and Danny Koren, "Revisiting Poor Insight into Illness in Anorexia Nervosa," *Journal of Psychiatric Practice* 20 (Spring 2014): 85–93.

72 *Our interactions reflected a common but underdiscussed criticism*: Walter Vandereycken, "Can Eating Disorders Become 'Contagious' in Group Therapy and Specialized Inpatient Care?" *European Eating Disorders Review* 19 (Spring 2011): 289–95.

72 *social contagion*: Andrea E. Hamel, Shannon L. Zaitsoff, Andrew Taylor, Rosanne Menna, and Daniel Le Grange, "Body-Related Social Comparison and Disordered Eating Among Adolescent Females with an Eating Disorder, Depressive Disorder, and Healthy Controls," *Nutrients* 4 (Fall 2012): 1260–72.

72 *comparison*: Vandereycken, "Can Eating Disorders Become 'Contagious.'"

72 *Once exposed to these tricks*: Valerie L. Forman-Hoffman and Cassie L. Cunningham. "Geographical Clustering of Eating Disordered Behaviors in U.S. High School Students," *International Journal of Eating Disorders* 41 (Spring 2008): 209–14.

74 *starvation distorts the mind*: Brooks B. Brodrick, Mallory A. Jacobs, and Carrie J. McAdams. "Psychosis in Anorexia Nervosa: A Case Report and Review of the Literature," *Psychosomatics* 61 (Spring 2020): 181–87.

74 *delusions about food and weight*: Joanna E. Steinglass, Jane L. Eisen, Evelyn Attia, Laurel Mayer, and Timothy B. Walsh, "Is Anorexia Nervosa a Delusional Disorder? An Assessment of Eating Beliefs in Anorexia Nervosa," *Journal of Psychiatric Practice* 13 (Spring 2007): 65–71.

76 *Doing origami also made me*: Mallary Tenore Tarpley, "How to Use Origami to Celebrate Small Victories and Love," *Los Angeles Times*,

February 14, 2023, https://www.latimes.com/lifestyle/story/2023-02-14/how-to-use-origami-to-celebrate-small-victories-and-self-love.

78 *comorbid mood and anxiety disorders*: Cheri A. Levinson, Stephanie C. Zerwas, Leigh C. Brosof, Laura M. Thornton, Michael Strober, Bernadette Pivarunas, et al., "Associations Between Dimensions of Anorexia Nervosa and Obsessive–Compulsive Disorder: An Examination of Personality and Psychological Factors in Patients with Anorexia Nervosa," *European Eating Disorders Review* 27 (March 2019): 161–72; Walter H. Kaye, Cynthia M. Bulik, Laura Thornton, Nicole Barbarich, and Kim Masters, "Comorbidity of Anxiety Disorders with Anorexia and Bulimia Nervosa," *American Journal of Psychiatry* 161 (Winter 2004): 2215–21.

78 *more likely to also develop OCD*: Laura Mandelli, Stefano Draghetti, Umerto Albert; Diana de Ronchi, and Anna-Rita Atti, "Rates of Comorbid Obsessive-Compulsive Disorder in Eating Disorders: A Meta-Analysis of the Literature," *Journal of Affective Disorders* 277 (Winter 2020): 927–39.

78 *the strong genetic overlap*: Cynthia Bulik, Martin Kennedy, and Tracey Wade, "ANGI—Anorexia Nervosa Genetics Initiative," *Twin Research and Human Genetics* 23 (Spring 2020): 135–36.

78 *between the two disorders*: Yilmaz Zeynep, Matthew Halvorsen, Julien Bryois, Dongmei Yu, Laura Thornton, Stephanie Zerwas, et al., "Examination of the Shared Genetic Basis of Anorexia Nervosa and Obsessive-Compulsive Disorder," *Molecular Psychiatry* 25 (Fall 2020): 2036–46.

78 *average seven- to ten-day stay nowadays*: "Your Child's Psychiatric Hospitalization: A Practical Guide for Caregivers," Boston Children's Hospital, https://www.childrenshospital.org/sites/default/files/media_migration/cbfe7135-8245-4e19-9ff0-6097b850a462.pdf: 6.

78 Prozac Nation, *published four years earlier*: Elizabeth Wurtzel, *Prozac Nation: Young and Depressed in America* (Riverhead Books, 1995).

78 *The medication had been on the market*: Timothy B. Walsh, Allan Kaplan, Evelyn Attia, Marion Olmsted, Michael Parides, Jacqueline C. Carter, et al., "Fluoxetine After Weight Restoration in Anorexia Nervosa: A Randomized Controlled Trial," *Journal of the American Medicine Association* 295 (Summer 2006): 2605–12.

79 *long-term use of some psychiatric drugs*: Elyse M. Cornett, Matthew Novitch, Alan David Kaye, Vijay Kata, and Adam M. Kaye, "Medication-Induced Tardive Dyskinesia: A Review and Update," *Ochsner Journal* 17 (Summer 2017): 162–74.

81 *get the care they needed*: Lynn Jolicoeur and Lisa Mullins, "'This Is a Crisis': Mom Whose Son Has Boarded 33 Days for Psych Bed Calls for State Action," *WBUR*, March 2, 2021, https://www.wbur.org/news/2021/02/26/mental-health-boarding-hospitals.

82 *sufferers who die from the disorder*: Nathalie Auger, Brian J. Potter, Ugochinyere Vivian Ukah, Nancy Low, Mimi Israël, Howard Steiger, et al., "Anorexia Nervosa and the Long-Term Risk of Mortality in Women," *World Psychiatry* 20 (Fall 2021): 448–49.

85 *According to one study*: Anna M. Bardone-Cone, Ellen E. Fitzsimmons-Craft, Megan B. Harney, Christine R. Maldonado, Melissa A. Lawson, Roma Smith, et al., "The Inter-Relationships Between Vegetarianism and Eating Disorders Among Females," *Journal of the Academy of Nutrition and Dietetics* 112 (2012): 1247–52.

86 *One of her recent studies*: Joanna E. Steinglass, Wenbo Fei, Karin Foerde, Caroline Touzeau, Julia Ruggiero, Caitlin Lloyd, et al., "Change in Food Choice During Acute Treatment and the Effect on Longer-Term Outcome in Patients with Anorexia Nervosa," *Psychological Medicine* 54 (Spring 2024): 1133–41.

86 *outside of binge-eating episodes*: Kayla Bjorlie, Kelsie T. Forbush, Danielle A. N. Chapa, Brianne N. Richson, Sarah N. Johnson, and Tera L. Fazzino, "Hyper-Palatable Food Consumption During Binge-eating Episodes: A Comparison of Intake During Binge

Eating and Restricting." *International Journal of Eating Disorders* 55 (Spring 2022): 688–96.

87 *a task designed to measure food choice*: Loren Gianini, Karin Foerde, Timothy B. Walsh, Melissa Riegel, Allegra Broft, and Joanna E. Steinglass, "Negative Affect, Dietary Restriction, and Food Choice in Bulimia Nervosa," *Eating Behaviors: An International Journal* 33 (Spring 2019): 49–54.

87 *This region is known to*: Karin Foerde, Joanna E. Steinglass, Daphna Shohamy, and Timothy B. Walsh, "Neural Mechanisms Supporting Maladaptive Food Choices in Anorexia Nervosa," *Nature Neuroscience,* vol. 18 (Winter 2015): 1571–73.

88 *48 percent increase in hospital admissions*: Daniel Devoe, Angela Han, Alida Anderson, Debra K. Katzman, Scott Patten, Andrea Soumbasis, et al., "The Impact of the COVID-19 Pandemic on Eating Disorders: A Systematic Review," *International Journal of Eating Disorders* 56 (Spring 2022): 5–25.

89 *"relations and friends [are] generally the worst attendants"*: Sir William Gull Withey, *Anorexia Nervosa (Apepsia Hysterica, Anorexia Hysterica)*, Clinical Society of London Transactions 7 (1873).

90 *Charcot went so far as to say*: Joan Jacobs Brumberg, *Fasting Girls: The Emergence of Anorexia Nervosa as a Modern Disease* (Harvard University Press, 1998), 142.

90 *used to treat other eating disorders*: James D. Lock, *Family-Based Treatment for Avoidant/Restrictive Food Intake Disorder* (Routledge, 2022).

90 *as well as young adults*: Eunice Y. Chen, Jessica A. Weissman, Thomas A. Zeffiro, Angelina Yiu, Kalina T. Eneva, Jean M. Arlt, et al., "Family-Based Therapy for Young Adults with Anorexia Nervosa Restores Weight," *International Journal of Eating Disorders* 49 (Summer 2016): 701–707.

91 *When a smoker is diagnosed with lung cancer*: Lauren Muhlheim, *When Your Teen Has an Eating Disorder: Practical Strategies to Help*

Your Teen Recover from Anorexia, Bulimia & Binge Eating (New Harbinger Publications, 2018), 32.

91 *FBT ideally happens at home*: James Lock, Daniel Le Grange, W. Stewart Agras, and Christopher Dare, *Treatment Manual for Anorexia Nervosa: A Family-Based Approach* (Guilford Press, 2001): 24.

92 *The researchers cited the "clinical conundrum"*: Jason M. Nagata, Andrea K. Garber, and Sara M. Buckelew. "Weight Restoration in Atypical Anorexia Nervosa: A Clinical Conundrum," *International Journal of Eating Disorders* 51 (Winter 2018): 1290–93.

93 *impedes recovery from eating disorders*: Christine C. Call, Laura D'Adamo, Meghan L. Butryn, and Eric Stice, "Examining Weight Suppression as a Predictor and Moderator of Intervention Outcomes in an Eating Disorder and Obesity Prevention Trial: A Replication and Extension Study," *Behaviour Research and Therapy* 141 (Summer 2021): 1-6; Meghan L. Butryn, Adrienne Juarascio, and Michael R. Lowe, "The Relation of Weight Suppression and BMI to Bulimic Symptoms," *International Journal of Eating Disorders* 44 (Winter 2011): 612–17.

93 *Knowing that weight suppression*: Mindy L. McEntee, Samantha R. Philip, and Sean M. Phelan, "Dismantling Weight Stigma in Eating Disorder Treatment: Next Steps for the Field," *Frontiers in Psychiatry* 14 (Spring 2023): 1–7.

Chapter Five: A Higher Level of Care

96 *Just a few miles away was McLean*: Susanna Kaysen, *Girl, Interrupted* (Vintage Books, 1994).

97 *The school eventually separated*: "Youth Villages and Germaine Lawrence Merge to Better Meet Needs of Massachusetts Children and Families," Youth Villages website, September 2012, https://youthvillages.wordpress.com/2012/09/12/youth-villages-and-germaine-lawrence-merge-to-better-meet-needs-of-massachusetts-children-and-families/.

97 Seventeen *magazine article*: Sabrina Solin, "A Home of Their Own," *Seventeen*, September 1996.

104 *self-harm, which is common among people with eating disorders*: Ryan H. Kirkpatrick, Edith Breton, Aleksandar Biorac, Douglas Munoz, and Linda Booji, "Non-Suicidal Self-Injury Among Individuals with an Eating Disorder: A Systematic Review and Prevalence Meta-analysis," *International Journal of Eating Disorders* 57 (Winter 2024): 223–48.

104 *Sometimes, the girls would run away*: Paul A. Sunseri, "Predicting Treatment Termination Due to Running Away Among Adolescents in Residential Care," *Residential Treatment for Children & Youth* 21 (Winter 2003): 43–60.

107 *For all the advances in treatment*: Cynthia M. Bulik, "From Awareness to Action: An Urgent Call to Address the Inadequacy of Treatment for Anorexia Nervosa," *American Journal of Psychiatry* 178 (Fall 2021): 786–88.

107 *comorbidities that often accompany anorexia*: Mae Lynn Reyes-Rodríguez, Ann Von Holle, Teresa Frances Ulman, Laura M. Thornton, Kelly L. Klump, Harry Brandt, et al., "Posttraumatic Stress Disorder in Anorexia Nervosa," *Psychosomatic Medicine* 73 (Summer 2011): 491–97.

108 *marketing materials can impact patient referrals*: Evelyn Attia, Kristy L. Blackwood, Angela S. Guarda, Marsha D. Marcus, and David J. Rothman, "Marketing Residential Treatment Programs for Eating Disorders: A Call for Transparency," *Psychiatric Services* 67 (Summer 2016): 664–66.

108 *swayed by treatment centers' incentives*: Erica Goode, "Centers to Treat Eating Disorders Are Growing, and Raising Concerns," *New York Times*, March 14, 2016, https://www.nytimes.com/2016/03/15/health/eating-disorders-anorexia-bulimia-treatment-centers.html.

108 *But studies of the pharmaceutical industry*: But studies of the pharmaceutical industry: M. King and P. S. Bearman, "Gifts and Influence: Conflict of Interest Policies and Prescribing of Psychotropic Medi-

cations in the United States," *Social Science & Medicine* 172 (Winter 2017): 153–62.

108 *now goes by the acronym REDC*: "What Is REDC?" Residential Eating Disorder Consortium website, https://redcconsortium.org/what-is-redc/.

109 *In response to criticism in the field*: "REDC Marketing Best Practices," Residential Eating Disorders Consortium website, updated June 2021, https://redcconsortium.org/wp-content/uploads/2021/06/REDC-Marketing-Best-Practices-FINAL-06.2021.pdf.

109 *The guidelines encourage members to*: "REDC Code of Ethics," Residential Eating Disorders Consortium website, updated May 2021, https://redcconsortium.org/wp-content/uploads/2021/06/REDC-Code-of-Ethics-FINAL-05.28.21.pdf.

110 *treatment could cost upwards of $60,000*: Christie Calucchia, "The Alarming Cost of Eating Disorder Treatment in America," *Glamour*, March 7, 2023, https://www.glamour.com/story/getting-eating-disorder-treatment-in-america.

110 *"maximum feasible benefit"*: Nora Todd, "Special Education: Understanding Federal and State Statutory Requirements," Massachusetts Teacher Association website, 2008, https://campussuite-storage.s3.amazonaws.com/prod/1213978/583ade96-581b-11e7-99ef-124f7febbf4a/1627673/809e4c6c-9441-11e7-8d7b-0a840aaa54e6/file/Sped_primer.pdf.

110 *Passed in 1972*: "A History of the Individuals with Disabilities Education Act," Individuals with Disabilities Education Act, https://sites.ed.gov/idea/IDEA-History#:~:text=On%20November%2029%2C%201975%2C%20President,and%20locality%20across%20the%20country.

111 *the then state commissioner told a local news outlet*: Michelle Galley, "Mass. Lawmakers Vote to Change Special Ed. Standard," *Education Week*, August 2, 2000, https://www.edweek.org/teaching-learning/mass-lawmakers-vote-to-change-special-ed-standard/2000/08.

111 *legal action against school districts*: Kristen Taketa, "Families Endure Costly Legal Fights Trying to Get the Right Special Education Services," *San Diego Union-Tribune*, October 6, 2019, https://www.latimes.com/california/story/2019-10-06/legal-fights-families-special-education-services.

112 *41 percent of Americans with public insurance*: Robin A. Cohen and Michael E. Martinez, "Health Insurance Coverage: Early Release of Estimates from the National Health Interview Survey, January–June 2023," National Center for Health Statistics website, https://www.cdc.gov/nchs/data/nhis/earlyrelease/insur202312.pdf.

112 *According to a 2023 study*: Ruby Moreno, Sara M. Buckelew, Erin C. Accurso, and Marissa Raymond-Flesch, "Disparities in Access to Eating Disorders Treatment for Publicly Insured Youth and Youth of Color: A Retrospective Cohort Study," *Journal of Eating Disorders* 11 (Winter 2023): 10.

114 *Colorado passed a new law*: See First Regular Session, Seventy-Fourth General Assembly, State of Colorado, Colorado General Assembly, 2023, State of Colorado government website, https://leg.colorado.gov/sites/default/files/documents/2023A/bills/2023a_176_01.pdf.

115 *Dr. Lester, who wrote the book*: Rebecca J. Lester, *Famished: Eating Disorders and Failed Care in America* (University of California Press, 2019).

115 *the limits of insurance coverage*: Margaret Sala, Ani Keshishian, Sarah Song, Rivka Moskowitz, Cynthia M. Bulik, Corey R. Roos, et al., "Predictors of Relapse in Eating Disorders: A Meta-Analysis," *Journal of Psychiatric Research* 158 (Winter 2023): 281–99.

115 *needed to be readmitted at least once*: Enrica Marzola, Paola Longo, Federica Sardella, Nadia Delsedime, and Giovanni Abbate-Daga, "Rehospitalization and 'Revolving Door' in Anorexia Nervosa: Are There Any Predictors of Time to Readmission?" *Frontiers in Psychiatry* 12 (Summer 2012): 694, 223.

Chapter Six: The Possibility of Recovery

129 *CBT is one of the most widely used therapies*: Alexandra F. Muratore and Evelyn Attia, "Current Therapeutic Approaches to Anorexia Nervosa: State of the Art," *Clinical Therapeutics* 43 (Winter 2021): 85–94.

129 *CBT-E was modified in the early 2000s*: Christopher G. Fairburn, Zafra Cooper, and Roz Shafran, "Cognitive Behaviour Therapy for Eating Disorders: A 'Transdiagnostic' Theory and Treatment," *Behaviour Research and Therapy* 41 (Spring 2003): 509–28.

130 *Patients are encouraged to monitor thoughts*: Rebecca Murphy, Suzanne Straebler, Zafra Cooper, and Christopher Fairburn, "Cognitive Behavioral Therapy for Eating Disorders," *Psychiatric Clinics of North America* 33 (Fall 2010): 611–27.

131 *In their book:* Carolyn Costin and Gwen Grabb, *8 Keys to Recovery from an Eating Disorder: Effective Strategies from Therapeutic Strategies and Personal Experience* (W. W. Norton, 2011), 72.

132 "*Let your eating-disorder self know*": Costin and Grabb, *8 Keys to Recovery from an Eating Disorder*, 41.

132 "*Let it know you will not*": Costin and Grabb, *8 Keys to Recovery from an Eating Disorder*, 61.

134 *we inherit a vulnerability to them*: Cynthia M. Bulik, Lauren Blake, and Jehannine Austin, "Genetics of Eating Disorders: What the Clinician Needs to Know," *Psychiatric Clinics of North America* 42 (Spring 2019): 59–73.

134 *But a growing body of research shows*: Johanna Louise Keeler, Carol Kan, Janet Treasure, and Hubertus Himmerich, "Novel Treatments for Anorexia Nervosa: Insights from Neuroplasticity Research," *European Eating Disorders Review* 4 (Fall 2023): 1–16.

134 *to achieve and sustain recovery*: Walter H. Kaye, Christina E. Wierenga, Stephanie Knatz, June Liang, Kerri Boutelle, Laura Hill, et al., "Temperament-Based Treatment for Anorexia Nervosa," *European Eating Disorders Review* 23 (Winter 2015): 12–18.

135 *gaining attention from eating-disorder specialists*: Madeline Holcombe, "Orthorexia: An Eating Disorder That Few People Understand and Many Accidentally Applaud," CNN, March 14, 2024, https://www.cnn.com/2024/03/c1/health/orthorexia-eating-disorder-explained-wellness/index.html.

136 *a cultural manifestation of anorexia nervosa*: Anushua Bhattacharya, Marita Cooper, Carrie McAdams, Rebecka Peebles, and Alix C. Timko, "Cultural Shifts in the Symptoms of Anorexia Nervosa: The Case of Orthorexia Nervosa," *Appetite* 170 (Spring 2022): 10, 5869.

137 *In a study on perfectionism group treatment*: Cheri Levinson, Leigh Brosof, Irina Vanzhula, Laura Bumberry, Stephanie Zerwas, and Cynthia M. Bulik, "Perfectionism Group Treatment for Eating Disorders in an Inpatient, Partial Hospitalization, and Outpatient Setting," *European Eating Disorders Review*, vol. 25 (Fall 2017): 579–85.

138 *traits to be expressed destructively*: Laura Hill, Stephanie Peck Knatz, and Christina Wierenga, *Temperament Based Therapy with Support for Anorexia Nervosa: A Novel Treatment* (Cambridge University Press, 2022): 42–49.

139 *TBT-S patients work closely with "supports"*: Kristin Stedal, Ingrid Funderud, Christina Wierenga, Stephanie Knatz-Peck, and Laura Hill, "Acceptability, Feasibility and Short-term Outcomes of Temperament Based Therapy with Support (TBT-S): A Novel 5-day Treatment for Eating Disorders," *Journal of Eating Disorders* 11 (Fall 2023): 1–156.

139 *the repeated practice of healthy behaviors*: Hill et al., *Temperament Based Therapy with Support for Anorexia Nervosa*, 17.

Chapter Seven: Slips

147 *perfectionism that began with my writing*: Randy O. Frost and Patricia A. Marten, "Perfectionism and Evaluative Threat," *Cognitive Therapy and Research* 14 (Winter 1990): 559–72.

153 *Dr. Carrie McAdams has observed*: Carrie J. McAdams, Haekyung Jeon-Slaughter, Terry Lohrenz, P. Read Montague, and Daniel C. Krawczyk, "Neural Differences in Self-Perception During Illness and After Weight-Recovery in Anorexia Nervosa," *Social Cognitive and Affective Neuroscience* 11 (Winter 2016): 1823–31.

153 *healthy controls who engage in positive self-talk*: Carlisdania J. Mendoza, Jayme M. Palka, Sarah E. Pelfrey, Bethany J. Hunt, Daniel C. Krawczyk, and Carrie J. McAdams, "Neural Processes Related to Negative Self-Concept in Adult and Adolescent Anorexia Nervosa," *European Eating Disorders Review* 30 (Winter 2022): 23–35.

153 *use those skills to reduce self-blame*: Whitney Smith Hagan, Susan Mericle, Bethany J. Hunt, Jessica A. Harper, Jayme M. Palka, Sarah Pelfrey, et al., "Qualitative Patient Experiences from the Self-Blame and Perspective-Taking Intervention for Eating Disorders," *Journal of Eating Disorders* 9 (Fall 2021): 1–127.

153 *the last symptoms to wane*: Elena Tomba, Lucia Tecuta, Elisabetta Crocetti, Fabio Squarcio, and Giuliano Tomei, "Residual Eating Disorder Symptoms and Clinical Features in Remitted and Recovered Eating Disorder Patients: A Systematic Review with Meta-Analysis," *International Journal of Eating Disorders* 52 (Summer 2019): 759–76.

153 *are known to contribute to relapse*: Pamela Keel, David J. Dorer, Debra L. Franko, Safia C. Jackson, and David B. Herzog, "Post-remission Predictors of Relapse in Women with Eating Disorders," *American Journal of Psychiatry* 162 (December 2005): 2263–68.

155 *demonizes weight gain and people in larger bodies*: Kate Manne, *Unshrinking: How to Face Fatphobia* (Crown, 2024): 3–8.

156 *implicit bias test for weight*: For information on this, see Project Implicit, Harvard Implicit Bias Tests, https://implicit.harvard.edu/implicit/selectatest.html.

156 *to gauge how she's doing*: Tessa E. S. Charlesworth and Mahzarin R. Banaji, "Patterns of Implicit and Explicit Attitudes: I. Long-Term

Change and Stability From 2007 to 2016," *Psychological Science* 30 (Winter 2019): 174–92.

157 *helps decrease these fears and related symptoms*: Cheri A. Levinson, Caroline Christian, Shruti Shankar Ram, Irina Vanzhula, Leigh C. Brosof, Lisa P. Michelson, et al., "Eating Disorder Symptoms and Core Eating Disorder Fears Decrease During Online Imaginal Exposure Therapy for Eating Disorders," *Journal of Affective Disorders* 276 (Winter 2020): 585–91.

157 *body dissatisfaction among those with eating disorders*: Trevor C. Griffen, Eva Naumann, and Tom Hildebrandt, "Mirror Exposure Therapy for Body Image Disturbances and Eating Disorders: A Review," *Clinical Psychology Review* 65 (Winter 2018): 163–74.

157 *Dr. Deliberto, co-author of the book*: Tara L. Deliberto and Dina Hirsch, *Treating Eating Disorders in Adolescents: Evidence-Based Interventions for Anorexia, Bulimia, and Binge Eating* (Context Press, 2019).

157 *as many definitions of "full recovery"*: Lydia Maurel, Molly MacKean, and Lacey J. Hubert, "Factors Predicting Long-Term Weight Maintenance in Anorexia Nervosa: A Systematic Review," *Eating and Weight Disorders* 29 (Spring 2024): 16–24.

158 *57 to 94 percent for anorexia*: Jennifer Couturier and James Lock, "What Is Recovery in Adolescent Anorexia Nervosa?" *International Journal of Eating Disorders* 39 (Winter 2006): 550–55.

158 *13 to 74 percent for bulimia*: Sarah E. Williams, Thomas K. O. Watts, and Tracey D. Wade, "A Review of the Definitions of Outcome Used in Treatment of Bulimia Nervosa," *Clinical Psychology Review* 32 (Summer 2012): 292–300.

158 *And the duration of illness studied*: Kamryn T. Eddy, Nassim Tabri, Jennifer J. Thomas, Helen B. Murray, Aparna Keshaviah, Elizabeth Hastings, et al., "Recovery from Anorexia Nervosa and Bulimia Nervosa at 22-Year Follow-Up," *Journal of Clinical Psychiatry* 78 (Winter 2017): 184–89.

158 *a book chapter on the topic*: Margo Maine, Beth Hartman McGilley, and Douglas W. Bunnel, "Treatment of Eating Disorders: Bridging the Research-Practice Gap," *Eating Disorders*, vol. 19 (2011): 210.

159 *"elevated risk of recurrence throughout life"*: Cynthia M. Bulik, "From Awareness to Action: An Urgent Call to Address the Inadequacy of Treatment for Anorexia Nervosa," *American Journal of Psychiatry* 178 (Fall 2021): 786.

159 *A study of nearly 400 caregivers*: Erin C. Accurso, Leslie Sim, Lauren Muhlheim, and Jocelyn Lebow, "Parents Know Best: Caregiver Perspectives on Eating Disorder Recovery," *International Journal of Eating Disorders* 53 (Summer 2020): 1252–60.

160 *clinicians define recovery*: Tracy K. Richmond, Alice G. Woolverton, Kathy Mammel, Rollyn M. Ornstein, Allegra Spalding, Elizabeth R. Woods, et al., "How Do You Define Recovery? A Qualitative Study of Patients with Eating Disorders, Their Parents, and Clinicians," *International Journal of Eating Disorders* 53 (Summer 2020): 1209–18.

160 *"Adopting a consensus definition of recovery"*: Anna M. Bardone-Cone, Megan B. Harney, Christine R. Maldonado, Melissa A. Lawson, D. Paul Robinson, Roma Smith, et al., "Defining Recovery from an Eating Disorder: Conceptualization, Validation, and Examination of Psychosocial Functioning and Psychiatric Comorbidity," *Behaviour Research and Therapy* 48 (Spring 2010): 194.

160 *the Eating Disorder Examination Questionnaire*: J. M. Mond, P. J. Hay, B. Rodgers, C. Owen, "Eating Disorder Examination Questionnaire (EDE-Q): Norms for Young Adult Women," *Behaviour Research and Therapy* 44 (Winter 2006): 53–62.

161 *In a comprehensive review*: Anna M. Bardone-Cone, Stephen A. Wonderlich, Randy O. Frost, Cynthia M. Bulik, James E. Mitchell, Saritha Uppala, et al., "Perfectionism and Eating Disorders: Current Status and Future Directions," *Clinical Psychology Review* 27 (Spring 2007): 384–405.

161 *She predictably found*: Anna M. Bardone-Cone, Jennifer P. White, Katherine A. Thompson, Nancy Zucker, Hunna J. Watson, and Cynthia M. Bulik, "Examination of Perfectionism and Self-Concept Constructs across Stages of Eating Disorder Recovery in Men: An Exploratory Study," *Eating Behaviors: An International Journal* 46 (Summer 2022): 101, 658.

Chapter Eight: Relapse

163 *the Freshman Fifteen is a myth*: Jay L. Zagorsky and Patricia K. Smith, "The Freshman 15: A Critical Time for Obesity Intervention or Media Myth?" *Social Science Quarterly*, vol. 92 (Winter 2011): 1389–407.

163 *The average weight gain*: Nicole L. Mihalopoulos, Peggy Auinger, and Jonathan D. Klein, "The Freshman 15: Is It Real?" *Journal of American College Health* 56 (Spring 2008): 531–33.

163 *the median age of onset for eating disorders*: Anne C. Grammer AC, Ellen E. Fitzsimmons-Craft, Olivia Laing, Bianco De Pietro, and Denise E. Wilfley, "Eating Disorders on College Campuses in the United States: Current Insight on Screening, Prevention, and Treatment," *Current Psychopharmacology* 9 (2020): 91–102.

166 *Saint Benedict had advised*: Benedict of Nursia, *The Rule of St. Benedict*, trans. Anthony C. Meisel and M. L. del Mastro (Image Books, 1975).

167 *"the vice of gluttony"*: Robert B. Kruschwitz, *Virtues and Their Vices* (Oxford University Press, 2014): 136–155.

167 *170 female religious figures*: Rudolph M. Bell, *Holy Anorexia* (University of Chicago Press, 1985): x.

167 *Among them was Saint Veronica*: Joan Jacobs Brumberg, *Fasting Girls: The Emergence of Anorexia Nervosa as a Modern Disease* (Harvard University Press, 1998), 43.

167 *"There is nothing we can desire"*: Catherine of Siena, *Catherine*

of Sienna: The Dialogue, trans. Suzanne Noffke (Paulist Press, 1980).

167 *Catherine died when she was thirty-three*: J. C. Harris, "Anorexia Nervosa and Anorexia Mirabilis: Miss K. R—and St. Catherine of Siena," *Journal of the American Medical Association* 71 (Winter 2014): 1212–13.

167 *died from starvation at age thirty-four*: Joan Jacobs Brumberg, *Fasting Girls: The Emergence of Anorexia Nervosa as a Modern Disease* (Harvard University Press, 1998), 43.

170 *much less that the risk was high*: Margaret Sala, Ani Keshishian, Sarah Song, Rivka Moskowitz, Cynthia M. Bulik, Corey R. Roos, et al., "Predictors of Relapse in Eating Disorders: A Meta-Analysis," *Journal of Psychiatric Research* 158 (Winter 2023): 281–99.

170 *40 to 50 percent for anorexia nervosa*: L. M. McCormick, P. K. Keel, M. C. Brumm, D. B. Watson, V. L. Forman-Hoffman, and W. A. Bowers, "A Pilot Study of Personality Pathology in Patients with Anorexia Nervosa: Modifiable Factors Related to Outcome After Hospitalization," Eating and Weight Disorders, *Studies on Anorexia, Bulimia and Obesity* 14 (Summer 2009): 113–20.

170 *41 percent for OSFED*: Traci McFarlane, Marion P. Olmsted, and Kathryn Trottier, "Timing and Prediction of Relapse in a Transdiagnostic Eating Disorder Sample," *International Journal of Eating Disorders* 41 (Winter 2008): 587–93.

170 *around 30 percent for bulimia*: Marion P. Omsted, Danielle E. MacDonald, Traci McFarlane, Kathryn Trottier, and Patricia Colton, "Predictors of Rapid Relapse in Bulimia Nervosa," *International Journal of Eating Disorders* 48 (Spring 2015): 337–40.

170 *and binge-eating disorder*: Giovanni Castellini, Edoardo Mannucci, Carolina Lo Sauro, Laura Benni, Lisa Lazzeretti, Claudia Ravaldi, et al., "Different Moderators of Cognitive-Behavioral Therapy on Subjective and Objective Binge Eating in Bulimia Nervosa and Binge Eating Disorder: A Three-Year Follow-Up Study," *Psychotherapy*

and Psychosomatics 81 (Winter 2012): 11–20; Debra L. Safer, Teresa J. Lively, Christy F. Telch, and Stewart W. Agras, "Predictors of Relapse Following Successful Dialectical Behavior Therapy for Binge Eating Disorder," *International Journal of Eating Disorders* 32 (Fall 2002): 155–63.

170 *The greatest risk for relapse*: Timothy B. Walsh, Tianchen Xu, Yuanjia Wang, Evelyn Attia, and Allan S. Kaplan, "Time Course of Relapse Following Acute Treatment for Anorexia Nervosa," *American Journal of Psychiatry* 178 (Fall 2021): 848–53.

171 *Slips are bound to happen in recovery*: Britt Berg, "Eating Disorder Relapse Is Common: Here's Why and What to Do About It," Eating Recovery Center website, blog, May 22, 2023: https://www.eatingrecoverycenter.com/blog/eating-disorder-relapse-common.

172 "*When the pendulum swings*": Christy Harrison, "The Life Thief: How Diet Culture Steals Your Time, Energy, and Your Health—and How You Can Take Them Back," ChristyHarrison.com, blog, December 6, 2017, https://christyharrison.com/blog/the-life-thief.

172 *Research shows that*: Savannah C. Hooper, Lisa Kilpela, Francesca Gomez, Keesha M. Middlemass, and Carolyn Black Becker, "Eating Disorder Pathology in a Sample of Midlife and Older Adults Experiencing Food Insecurity," *Eating Behaviors: An International Journal* 49 (Spring 2023): 101, 742.

172 *food insecurity contributes to weight stigma*: Carolyn Black Becker, Keesha M. Middlemass, Francesca Gomez, and Andrea Abrego-Martinez, "Eating Disorder Pathology Among Individuals Living with Food Insecurity: A Replication Study." *Clinical Psychological Science* 7 (Fall 2019): 1144–158; Carolyn Black Becker, Keesha Middlemass, Brigitte Taylor, Clara Johnson, and Francesca Gomez, "Food Insecurity and Eating Disorder Pathology," *International Journal of Eating Disorders*: 1031–40.

172 *50 percent of people with anorexia*: Franziska Plessow and Kamryn T.

Eddy, "Diagnostic Crossover," in *Encyclopedia of Feeding and Eating Disorders*, ed. Tracey Wade (Springer, 2017), 203–206.

172 *It's a phenomenon specific to eating disorders*: Kamryn T. Eddy, David Dorer, Debra L. Franko, Kavita Tahilani, Heather Thompson-Brenner, and David B. Herzog, "Diagnostic Crossover in Anorexia Nervosa and Bulimia Nervosa: Implications for DSM-V," *American Journal of Psychiatry* 165 (Winter 2008): 245–50.

174 *a binge-eating episode is defined by*: American Psychiatric Association, *Diagnostic and Statistical Manual of Mental Disorders: DSM-5-TR*, 5th ed., text rev. (American Psychiatric Association, 2022).

174 *One man even went to the hospital*: Leah M. Kalm and Richard D. Semba, "They Starved So That Others Be Better Fed: Remembering Ancel Keys and the Minnesota Experiment," *Journal of Nutrition* 135 (Summer 2005): 1347–52.

174 *"failing to live up to high standards and expectations"*: Todd F. Heatherton and Roy F Baumeister, "Binge Eating as Escape from Self-Awareness," *Psychological Bulletin* 110 (Summer 1991): 86–108.

175 *stuck in a binge-and-purge cycle*: Margo Maine, Beth Hartman McGilley, and Douglas W. Bunnell, "Treatment of Eating Disorders: Bridging the Research-Practice Gap," *Eating Disorders* 19 (2011): 286–88.

175 *neurobiological factors at play*: Walter H. Kaye, Christina Wierenga, Ursula F. Bailer, Alan N. Simmons, and Amanda Bischoff-Grethe, "Nothing Tastes as Good as Skinny Feels: The Neurobiology of Anorexia Nervosa," *Trends in Neurosciences* 36 (Winter 2013): 110–20.

175 *Laura Berner, PhD, is working on new research*: Laura A. Berner, Katia M. Harlé, Alan N. Simmons, Angela Yu, Martin P. Paulus, Amanda Bischoff-Grethe, et al., "State-Specific Alterations in the Neural Computations Underlying Inhibitory Control in Women Remitted from Bulimia Nervosa," *Nature's Molecular Psychiatry* 28 (Spring 2023): 3055–62.

175 *One study found that people with anorexia*: Lauren R. Godier and Rebecca J. Park, "Does Compulsive Behavior in Anorexia Nervosa Resemble an Addiction? A Qualitative Investigation," *Frontiers in Psychology* 6 (Fall 2015): 1608.

175 *hesitate to classify anorexia as an* actual *addiction*: Nicole C. Barbarich-Marsteller, Richard W. Foltin, and Timothy B. Walsh, "Does Anorexia Nervosa Resemble an Addiction?" *Current Drug Abuse Reviews* 4 (Fall 2011): 197–200.

175 *Some top researchers have urged*: Kristen Rogers, "Why a food addiction many Americans say they struggle with is one experts can't agree on," CNN, June 15, 2023, https://www.cnn.com/2023/06/15/health/food-addiction-help-symptoms-wellness/index.html.

175 *A recent University of Michigan poll*: "Addiction to Highly Processed Foods Among Older Adults," University of Michigan Institute for Healthcare Policy and Innovation website, January/February 2023, https://deepblue.lib.umich.edu/bitstream/handle/2027.42/175578/0298_NPHA-Addictive-Eating-report-FINAL-doi.pdf?sequence=4&isAllowed=y.

176 *And research suggests that ultra-processed foods*: Ashley N. Gearhardt, Nassib B. Bueno, Alexandra G. DiFeliceantonio, Christina A. Roberto, Susana Jiménez-Murcia, and Fernando Fernandez-Aranda, "Social, Clinical, and Policy Implications of Ultra-Processed Food Addiction," *BMJ* 383 (Fall 2023): e07535.

176 *are by no means an addiction*: Graham Finlayson, "Food Addiction and Obesity: Unnecessary Medicalization of Hedonic Overeating," *Nature Reviews, Endocrinology* 18 (Summer 2017): 493–98; Margaret L. Westwater, Paul C. Fletcher, and Hisham Ziauddeen. "Sugar Addiction: The State of the Science," *European Journal of Nutrition* 55 (Winter 2016): 55–69.

176 *They point to research showing*: Finlayson, "Food Addiction and Obesity."

176 *"another example of modern-day pseudoscience"*: Jennifer Gaudiani,

Sick Enough: A Guide to the Medical Complications of Eating Disorders (Routledge, 2018), 228.

176 *But recent data*: Megan E. Mikhail, "Affect Dysregulation in Context: Implications and Future Directions of Experience Sampling Research on Affect Regulation Models of Loss of Control Eating," *Frontiers in Psychiatry* 12 (Fall 2021): 1–17.

176 *binge eating actually makes them feel worse*: Alissa A. Haedt-Matt and Pamela K. Keel, "Revisiting the Affect Regulation Model of Binge Eating: A Meta-Analysis of Studies Using Ecological Momentary Assessment," *Psychological Bulletin* 137 (Summer 2011): 660–81.

177 *both substance-use disorders and eating disorders*: N. Noha Eskander, Sumita Chakrapani, and Mohammad R. Ghani, "The Risk of Substance Use Among Adolescents and Adults with Eating Disorders," *Cureus* 12 (Fall 2020): 10, 309.

177 *A major study conducted*: Joseph A. Califano, "Food for Thought: Substance Abuse and Eating Disorders," National Center on Addiction and Drug Abuse (CASA), Columbia University Conference, U.S. Department of Justice, December 2003, https://www.ojp.gov/ncjrs/virtual-library/abstracts/food-thought-substance-abuse-and-eating-disorders.

177 *"Trying to control my drinking"*: Leslie Jamison, *The Recovering: Intoxication and its Aftermath* (Hachette, 2019), 256–57.

178 *a typical precursor to osteoporosis*: Nurgun Kandemir, Kendra Becker, Meghan Slattery, Shreya Tulsiani, Vibha Singhal, Jennifer J. Thomas, et al., "Impact of Low-Weight Severity and Menstrual Status on Bone in Adolescent Girls with Anorexia Nervosa," *International Journal of Eating Disorders* 50 (Spring 2017): 359–69.

179 *In reading the 1988 book*: Dana Mira and Marilyn Lawrence, *Women's Secret Disorder: A New Understanding of Bulimia* (Grafton Books, 1988).

179 *one book did lead her to stop drinking*: Ann Dowsett Johnson, *Drink: The Intimate Relationship Between Women and Alcohol* (Harper Wave, 2014), 267.

180 *Researchers have found that people with eating disorders*: Molly McDonough, "Making Sense of Interoception," *Harvard Medicine*, Spring 2024, https://magazine.hms.harvard.edu/articles/making-sense-interoception.

180 *These alterations may help explain*: L. A. Berner, A. N. Simmons, C. E. Wierenga, A. Bischoff-Grethe, M. P. Paulus, U. F. Bailer, et al., "Altered Interoceptive Activation Before, During, and After Aversive Breathing Load in Women Remitted from Anorexia Nervosa," *Psychological Medicine* 48 (Winter 2018): 142–54; Sahib S. Khalsa, Laura A. Berner, and Lisa M. Anderson, "Gastrointestinal Interoception in Eating Disorders: Charting a New Path," *Current Psychiatry Reports* 24 (Winter 2022): 47–60.

181 *the case for many people with eating disorders*: Deborah Mitchison, Christopher Basten, Scott Griffiths, and Stuart B. Murray, "Beneath the Tip of the Iceberg: Why So Many People with Eating Disorders Are Not Referred for Treatment," *Australian Family Physician* 46 (Summer 2017): 539–40.

Chapter Nine: The Middle Place

187 *books, newspapers, magazines, television, and social media*: Pilar Aparicio-Martinez, Alberto-Jesus Perea-Moreno, María Pilar Martinez-Jimenez, María Dolores Redel-Macías, Claudia Pagliari, and Manuel Vaquero-Abellan, "Social Media, Thin-Ideal, Body Dissatisfaction and Disordered Eating Attitudes: An Exploratory Analysis," *International Journal of Environmental Research and Public Health* 16 (Fall 2019): 4177; Alexandra Dane and Komal Bhatia, "The Social Media Diet: A Scoping Review to Investigate the Association between Social Media, Body Image and Eating Disorders Amongst Young People," *PLOS Global Public Health* 3 (Spring 2023): e0001091.

188 *the rise of "thinspiration" content online*: Jane C. Silva Ramirez,

"Pro-Anorexia Website Harm," *Journal of Critical Issues in Educational Practice*, vol. 9 (Spring 2019): 1–6.

188 *YouTube glamorized these illnesses*: Debbie Ging and Sarah Garvey, "'Written in These Scars Are the Stories I Can't Explain': A Content Analysis of Pro-Ana and Thinspiration Image Sharing on Instagram," *New Media & Society* 20 (Spring 2018): 1181–1200.

188 *an untold—or at best half-told—story*: Mallary Tenore Tarpley, "What the News Media Get Wrong in Coverage of Eating Disorders and How They Can Improve," Poynter Institute website, January 31, 2023:https://www.poynter.org/ethics-trust/2023/responsible-media-coverage-eating-disorders/.

189 *"crafting a redemptive narrative"*: Rachel Aviv, "Local Story," *The New Yorker*, March 4, 2013, https://www.newyorker.com/magazine/2013/03/04/local-story.

189 *in those consuming the stories*: "The Burden of Stress in America," NPR/Robert Wood Johnson Foundation/Harvard School of Public Health website, July 7, 2014, https://media.npr.org/documents/2014/july/npr_rwfj_harvard_stress_poll.pdf.

189 *in those telling them*: River J. Smith, Susan Drevo, and Elana Newman, "Covering Traumatic News Stories: Factors Associated with Post-Traumatic Stress Disorder among Journalists," *Stress and Health* 34 (Spring 2018): 218–26.

191 *outlines three types of illness narratives*: Arthur W. Frank, *The Wounded Storyteller: Body, Illness, and Ethics* (University of Chicago Press, 2013), 75–136.

192 *"Its plot imagines life"*: Frank, *The Wounded Storyteller*, 102.

192 *"the hero's journey"*: Joseph Campbell, Stuart L. Brown, et al., *The Hero's Journey: Joseph Campbell on His Life and Work* (Collected Works of Joseph Campbell), 3rd ed. (New World Library, 2003).

192 *"Quest stories tell of searching"*: Frank, *The Wounded Storyteller*, 53.

193 *"multiple selves available to themselves"*: Frank, *The Wounded Storyteller*, 66.

193 *The late journalist*: Stewart Alsop, *Stay of Execution: A Sort of Memoir* (Lippincott, 1973), 18.

193 *"If I didn't define myself for myself"*: "Audre Lorde, 'Learning from the 60s,'" BlackPast website, August 12, 2012, https://www.blackpast.org/african-american-history/1982-audre-lorde-learning-60s/.

194 *"Everyone who is born holds dual citizenship"*: Sontag, *Illness as Metaphor*, 3.

194 *cross that space in between*: Suleika Jaouad, *Between Two Kingdoms: A Memoir of a Life Interrupted* (Random House, 2022), 213.

194 *cross that space in between*: Meghan O'Rourke, *The Invisible Kingdom: Reimagining Chronic Illness* (Riverhead Books, 2022), 8-9.

194 *"long-term course" of the disorder*: Walter Vandereycken and Rolf Meermann, *Anorexia Nervosa: A Clinician's Guide to Treatment* (Walter de Gruyter GmbH, 1984).

195 *The treatment community has yet to reach*: Phillipa Hay and Stephen Touyz, "Classification Challenges in the Field of Eating Disorders: Can Severe and Enduring Anorexia Nervosa Be Better Defined?" *Journal of Eating Disorders* 6 (Winter 2018): 41.

195 *"How, precisely, should this stage of illness be defined?"*: Stephen W. Touyz et al., eds., *Managing Severe and Enduring Anorexia Nervosa: A Clinician's Guide* (Routledge, 2016): xviii.

195 *One team of researchers*: Stephen A. Wonderlich, Cynthia M. Bulik, Ulrike Schmidt, Howard Steiger, Hans W. Hoek, "Severe and Enduring Anorexia Nervosa: Update and Observations about the Current Clinical Reality," *The International Journal of Eating Disorders*, 53 (Summer 2020): 1303–12.

195 *In one of the more interesting studies*: Kamryn T. Eddy, Nassim Tabri, Jennifer J. Thomas, Helen B. Murray, Aparna Keshaviah, Elizabeth Hastings, et al., "Recovery from Anorexia Nervosa and Bulimia Nervosa at 22-Year Follow-Up," *Journal of Clinical Psychiatry* 78 (Winter 2017): 184–89.

196 *adolescents' development of self*: Jennifer H. Pfeifer and Elliot T.

Berkman, "The Development of Self and Identity in Adolescence: Neural Evidence and Implications for a Value-Based Choice Perspective on Motivated Behavior," *Child Development Perspectives* 12 (Fall 2018): 158–64.

196 *connections are formed in the brain*: Carrie J. McAdams and Daniel C. Krawczyk, "Who Am I? How Do I Look? Neural Differences in Self-Identity in Anorexia Nervosa," *Social Cognitive and Affective Neuroscience* 9 (Winter 2014): 12–21.

196 *the brain's white matter*: Daniel Geisler, Joseph A. King, Klaas Bahnsen, Fabio Bernardoni, Arne Doose, Dirk K. Müller, et al., "Altered White Matter Connectivity in Young Acutely Underweight Patients with Anorexia Nervosa," *Journal of the American Academy of Child and Adolescent Psychiatry* 61, no. 2 (2022): 331–40.

197 *reminds me of the book*: Rachel Aviv, *Strangers to Ourselves: Unsettled Minds and the Stories That Make Us* (Farrar, Straus and Giroux, 2022).

197 *"There are stories that save us"*: Aviv, *Strangers to Ourselves*, 22, 24.

197 *anorexia can be divided into two phases*: Joan Jacobs Brumberg, *Fasting Girls: The Emergence of Anorexia Nervosa as a Modern Disease* (Harvard University Press, 1998), 41.

197 *"find redemptive meanings in suffering"*: Dan P. McAdams and Kate C. McLean. "Narrative Identity," *Current Directions in Psychological Science: A Journal of the American Psychological Society* 22 (Summer 2013): 233–38.

198 *where we place the chapter breaks*: Jonathan Adler, Jennifer Lodi-Smith, Frederick L. Philippe, and Iliane Houle, "The Incremental Validity of Narrative Identity in Predicting Well-Being: A Review of the Field and Recommendations for the Future," Personality and Social Psychology Review 20 (Spring 2016): 142-175.

198 *research about the restorative narrative genre*: Kaitlin Fitzgerald, Elaine Paravati, Melanie C. Green, Melissa M. Moore, and Jeffrey L. Qian, "Restorative Narratives for Health Promotion," *Health Communication* 35 (Winter 2020): 356–63.

198 *"In many ways, it's just beginning"*: Kaitlin Fitzgerald, Melanie C. Green, and Elaine Paravati, "Restorative Narratives," *Journal of Public Interest Communications* 4 (Winter 2020): 51–74.

198 *"a very wordless time"*: Marya Hornbacher, *Wasted: A Memoir of Anorexia and Bulimia* (HarperFlamingo, 1998), 279.

201 *If I had to pick a poem*: "Risk," by Anaïs Nin, Goodreads, https://www.goodreads.com/quotes/876911-and-the-day-came-when-the-risk-to-remain-tight.

203 *"When you are recovered"*: Carolyn Costin and Gwen Grabb, *8 Keys to Recovery from an Eating Disorder: Effective Strategies from Therapeutic Strategies and Personal Experience* (W. W. Norton, 2011), 16–17.

205 *the famous Viktor Frankl book title*: Viktor Emil Frankl, *Yes to Life: In Spite of Everything* (Beacon Press, 2021).

Chapter Ten: Love, Sex, and Marriage in the Middle Place

213 *"To lose balance sometimes"*: Elizabeth Gilbert, *Eat, Pray, Love* (Riverhead, 2007).

214 *"commitment to truth telling"*: bell hooks, *All About Love* (Perennial, 2001), 53.

215 *"This kind of unmasking"*: John Welwood, *Toward a Psychology of Awakening: Buddhism, Psychotherapy, and the Path of Personal and Spiritual Transformation* (Shambhala, 2000).

215 *"love is the great intangible"*: Diane Ackerman, *A Natural History of Love* (Random House, 1994): xvii.

218 *It raises its head at social gatherings*: Mallary Tenore Tarpley, "When Recovering from an Eating Disorder, Vegetarianism Can Be Complicated," *Tampa Bay Times*, September 21, 2021, https://www.tampabay.com/life-culture/food/2021/09/28/recovering-from-an-eating-disorder-being-vegetarian-can-be-complicated/.

219 *In her book* Life Without Ed: Jenni Schaefer and Thomas Rutledge, *Life Without Ed*, 10th anniversary edition (McGraw-Hill, 2014), xxi.

221 *teamed up to create UNITE*: Jennifer S. Kirby, Cristin D. Runfola, Melanie S. Fischer, Donald H. Baucom, and Cynthia M. Bulik, "Couples-Based Interventions for Adults with Eating Disorders," *Eating Disorders* 23 (Summer 2015): 356–65.

221 *This treatment model is considered effective*: Jennifer S. Kirby, Melanie S. Fischer, Thomas J. Raney, Donald H. Baucom, Cynthia M. Bulik, Heather Thompson-Brenner, et al., "Couple-Based Interventions in the Treatment of Adult Anorexia Nervosa: A Brief Case Example of UCAN," *Psychotherapy* 53 (Summer 2016): 241–50.

221 *loving relationships can improve recovery outcomes*: Federica Tozzi, Patrick F. Sullivan, Jennifer L. Fear, Jan McKenzie, and Cynthia M. Bulik, "Causes and Recovery in Anorexia Nervosa: The Patient's Perspective," *International Journal of Eating Disorders* 33 (Spring 2003): 143–54.

221 *"closely linked to body acceptance"*: Gunn Pettersen, Jan H. Rosenvinge, "Improvement and Recovery from Eating Disorders: A Patient Perspective," *Eating Disorders* 10 (Spring 2002): 61–71.

221 *"What does a lack of appetite* mean?": Joan Jacobs Brumberg, *Fasting Girls: The Emergence of Anorexia Nervosa as a Modern Disease* (Harvard University Press, 1998), 213.

222 *"where sexuality is underdeveloped"*: Joan Jacobs Brumberg, *Fasting Girls*, 30.

222 *"a deep psychological disturbance"*: Pierre Janet, *The Major Symptoms of Hysteria: Fifteen Lectures Given in the Medical School of Harvard University* (Macmillan, 1920), 233.

222 *"I would have liked always to stay a little girl"*: Joan Jacobs Brumberg, *Fasting Girls*, 216.

222 *she wrote in her seminal 1973 book*: Hilde Bruch, *Eating Disorders; Obesity, Anorexia Nervosa, and the Person Within* (Basic Books, 1973), 276–77.

222 *That's been changing in recent years*: Matt Richtel, "More Adolescent Boys Have Eating Disorders, Two Experts Discuss Why," *New York*

Times, February 8, 2024, https://www.nytimes.com/2024/02/08/health/adolescents-boys-eating-disorders.html.

223 *transgender people also struggle with eating disorders*: Anna Keski-Rahkonen, "Eating Disorders in Transgender and Gender Diverse People: Characteristics, Assessment, and Management," *Current Opinion in Psychiatry* 36 (Fall 2023): 412–18.

225 *One study of women*: Andréa Poyastro Pinheiro, T. J. Raney, Laura M. Thornton, Manfred M. Fichter, Wade H. Berrettini, David Goldman, et al., "Sexual Functioning in Women with Eating Disorders," *International Journal of Eating Disorders* 43 (Spring 2010): 123–29.

226 *has never had an official diagnosis*: Jason M. Nagata, Andrea K. Garber, Jennifer L. Tabler, Stuart B. Murray, and Kirsten Bibbins-Domingo, "Prevalence and Correlates of Disordered Eating Behaviors Among Young Adults with Overweight or Obesity," *Journal of General Internal Medicine* 33 (Summer 2018): 1337–43.

Chapter Eleven: Pregnancy in the Middle Place

233 *reduce my risk of breast cancer by 4.3 percent*: Britta Stordal, "Breastfeeding Reduces the Risk of Breast Cancer: A Call for Action in High-income Countries with Low Rates of Breastfeeding," *Cancer Medicine* 12 (Winter 2023): 4616–25.

233 *two-thirds are women*: "About Eating Disorders," Columbia University Department of Psychiatry website, https://www.columbiapsychiatry.org/research-clinics/eating-disorders-clinic/about-eating-disorders.

237 *"feel the present sliding over the depths of the past"*: Virginia Woolf, *Moments of Being* (Mariner, 1985), 98.

244 *I wrote an article*: Mallary Tenore Tarpley, "How Donating Breast Milk Helped Me Heal and Nourished Babies in Need," *Dallas Morning News*, January 8, 2019, https://www.dallasnews.com/news

/healthy-living/2019/01/08/how-donating-breast-milk-helped-me-heal-and-nourished-babies-in-need/.

244 *"breast isn't always best"*: C. G. Colen and D. M. Ramey, "Is Breast Truly Best? Estimating the Effects of Breastfeeding on Long-Term Child Health and Wellbeing in the United States Using Sibling Comparisons," *Social Science & Medicine* 109 (Spring 2014): 55–65, https://doi: 10.1016/j.socscimed.2014.01.027, PMID: 24698713; PMCID: PMC4077166.

244 *perceived pressures to breastfeed*: Katherine A. Thompson, Jennifer P. White, and Anna M. Bardone-Cone, "Associations Between Pressure to Breastfeed and Depressive, Anxiety, Obsessive-Compulsive, and Eating Disorder Symptoms Among Postpartum Women," *Psychiatry Research* 328: (2023): 1–12.

245 *maladaptive breastfeeding and pumping*: Suzanne Bailey-Straebler, Leah C. Susser, and Zafra Cooper, "Breastfeeding and Pumping as Maladaptive Weight Control Behaviors," *International Journal of Eating Disorders*, vol. 56 (Fall 2023): 1683–87.

245 *Some patients view them*: Nial Wheate, Jessica Pace, and The Conversation US, "'Budget Ozempic' Weight-Loss Trend Raises Safety Concerns," *Scientific American*, September 16, 2023, https://www.scientificamerican.com/article/budget-ozempic-weight-loss-trend-raises-safety-concerns/.

246 *eating disorders can affect reproductive health*: Suzanne M. Bailey-Straebler and Leah C. Susser, "The Impact of Eating Disorders on Reproductive Health: Mitigating the Risk," *Primary Care Companion for CNS Disorders* 25 (2023).

246 *Specifically, malnourishment can suppress*: Sasha Mikhael, Advaita Punjala-Patel, and Larisa Gavrilova-Jordan, "Hypothalamic-Pituitary-Ovarian Axis Disorders Impacting Female Fertility," *Biomedicines* 7 (Winter 2019): 5.

246 *Two large population-based studies*: Abigail Easter, Janet Treasure, and Nadia Micali, "Fertility and Prenatal Attitudes Towards Pregnancy

in Women with Eating Disorders: Results from the Avon Longitudinal Study of Parents and Children," *BJOG* 118 (Winter 2011): 1491–98; Nadia Micali, I. dos-Santos-Silva, B. De Stavola, J. Steenweg-de Graaff, V. Jaddoe, A. Hofman, et al., "Fertility Treatment, Twin Births, and Unplanned Pregnancies in Women with Eating Disorders: Findings from a Population-Based Birth Cohort," *BJOG* 121 (Spring 2014): 408–16.

246 *ill-equipped to detect these disorders*: Meaghan A. Leddy, Candace Jones, Maria A. Morgan, and Jay Schulkin, "Eating Disorders and Obstetric-Gynecologic Care," *Journal of Women's Health* 18 (Fall 2009): 1395–401.

247 *One such tool was developed in 2022*: Elizabeth A. Claydon, Christa L. Lilly, Jordan Z. Ceglar, and Omar F. Dueñas-Garcia, "Development and Validation Across Trimester of the Prenatal Eating Behaviors Screening Tool," *Archives of Women's Mental Health* 25 (August 2022): 705–16.

247 *Studies suggest that most OB/GYNs report*: Leddy, et al., "Eating Disorders and Obstetric-Gynecologic Care."

247 *That avoidance can lead to serious complications*: Mary C. Kimmel, E. H. Ferguson, Stephanie Zerwas, Cynthia M. Bulik, and Samantha Meltzer-Brody, "Obstetric and Gynecologic Problems Associated with Eating Disorders," *International Journal of Eating Disorders* 49 (Spring 2016): 260–75.

247 *Women with anorexia are at higher risk of*: Milla S. Linna, Anu Raevuori, Jari Haukka, Jaana M. Suvisaari, Jaana T. Suokas, and Mika Gissler, "Pregnancy, Obstetric, and Perinatal Health Outcomes in Eating Disorders," *American Journal of Obstetrics and Gynecology* 4 (Fall 2014): 392.

248 *lesser-known risks that are rarely discussed*: Cynthia M. Bulik, Frances A. Carter, and Patrick F. Sullivan, "Self-Induced Abortion in a Bulimic Woman," *International Journal of Eating Disorders* 15 (Spring 1994): 297–99.

248 *Some studies have found*: Abigal Easter, Francessca Solmi, Amanda Bye, Emma Taborelli, Freya Corfield, Ulrike Schmidt, et al., "Antenatal and Postnatal Psychopathology Among Women with Current and Past Eating Disorders: Longitudinal Patterns," *European Eating Disorders Review* 23 (Winter 2015): 19–27; Nadia Micali, Janet Treasure, and Emily Simonoff, "Eating Disorders Symptoms in Pregnancy: A Longitudinal Study of Women with Recent and Past Eating Disorders and Obesity," *Journal of Psychosomatic Research* 63 (Fall 2007): 297–303.

248 *a relapse rate as high as 33 percent*: Saloua Koubaa, Tore Hällström, Caroline Lindholm, and Angelica Lindén Hirschberg, "Pregnancy and Neonatal Outcomes in Women with Eating Disorders," *Obstetric Gynecology* 105 (Winter 2005): 255–60.

248 *the onset and continuation of binge-eating disorder*: Cynthia M. Bulik, Ann Von Holle, Robert Hamer, Cecile Knoph Berg, Leila Torgersen, Per Magnus, et al., "Patterns of Remission, Continuation and Incidence of Broadly Defined Eating Disorders During Early Pregnancy in the Norwegian Mother and Child Cohort Study," *Psychological Medicine* 37 (Summer 2007): 1109–18; H. J. Watson, Ann-Von Holle, Robert Hamer, Cecile Knoph Berg, Leila Torgersen, Per Magnus, et al., "Remission, Continuation and Incidence of Eating Disorders During Early Pregnancy: A Validation Study in a Population-Based Birth Cohort," *Psychological Medicine* 43 (Summer 2013): 1723–34.

248 *pregnancy can lead to a decrease in concerns*: Ida Ringsborg Madsen, Kirsten Hørder, and René Klinkby Støving, "Remission of Eating Disorder During Pregnancy: Five Cases and Brief Clinical Review," *Journal of Psychosomatic Obstetrics Gynaecology* 30 (Summer 2009): 122–26.

250 *Almost two-thirds of pregnant and postpartum women*: Nicola Heslehurst, Elizabeth H. Evans, Angela C. Incollingo Rodriguez, Taniya S. Nagpal, and Shelina Visram, "Newspaper Media Framing

of Obesity During Pregnancy in the UK: A Review and Framework Synthesis," *Obesity Reviews* 23 (Winter 2022): 13, 511.

250 *And an estimated 40 percent of women*: María Martínez-Olcina, Jacobo A. Rubio-Arias, Cristina Reche-García, Belén Leyva-Vela, María Hernández-García, Juan José Hernández-Morante, et al., "Eating Disorders in Pregnant and Breastfeeding Women: A Systematic Review," *Medicina* (Kaunas, Lithuania) 56 (Summer 2020): 352.

Chapter Twelve: Motherhood in the Middle Place

255 *During stressful stretches*: Mallary Tenore Tarpley, "When I Lost My Sense of Taste to Covid, Anorexia Stepped In," *New York Times*, March 3, 2021, https://www.nytimes.com/2021/03/03/well/mind/covid-anorexia-eating-disorder.html.

256 *The term first emerged in 1984*: Judith Rodin, Lisa Silberstein, and Ruth Striegel-Moore, "Women and Weight: A Normative Discontent," *Nebraska Symposium on Motivation* 32 (Winter 1984): 267–307. PMID: 6398857.

256 *this discontent is pervasive among men, too*: Stacey Tantleff-Dunn, Rachel D. Barnes, and Jessica Gokee Larose. "It's Not Just a 'Woman Thing': The Current State of Normative Discontent," *Eating Disorders* 19 (Fall 2011): 392–402.

256 *"social success, career success, academic success"*: José I. Baile, María J. González-Calderón, and María F. Rabito-Alcón, "Obesity Bias in the School Setting: A Brief Report," *Children* 9 (Summer 2022): 1067.

256 *"a bad way of attaining the ideal"*: Jacqueline Howard, "The History of the 'Ideal' Woman and Where That Has Left Us," CNN, March 9, 2018, https://www.cnn.com/2018/03/07/health/body-image-history-of-beauty-explainer-intl/index.html.

256 *a $76 billion diet industry*: Andrea Peterson, Rolfe Winkler, and Sara Ashley O'Brien, "The $76 Billion Diet Industry Ask: What to Do

About Ozempic?" *Wall Street Journal*, April 10, 2023, https://www.wsj.com/articles/ozempic-wegovy-mounjaro-weight-loss-industry-89419ecb.

257 *Research shows that females*: Laura M. Thornton, Suzanne E. Mazzeo, and Cynthia M. Bulik, "The Heritability of Eating Disorders: Methods and Current Findings," in *Behavioral Neurobiology of Eating Disorders: Current Topics in Behavioral Neurosciences*, vol. 6, ed. R. Adan and W. Kaye (Springer, 2010) 141–56.

258 *in a piece for* The Washington Post: Mallary Tenore Tarpley, "Healthy Eating Curriculum May Contribute to Eating Disorders in Kids," *Washington Post*, August 21, 2023, https://www.washingtonpost.com/parenting/2023/08/21/curriculum-trigger-eating-disorder/.

258 *public health interventions for children*: Tracy K. Richmond, Idia B. Thurston, and Kendrin R. Sonneville, "Weight-Focused Public Health Interventions—No Benefit, Some Harm," *Journal of American Medical Association, Pediatrics* 175 (Spring 2021): 238–39.

258 *rates have quadrupled since 1990*: "Obesity and Overweight," World Health Organization, fact sheet, March 1, 2024: https://www.who.int/news-room/fact-sheets/detail/obesity-and-overweight.

259 *Intuitive eating is about*: Evelyn Tribole, Elyse Resch, *Intuitive Eating: A Revolutionary Anti-Diet Approach* (St. Martin's Essentials, 2020): xx–xxi.

260 "*why young children prefer quickly digestible carbohydrates*": Sumner Brooks and Amee Severson, *How to Raise an Intuitive Eater: Raising the Next Generation with Food and Body Confidence* (St. Martin's, 2020), 235–37.

265 *Eating disorders always stem from a complex set of factors*: Thomas Vander Ven and Marikay Vander Ven, "Exploring Patterns of Mother-Blaming in Anorexia Scholarship: A Study in the Sociology of Knowledge," *Human Studies* 26 (Winter 2003): 97–119.

265 *Mother-blaming abounds*: David J. Lynn, "Madness on the Couch:

Blaming the Victim in the Heyday of Psychoanalysis," *Bulletin of the History of Medicine* 74 (Summer 2000): 407–408.

265 *"an insoluble conflict with the patient's mother"*: Melitta Sperling, "The Role of the Mother in Psychosomatic Disorders in Children," *Psychosomatic Medicine*, vol. 11 (Winter 1949): 377–386.

265 *A 1974* New York Times *article*: Sam Blum, "Anorexics Look Like Gorgeous Waifs, But They May Be Simply Trying Not to Grow Up," *New York Times*, November 10, 1974, https://www.nytimes.com/1974/11/10/archives/children-who-starve-themselves-anorexics-look-like-gorgeous-waifs.html.

265 *"frustrated" career women*: Hilde Bruch, "Perceptual and Conceptual Disturbances in Anorexia Nervosa," *Psychoanalytic Quarterly* 31 (Spring 1962): 588–89.

266 *"This is the psychological background"*: Kim Chernin, *The Hungry Self: Women, Eating and Identity* (Times Books, 1985), 81.

266 *away from theory and toward scientific testing*: Michele A. Crisafulli, Ann Von Holle, and Cynthia M. Bulik, "Attitudes Towards Anorexia Nervosa: The Impact of Framing on Blame and Stigma," *International Journal of Eating Disorders* 41 (Spring 2008): 333–39.

267 *a higher genetic* and *environmental risk*: Cynthia M. Bulik, "If We Build It, Will They Come? Commentary on 'Preventing Eating Disorders and Disordered Eating in High-risk Families,'" *International Journal of Eating Disorders* 56 (Spring 2023): 535–37.

267 *program for high-risk families*: Shiri Sadeh-Sharvit, Eynat Zubery, Esty Mankovski, Evelyne Steiner, and James D. Lock, "Parent-Based Prevention Program for the Children of Mothers with Eating Disorders: Feasibility and Preliminary Outcomes," *Eating Disorders* 24 (Summer 2016): 312–25.

267 *high-risk families with adolescent children*: Michael P. Levine and Shiri Sadeh-Sharvit, "Preventing Eating Disorders and Disordered Eating in Genetically Vulnerable, High-risk Families," *International Journal of Eating Disorders* 56 (Spring 2023): 523–34.

267 *fear of parent-blaming*: Shiri Sadeh-Sharvit and James Lock, *Parents with Eating Disorders: An Intervention Guide* (Routledge, 2018): 25.

269 *A large twin study has shown*: Lisa Dinkler, Marie-Louis Wronski, Paul Lichtenstein, Sebastian Lundström, Henrik Larsson, Nadia Micali, et al., "Etiology of the Broad Avoidant Restrictive Food Intake Disorder Phenotype in Swedish Twins Aged 6 to 12 Years," *Journal of American Medical Association, Psychiatry* 80 (Spring 2023): 260–69.

272 *Cancer research is so sophisticated*: Michael Snyder, *Genomics and Personalized Medicine: What Everyone Needs to Know* (Oxford University Press, 2020): 21–29.

272 *The complexity of polygenic risk scores*: "Polygenic Risk Scores," National Human Genome Research Institute, https://www.genome.gov/Health/Genomics-and-Medicine/Polygenic-risk-scores; Naomi R. Wray, Tian Lin, Jehannine Austin, John J. McGrath, Ian B. Hickie, Graham K. Murray, et al., "From Basic Science to Clinical Application of Polygenic Risk Scores: A Primer," *Journal of the American Medical Association, Psychiatry* 78 (Winter 2021): 101–109.

273 *ANGI compared the genomes*: Cynthia Bulik, Martin Kennedy, and Tracey Wade, "ANGI—Anorexia Nervosa Genetics Initiative," *Twin Research and Human Genetics* 23 (Spring 2020): 135–36.

273 *ANGI was groundbreaking*: Hunna J. Watson, Zeynep Yilmaz, Laura M. Thornton, Christopher Hubel, Jonathan Coleman, Helena Gaspart, et al., "Genome-Wide Association Study Identifies Eight Risk Loci and Implicates Metabo-Psychiatric Origins for Anorexia Nervosa," *Nature Genetics* 51, no. 8 (2019): 1207–14.

273 *"metabo-psychiatric disorder"*: Cynthia M. Bulik, Ian M. Carroll, and Philip Mehler, "Reframing Anorexia Nervosa as a Metabo-Psychiatric Disorder," *Trends in Endocrinology and Metabolism* 32 (Fall 2021): 752–61.

274 *greater risk of relapse metabolically*: Watson, et al. "Genome-Wide Association Study Identifies Eight Risk Loci."

274 *the downward metabolic pull*: Cynthia M. Bulik, Rachael Flatt, Afrouz Abbaspour, and Ian Carroll, "Reconceptualizing Anorexia Nervosa," *Psychiatry Clinical Neurosciences* 73 (Fall 2019): 518–25.

274 *Dr. Bulik and colleagues just completed a new study*: Kylie K. Reed, Emily C. Bulik-Sullivan, et. al, "Using Bomb Calorimetry to Investigate Intestinal Energy Harvest in Anorexia Nervosa: Preliminary Findings on Stool Calorie Loss," *The International Journal of Eating Disorders* (Fall 2024).

275 *Called the Eating Disorders Genetics Initiative (EDGI)*: Cynthia M. Bulik, Laura M. Thornton, Richard Parker, Hannah Kennedy, Jessica H. Baker, Casey MacDormo, et al., "The Eating Disorders Genetics Initiative (EDGI): Study Protocol," *BMC Psychiatry* 21 (Spring 2021): 234.

Further Resources

National Center of Excellence for Eating Disorders: nceedus.org

National Alliance for Eating Disorders' Resource Library: allianceforeatingdisorders.com/resource-library

National Association of Anorexia Nervosa and Associated Disorders (ANAD): anad.org

National Eating Disorders Association: nationaleatingdisorders.org

Multi-Service Eating Disorders Association (MEDA): medainc.org

Families Empowered And Supporting Treatment of Eating Disorders (F.E.A.S.T.): feast-ed.org/

Strategic Training Initiative for the Prevention of Eating Disorders: hsph.harvard.edu/striped/

Eating Disorders Coalition: eatingdisorderscoalition.org

Project Heal: theprojectheal.org

Academy for Eating Disorders: aedweb.org

International Association of Eating Disorders Professionals: iaedpfoundation.com

Body Equity Alliance: bodyequityalliance.com

Center for Body Trust: centerforbodytrust.com

Association for Size Diversity and Health (ASDAH): asdah.org

More Than a Body: morethanabody.org

The Association for Weight and Size Inclusive Medicine: weightinclusivemedicine.org

Index

About the Author

Mallary Tenore Tarpley is an award-winning author and journalism professor at the University of Texas at Austin's Moody College of Communication and McCombs School of Business. Her writing has appeared in *The New York Times*, *The Washington Post*, *The Los Angeles Times*, *The Wall Street Journal*, and *TIME* magazine, among other publications. She is the recipient of a prestigious Alfred P. Sloan Foundation grant, which has helped support her research and writing. Mallary holds bachelor's degrees from Providence College, as well as a master of fine arts in nonfiction writing from Goucher College. *Slip*, which is Mallary's first book, won the 2026 PROSE Award for Excellence in Biological and Life Sciences from the Association of American Publishers. Mallary lives outside of Austin, Texas, with her husband and two children.

Instagram: @MallaryTenoreTarpley
Substack: Mallary.substack.com
MallaryTenoreTarpley.com